CAPTAIN AMERICA
AND THE MIGHTY AVENGERS

LAST DAYS

COLLECTION EDITOR: ALEX STARBUCK   ASSISTANT EDITOR: SARAH BRUNSTAD
EDITORS, SPECIAL PROJECTS: JENNIFER GRÜNWALD & MARK D. BEAZLEY
SENIOR EDITOR, SPECIAL PROJECTS: JEFF YOUNGQUIST
SVP PRINT, SALES & MARKETING: DAVID GABRIEL
BOOK DESIGNER: ADAM DEL RE

EDITOR IN CHIEF: AXEL ALONSO   CHIEF CREATIVE OFFICER: JOE QUESADA
PUBLISHER: DAN BUCKLEY   EXECUTIVE PRODUCER: ALAN FINE

CAPTAIN AMERICA & THE MIGHTY AVENGERS VOL. 2: LAST DAYS. Contains material originally published in magazine form as CAPTAIN AMERICA & THE MIGHTY AVENGERS #8-9, CAPTAIN BRITAIN AND THE MIGHTY DEFENDERS #1-2 and AVENGERS ASSEMBLE #15AU. First printing 2015. ISBN# 978-0-7851-9803-1. Published by MARVEL WORLDWIDE, INC., a subsidiary of MARVEL ENTERTAINMENT, LLC. OFFICE OF PUBLICATION: 135 West 50th Street, New York, NY 10020. Copyright © 2015 MARVEL No similarity between any of the names, characters, persons, and/or institutions in this magazine with those of any living or dead person or institution is intended, and any such similarity which may exist is purely coincidental. **Printed in Canada.** ALAN FINE, President, Marvel Entertainment; DAN BUCKLEY, President, TV, Publishing and Brand Management; JOE QUESADA, Chief Creative Officer; TOM BREVOORT, SVP of Publishing; DAVID BOGART, SVP of Operations & Procurement, Publishing; C.B. CEBULSKI, VP of International Development & Brand Management; DAVID GABRIEL, SVP Print, Sales & Marketing; JIM O'KEEFE, VP of Operations & Logistics; DAN CARR, Executive Director of Publishing Technology; SUSAN CRESPI, Editorial Operations Manager; ALEX MORALES, Publishing Operations Manager; STAN LEE, Chairman Emeritus. For information regarding advertising in Marvel Comics or on Marvel.com, please contact Jonathan Rheingold, VP of Custom Solutions & Ad Sales, at jrheingold@marvel.com. For Marvel subscription inquiries, please call 800-217-9158. **Manufactured between 8/28/2015 and 10/5/2015 by SOLISCO PRINTERS, SCOTT, QC, CANADA.**

10 9 8 7 6 5 4 3 2 1

CAPTAIN AMERICA AND THE MIGHTY AVENGERS

LAST DAYS

WRITER
AL EWING

CAPTAIN AMERICA AND THE MIGHTY AVENGERS
ARTIST LUKE ROSS
COLOR ARTIST RACHELLE ROSENBERG
LETTERER TRAVIS LANHAM
COVER ART LUKE ROSS & FRANK MARTIN

CAPTAIN BRITAIN AND THE MIGHTY DEFENDERS
PENCILER ALAN DAVIS
INKER MARK FARMER
COLORIST WIL QUINTANA
LETTERER TRAVIS LANHAM
COVER ART ALAN DAVIS, MARK FARMER & JORDIE BELLAIRE (#1);
AND ALAN DAVIS, MARK FARMER & WIL QUINTANA (#2)

AVENGERS ASSEMBLE
PENCILER BUTCH GUICE
INKER TOM PALMER WITH RICK MAGYAR
COLORIST FRANK D'ARMATA
LETTERER CLAYTON COWLES
COVER ART NIC KLEIN

ASSISTANT EDITORS JON MOISAN & ALANNA SMITH
EDITORS TOM BREVOORT & WIL MOSS WITH LAUREN SANKOVITCH

CAPTAIN AMERICA CREATED BY JOE SIMON & JACK KIRBY

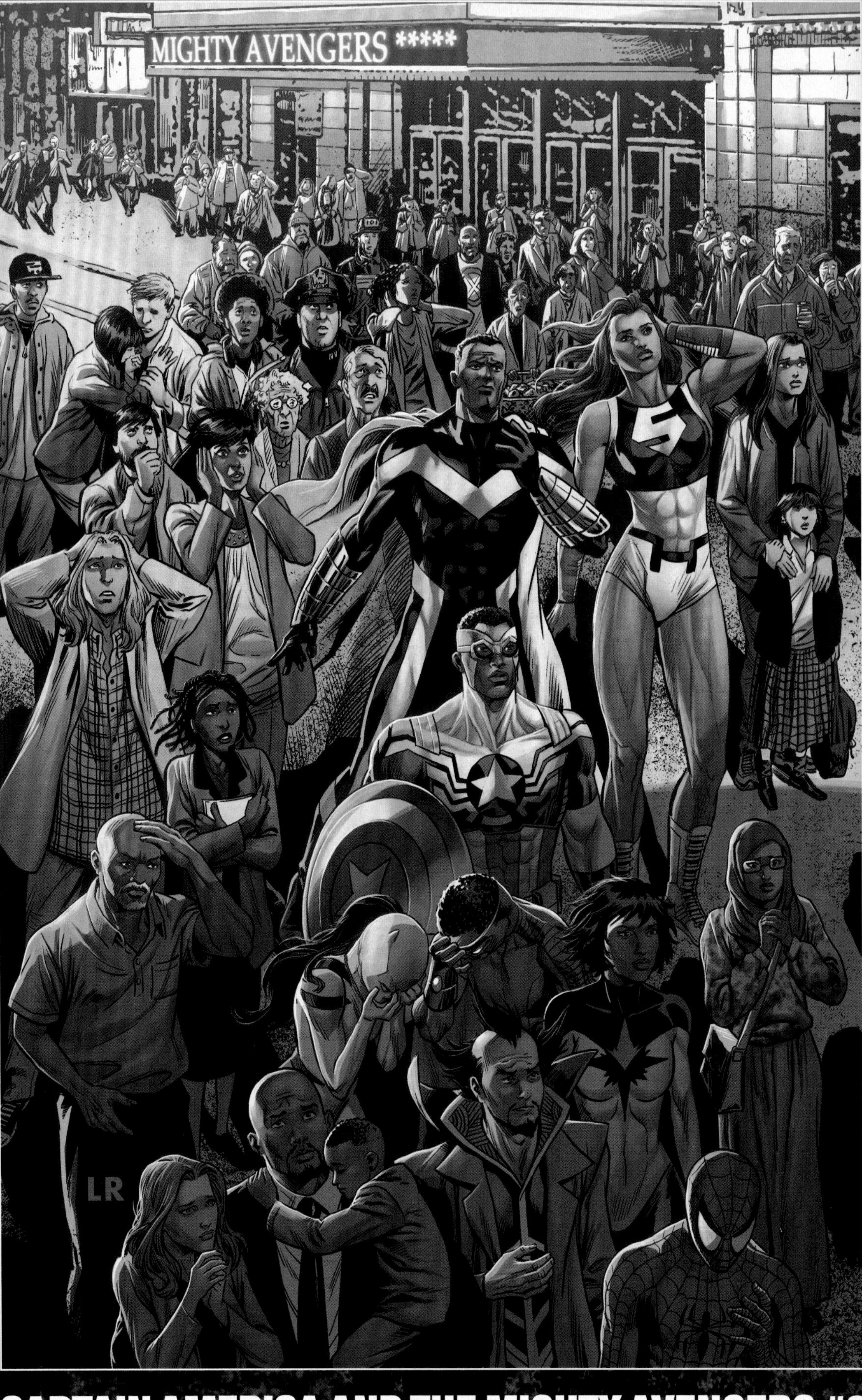
MIGHTY AVENGERS *****
LR

CAPTAIN AMERICA AND THE MIGHTY AVENGERS #8

CAPTAIN AMERICA AND THE MIGHTY AVENGERS

Dear Community,

We've had some setbacks recently, but our team (including Captain America, Power Man, She-Hulk, Kaluu, White Tiger, Blue Marvel, Spectrum, Jessica Jones and myself, Luke Cage) remains committed to working with you, the people, to help those in need. Legal difficulties, car trouble, rampaging super villains, you name it -- if you've got a problem, we're your guys.

Our volunteer call center is always looking for new recruits to answer calls from folks who need help. You could even end up fielding a call from Steve Rogers, the original Captain America, like our newest Mighty Avenger volunteer Soraya Khorasani recently did!

As always, thanks for your ongoing support and feedback.

Your neighbor,

Luke Cage

STEVE ROGERS STOPS BY MIGHTY AVENGERS HQ!

The Mighty Avengers are riding high after their victory over CORTEX CEO Jason Quantrell and the otherworldly Beyond Corporation, in large part thanks to the revitalized Spectrum. But there's no time to celebrate when former Captain America Steve Rogers calls on the Mighty Avengers to help with a problem that affects all of reality...

BAD NEWS and WORSE NEWS

178 DAYS to LIVE

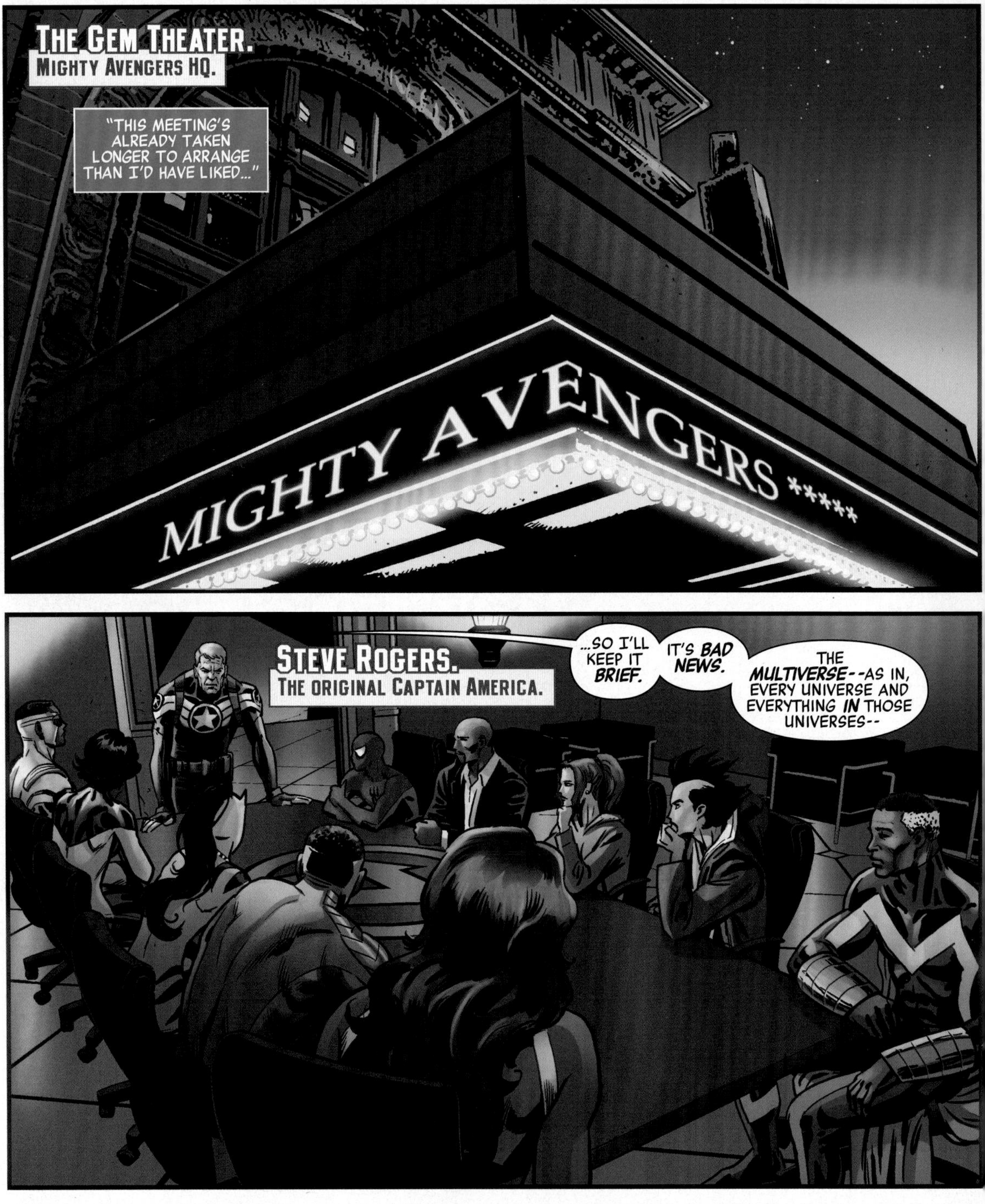
THE GEM THEATER.
MIGHTY AVENGERS HQ.
"THIS MEETING'S ALREADY TAKEN LONGER TO ARRANGE THAN I'D HAVE LIKED..."
MIGHTY AVENGERS
STEVE ROGERS.
THE ORIGINAL CAPTAIN AMERICA.
...SO I'LL KEEP IT BRIEF.
IT'S BAD NEWS.
THE MULTIVERSE--AS IN, EVERY UNIVERSE AND EVERYTHING IN THOSE UNIVERSES--

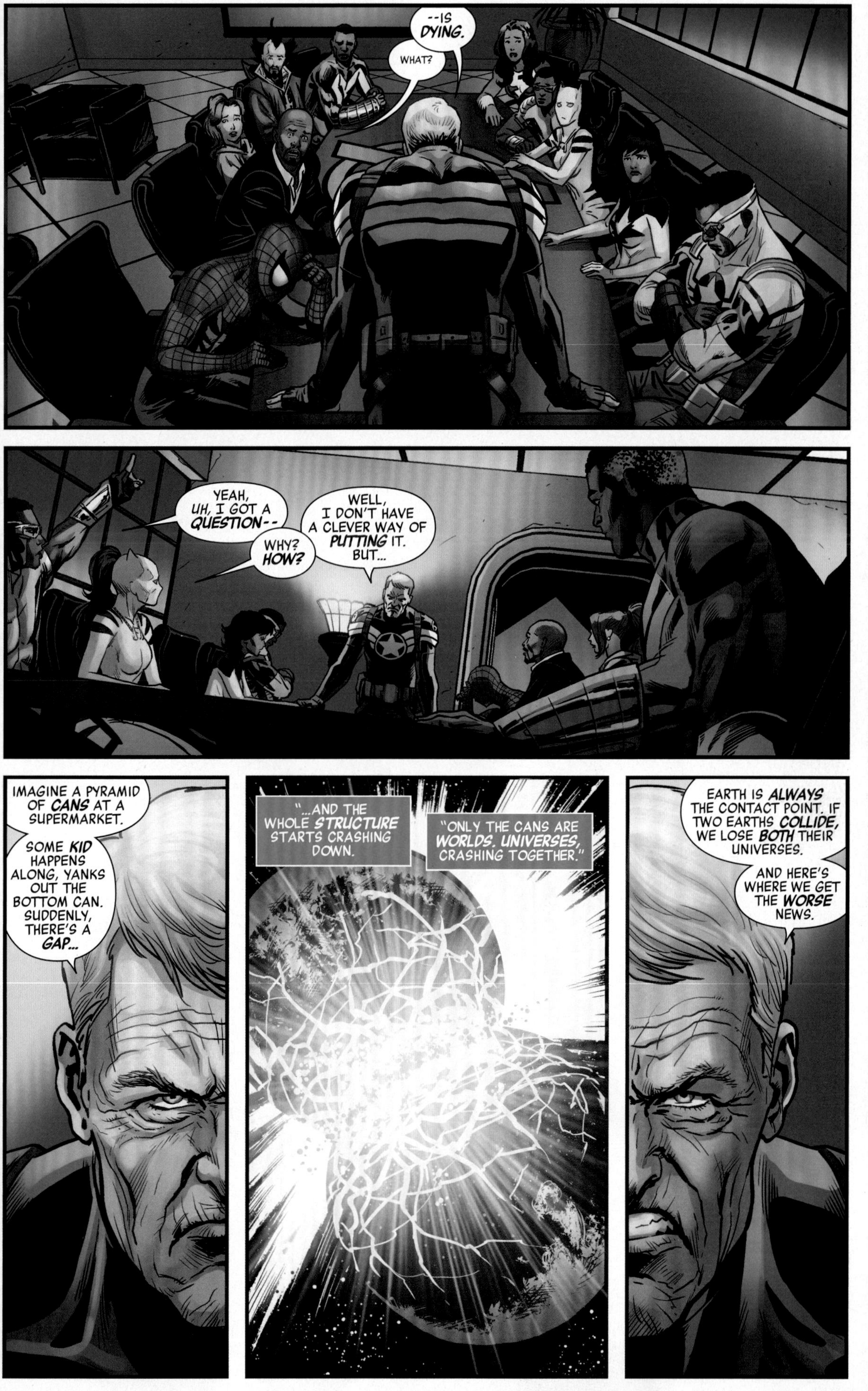
WHAT?
--IS DYING.
YEAH, UH, I GOT A QUESTION--
WHY? HOW?
WELL, I DON'T HAVE A CLEVER WAY OF PUTTING IT. BUT...
IMAGINE A PYRAMID OF CANS AT A SUPERMARKET.
SOME KID HAPPENS ALONG, YANKS OUT THE BOTTOM CAN. SUDDENLY, THERE'S A GAP...
"...AND THE WHOLE STRUCTURE STARTS CRASHING DOWN.
"ONLY THE CANS ARE WORLDS. UNIVERSES, CRASHING TOGETHER."
EARTH IS ALWAYS THE CONTACT POINT. IF TWO EARTHS COLLIDE, WE LOSE BOTH THEIR UNIVERSES.
AND HERE'S WHERE WE GET THE WORSE NEWS.

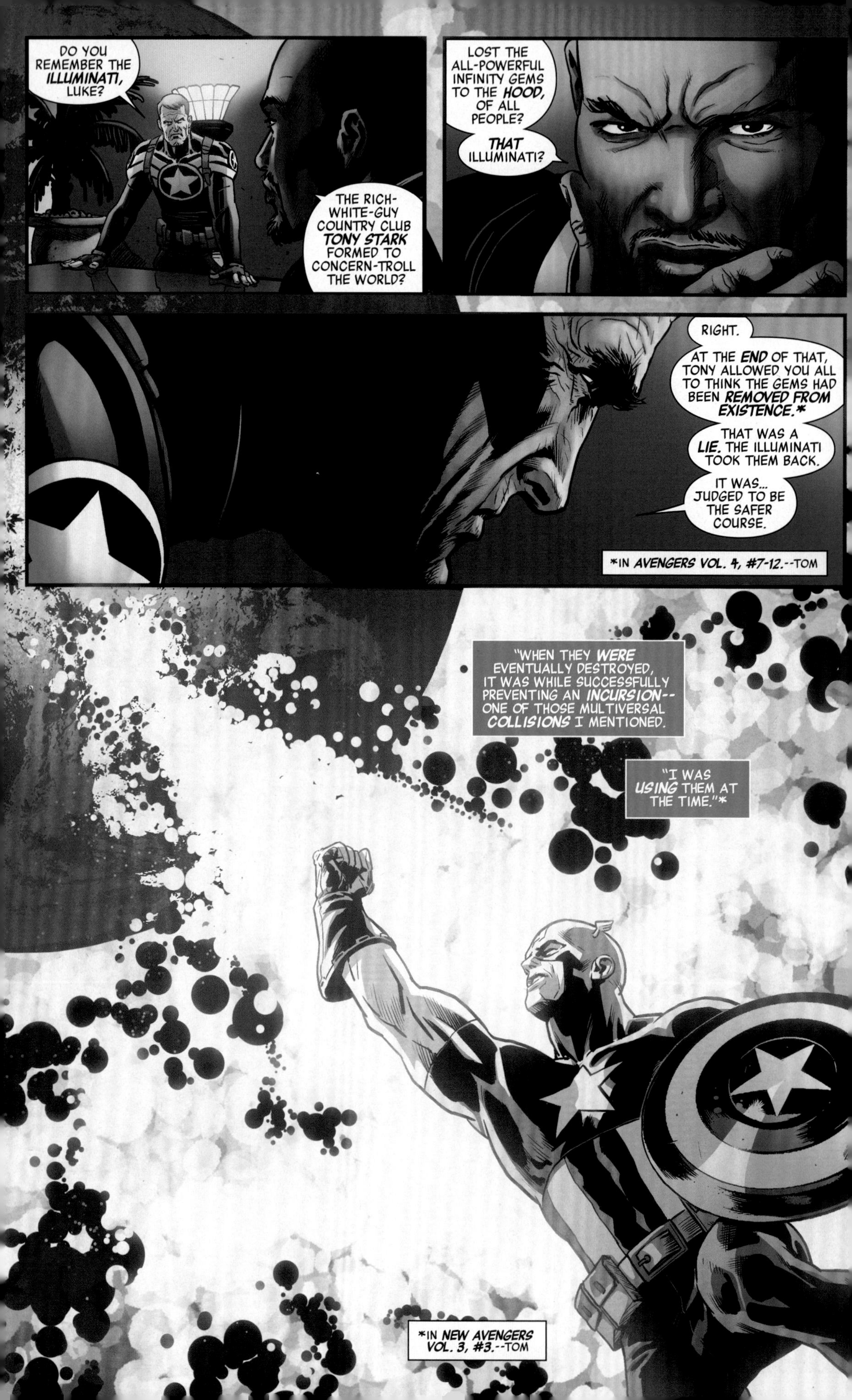

DO YOU REMEMBER THE ILLUMINATI, LUKE?
THE RICH-WHITE-GUY COUNTRY CLUB TONY STARK FORMED TO CONCERN-TROLL THE WORLD?
LOST THE ALL-POWERFUL INFINITY GEMS TO THE HOOD, OF ALL PEOPLE?
THAT ILLUMINATI?
RIGHT.
AT THE END OF THAT, TONY ALLOWED YOU ALL TO THINK THE GEMS HAD BEEN REMOVED FROM EXISTENCE.*
THAT WAS A LIE. THE ILLUMINATI TOOK THEM BACK.
IT WAS... JUDGED TO BE THE SAFER COURSE.
*IN AVENGERS VOL. 4, #7-12.--TOM
"WHEN THEY WERE EVENTUALLY DESTROYED, IT WAS WHILE SUCCESSFULLY PREVENTING AN INCURSION--ONE OF THOSE MULTIVERSAL COLLISIONS I MENTIONED.
"I WAS USING THEM AT THE TIME."*
*IN NEW AVENGERS VOL. 3, #3.--TOM

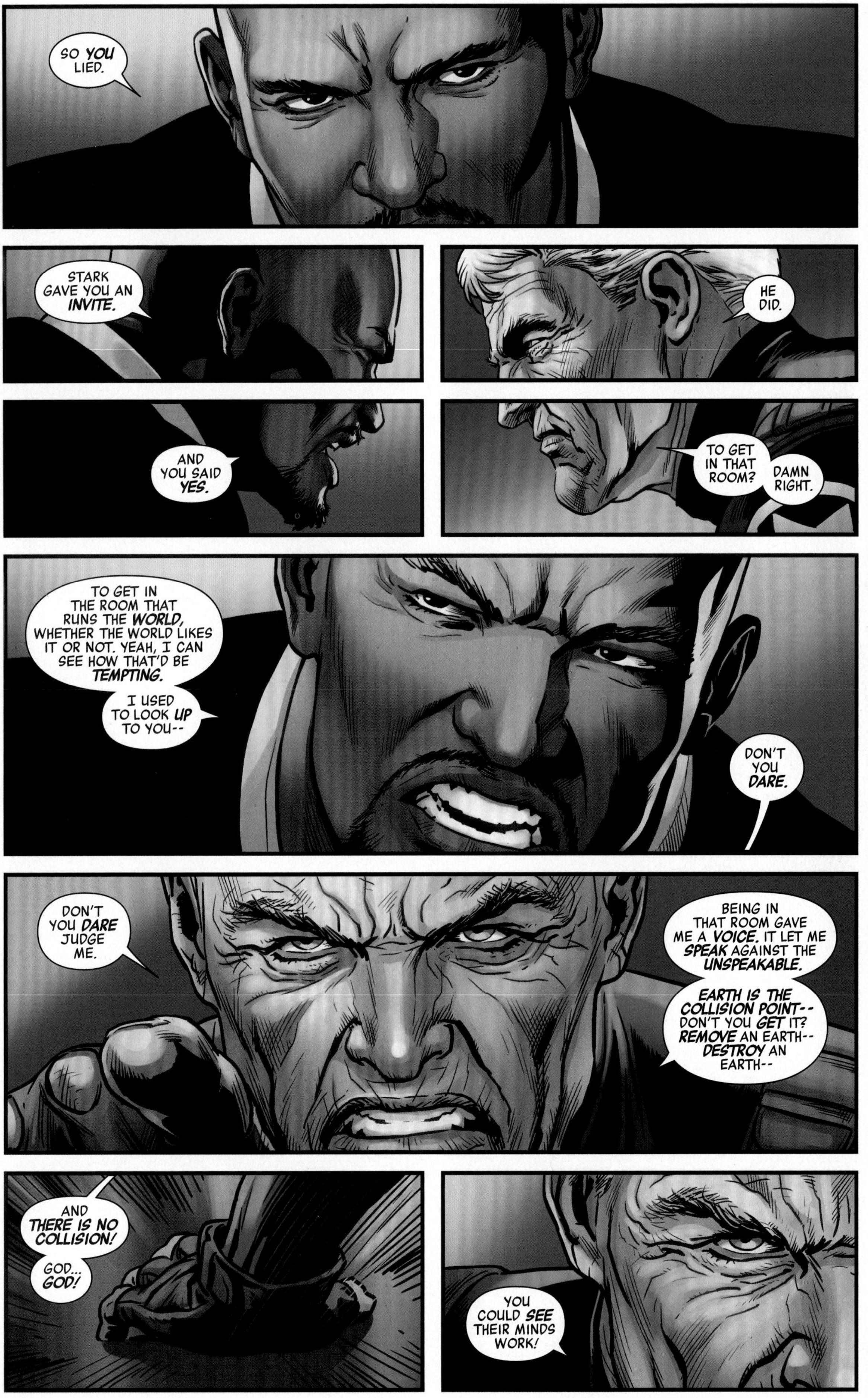
SO YOU LIED.
STARK GAVE YOU AN INVITE.
HE DID.
AND YOU SAID YES.
TO GET IN THAT ROOM?
DAMN RIGHT.
TO GET IN THE ROOM THAT RUNS THE WORLD, WHETHER THE WORLD LIKES IT OR NOT. YEAH, I CAN SEE HOW THAT'D BE TEMPTING.
I USED TO LOOK UP TO YOU--
DON'T YOU DARE.
DON'T YOU DARE JUDGE ME.
BEING IN THAT ROOM GAVE ME A VOICE. IT LET ME SPEAK AGAINST THE UNSPEAKABLE.
EARTH IS THE COLLISION POINT-- DON'T YOU GET IT? REMOVE AN EARTH-- DESTROY AN EARTH--
AND THERE IS NO COLLISION!
GOD... GOD!
YOU COULD SEE THEIR MINDS WORK!

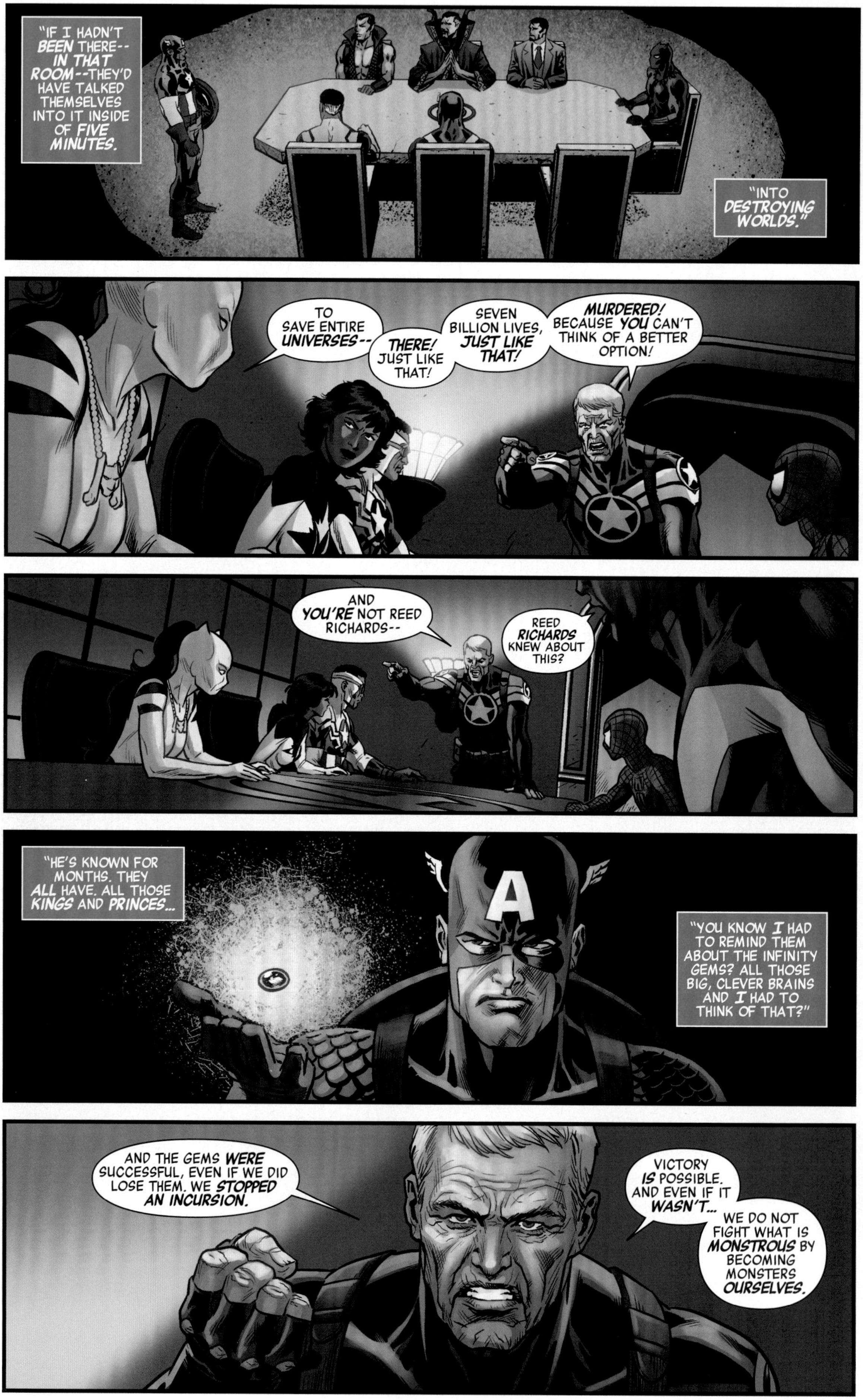
"IF I HADN'T BEEN THERE-- IN THAT ROOM--THEY'D HAVE TALKED THEMSELVES INTO IT INSIDE OF FIVE MINUTES.
"INTO DESTROYING WORLDS."
TO SAVE ENTIRE UNIVERSES--
THERE! JUST LIKE THAT!
SEVEN BILLION LIVES, JUST LIKE THAT!
MURDERED! BECAUSE YOU CAN'T THINK OF A BETTER OPTION!
AND YOU'RE NOT REED RICHARDS--
REED RICHARDS KNEW ABOUT THIS?
"HE'S KNOWN FOR MONTHS. THEY ALL HAVE. ALL THOSE KINGS AND PRINCES...
"YOU KNOW I HAD TO REMIND THEM ABOUT THE INFINITY GEMS? ALL THOSE BIG, CLEVER BRAINS AND I HAD TO THINK OF THAT?"
AND THE GEMS WERE SUCCESSFUL, EVEN IF WE DID LOSE THEM. WE STOPPED AN INCURSION.
VICTORY IS POSSIBLE. AND EVEN IF IT WASN'T...
WE DO NOT FIGHT WHAT IS MONSTROUS BY BECOMING MONSTERS OURSELVES.

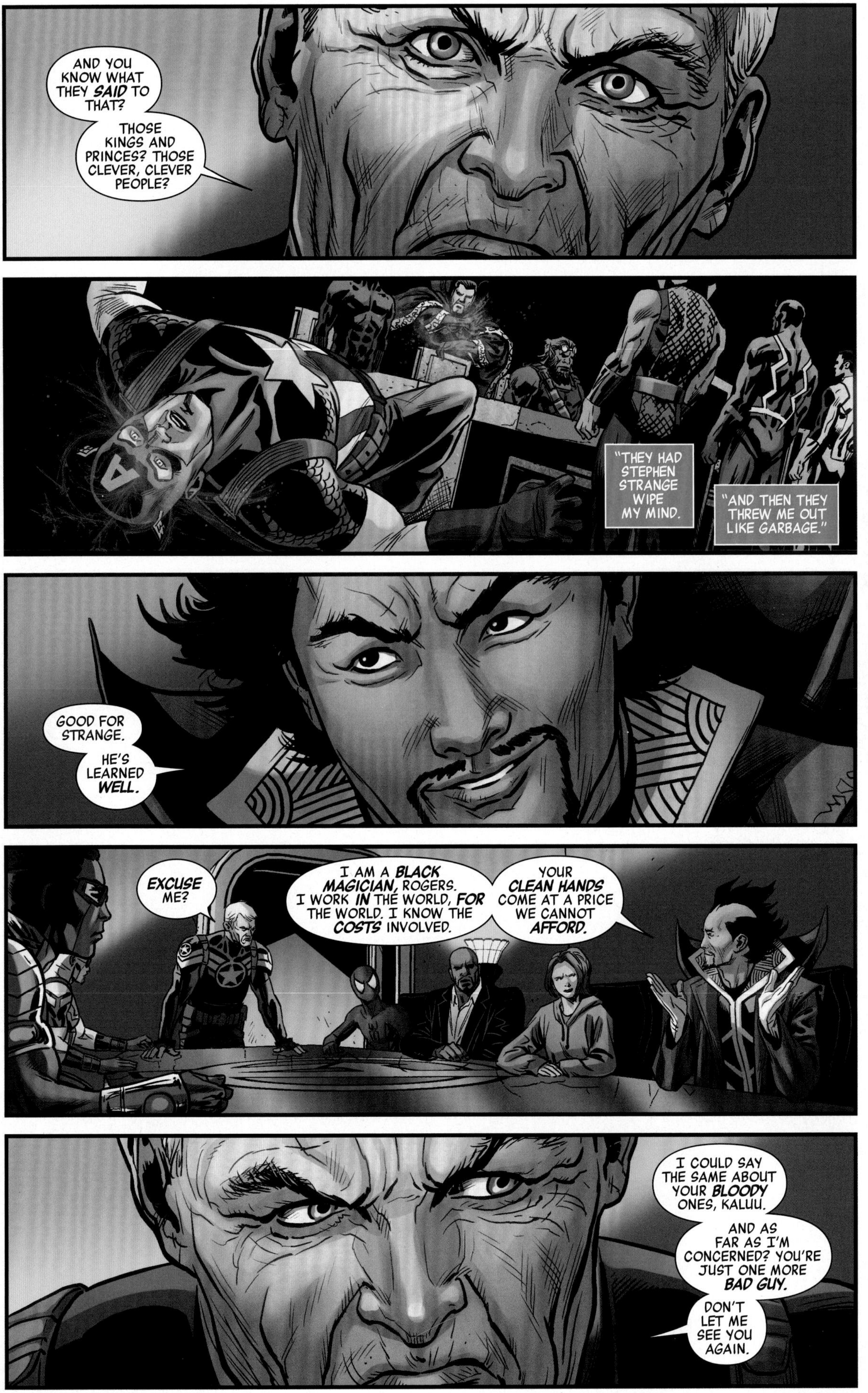
AND YOU KNOW WHAT THEY SAID TO THAT?
THOSE KINGS AND PRINCES? THOSE CLEVER, CLEVER PEOPLE?
"THEY HAD STEPHEN STRANGE WIPE MY MIND.
"AND THEN THEY THREW ME OUT LIKE GARBAGE."
GOOD FOR STRANGE.
HE'S LEARNED WELL.
EXCUSE ME?
I AM A BLACK MAGICIAN, ROGERS. I WORK IN THE WORLD, FOR THE WORLD. I KNOW THE COSTS INVOLVED.
YOUR CLEAN HANDS COME AT A PRICE WE CANNOT AFFORD.
I COULD SAY THE SAME ABOUT YOUR BLOODY ONES, KALUU.
AND AS FAR AS I'M CONCERNED? YOU'RE JUST ONE MORE BAD GUY.
DON'T LET ME SEE YOU AGAIN.

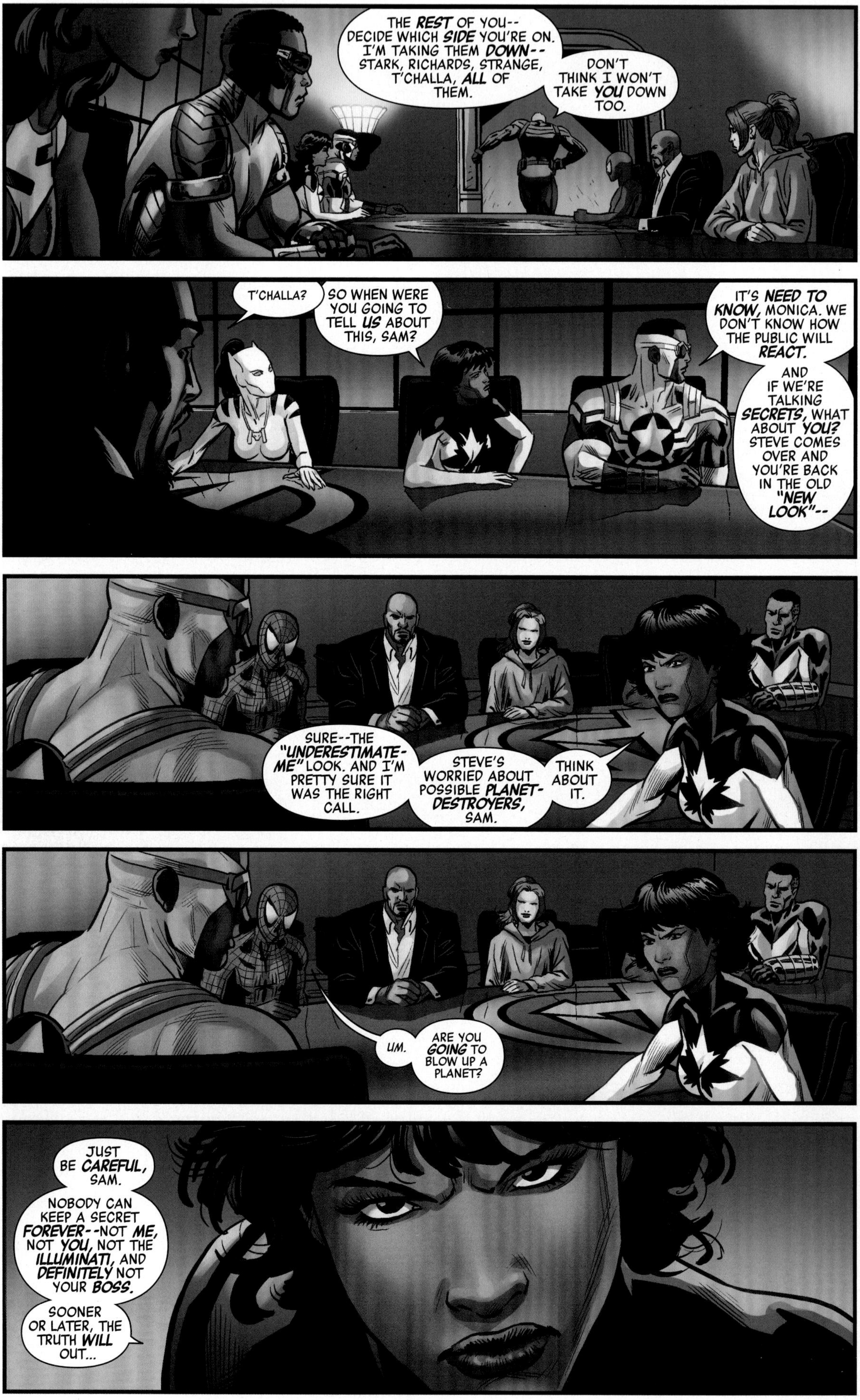

THE REST OF YOU-- DECIDE WHICH SIDE YOU'RE ON. I'M TAKING THEM DOWN-- STARK, RICHARDS, STRANGE, T'CHALLA, ALL OF THEM.
DON'T THINK I WON'T TAKE YOU DOWN TOO.
T'CHALLA?
SO WHEN WERE YOU GOING TO TELL US ABOUT THIS, SAM?
IT'S NEED TO KNOW, MONICA. WE DON'T KNOW HOW THE PUBLIC WILL REACT.
AND IF WE'RE TALKING SECRETS, WHAT ABOUT YOU? STEVE COMES OVER AND YOU'RE BACK IN THE OLD "NEW LOOK"--
SURE--THE "UNDERESTIMATE-ME" LOOK. AND I'M PRETTY SURE IT WAS THE RIGHT CALL.
STEVE'S WORRIED ABOUT POSSIBLE PLANET-DESTROYERS, SAM.
THINK ABOUT IT.
UM.
ARE YOU GOING TO BLOW UP A PLANET?
JUST BE CAREFUL, SAM.
NOBODY CAN KEEP A SECRET FOREVER--NOT ME, NOT YOU, NOT THE ILLUMINATI, AND DEFINITELY NOT YOUR BOSS.
SOONER OR LATER, THE TRUTH WILL OUT...

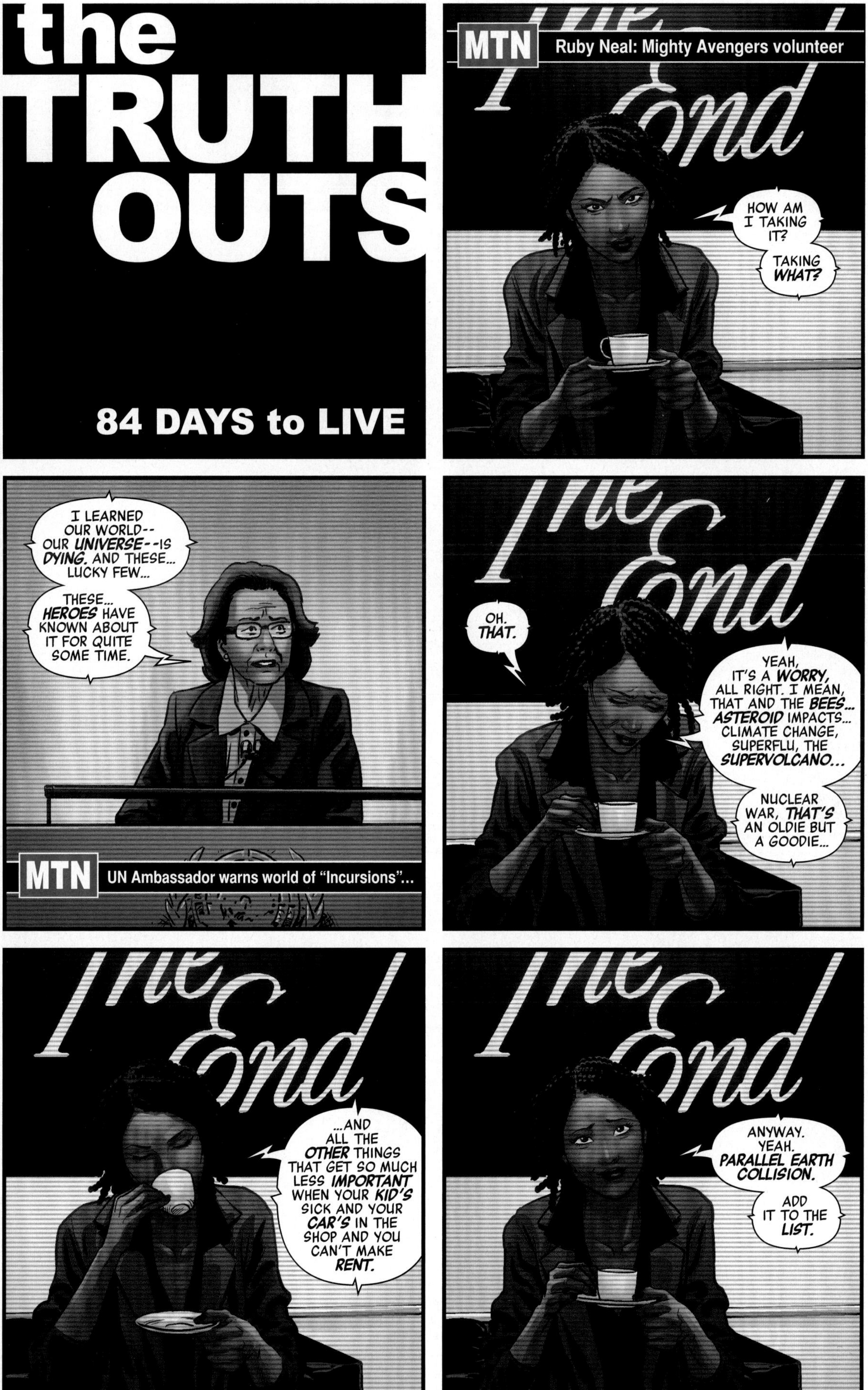

the TRUTH OUTS
84 DAYS to LIVE
MTN
Ruby Neal: Mighty Avengers volunteer
The End
HOW AM I TAKING IT?
TAKING WHAT?
I LEARNED OUR WORLD-- OUR UNIVERSE--IS DYING. AND THESE... LUCKY FEW...
THESE... HEROES HAVE KNOWN ABOUT IT FOR QUITE SOME TIME.
MTN
UN Ambassador warns world of "Incursions"...
The End
OH. THAT.
YEAH, IT'S A WORRY, ALL RIGHT. I MEAN, THAT AND THE BEES... ASTEROID IMPACTS... CLIMATE CHANGE, SUPERFLU, THE SUPERVOLCANO...
NUCLEAR WAR, THAT'S AN OLDIE BUT A GOODIE...
The End
...AND ALL THE OTHER THINGS THAT GET SO MUCH LESS IMPORTANT WHEN YOUR KID'S SICK AND YOUR CAR'S IN THE SHOP AND YOU CAN'T MAKE RENT.
The End
ANYWAY. YEAH. PARALLEL EARTH COLLISION.
ADD IT TO THE LIST.

MESSED-UP STUFF

39 DAYS to LIVE

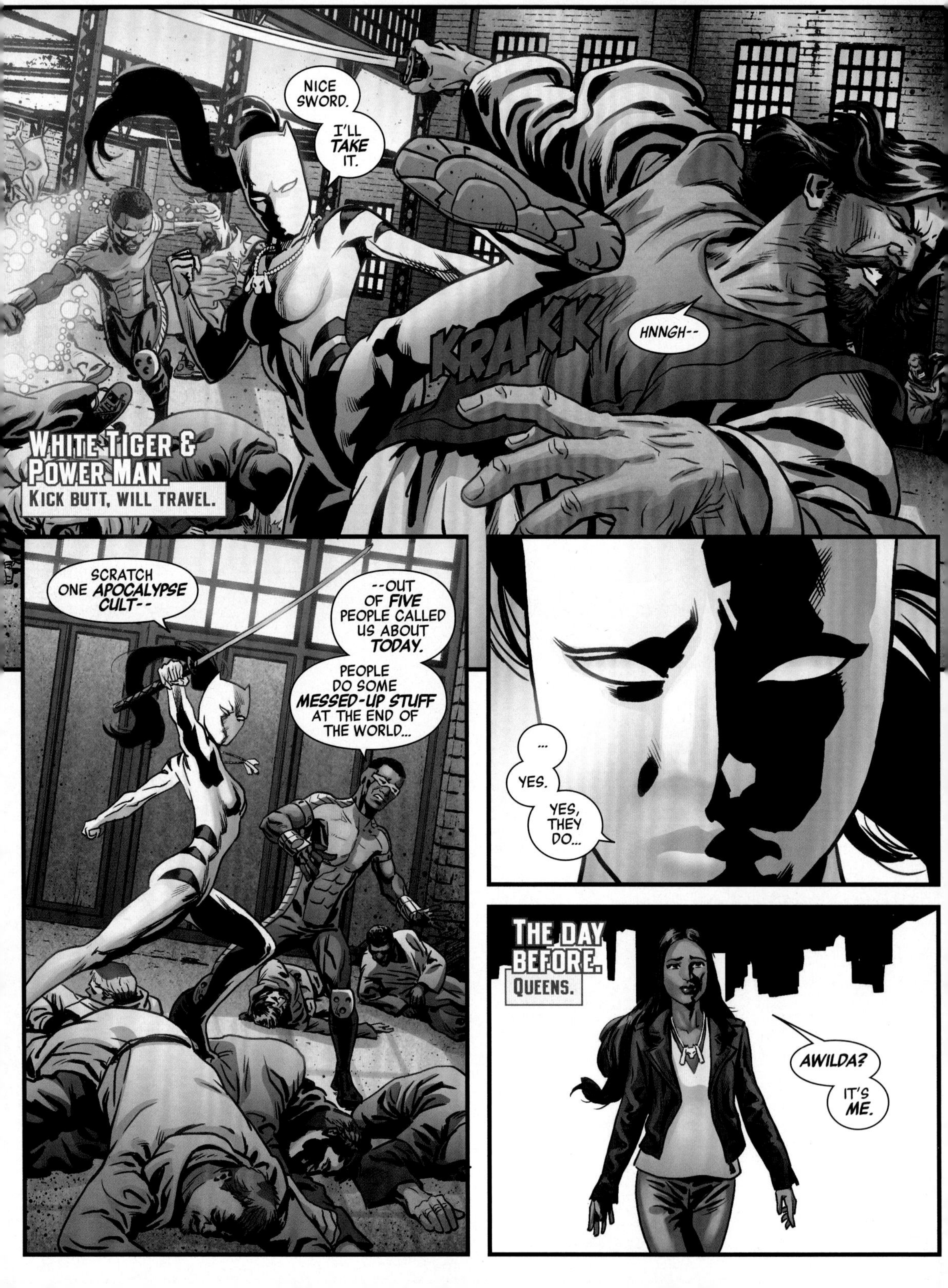

NICE SWORD.
I'LL TAKE IT.
KRAKK
HNNGH--
WHITE TIGER & POWER MAN.
KICK BUTT, WILL TRAVEL.
SCRATCH ONE APOCALYPSE CULT--
--OUT OF FIVE PEOPLE CALLED US ABOUT TODAY.
PEOPLE DO SOME MESSED-UP STUFF AT THE END OF THE WORLD...
...
YES.
YES, THEY DO...
THE DAY BEFORE.
QUEENS.
AWILDA?
IT'S ME.

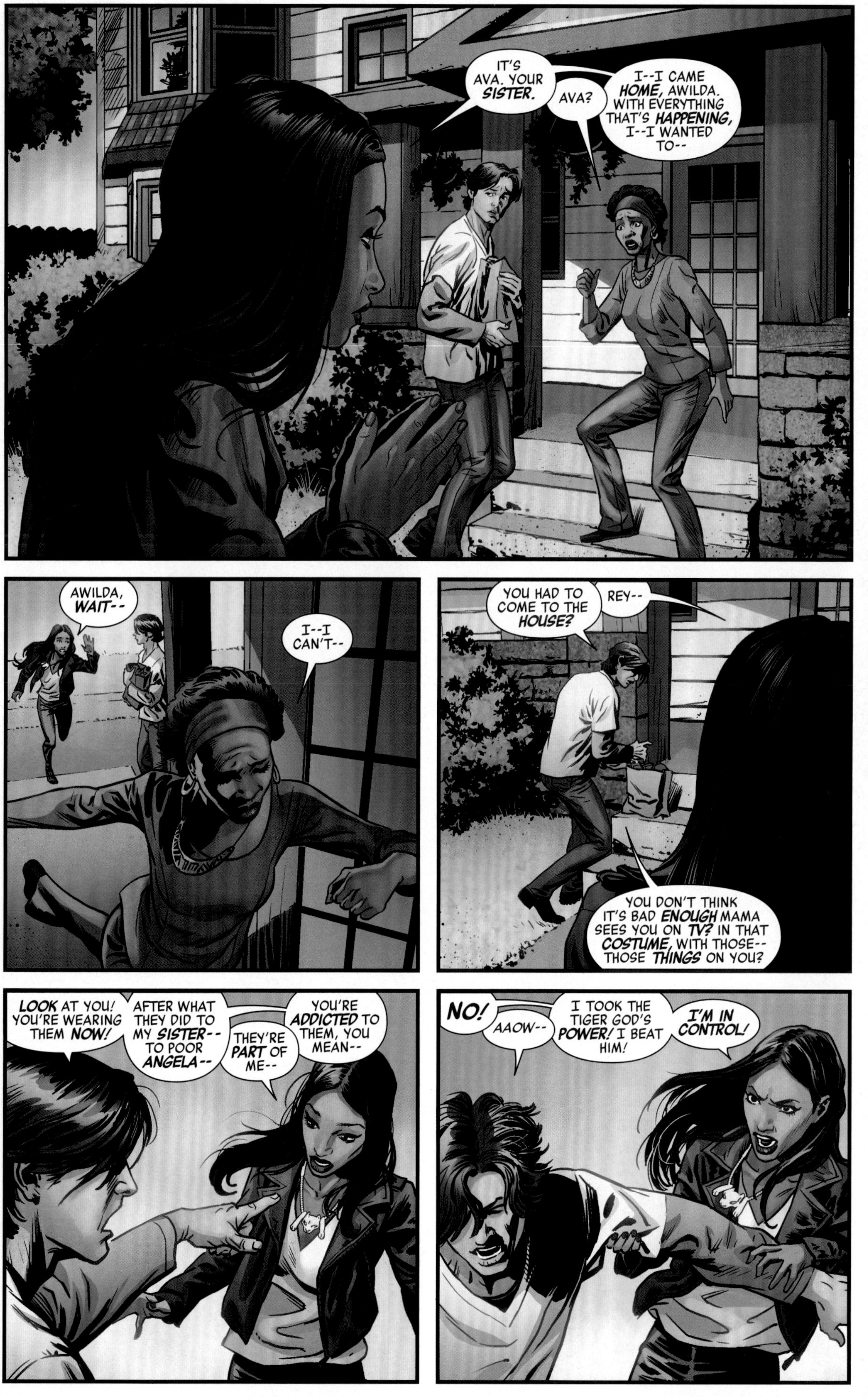
IT'S AVA. YOUR SISTER.
AVA?
I--I CAME HOME, AWILDA. WITH EVERYTHING THAT'S HAPPENING, I--I WANTED TO--
AWILDA, WAIT--
I--I CAN'T--
YOU HAD TO COME TO THE HOUSE?
REY--
YOU DON'T THINK IT'S BAD ENOUGH MAMA SEES YOU ON TV? IN THAT COSTUME, WITH THOSE-- THOSE THINGS ON YOU?
LOOK AT YOU! YOU'RE WEARING THEM NOW!
AFTER WHAT THEY DID TO MY SISTER-- TO POOR ANGELA--
THEY'RE PART OF ME--
YOU'RE ADDICTED TO THEM, YOU MEAN--
NO!
AAOW--
I TOOK THE TIGER GOD'S POWER! I BEAT HIM!
I'M IN CONTROL!

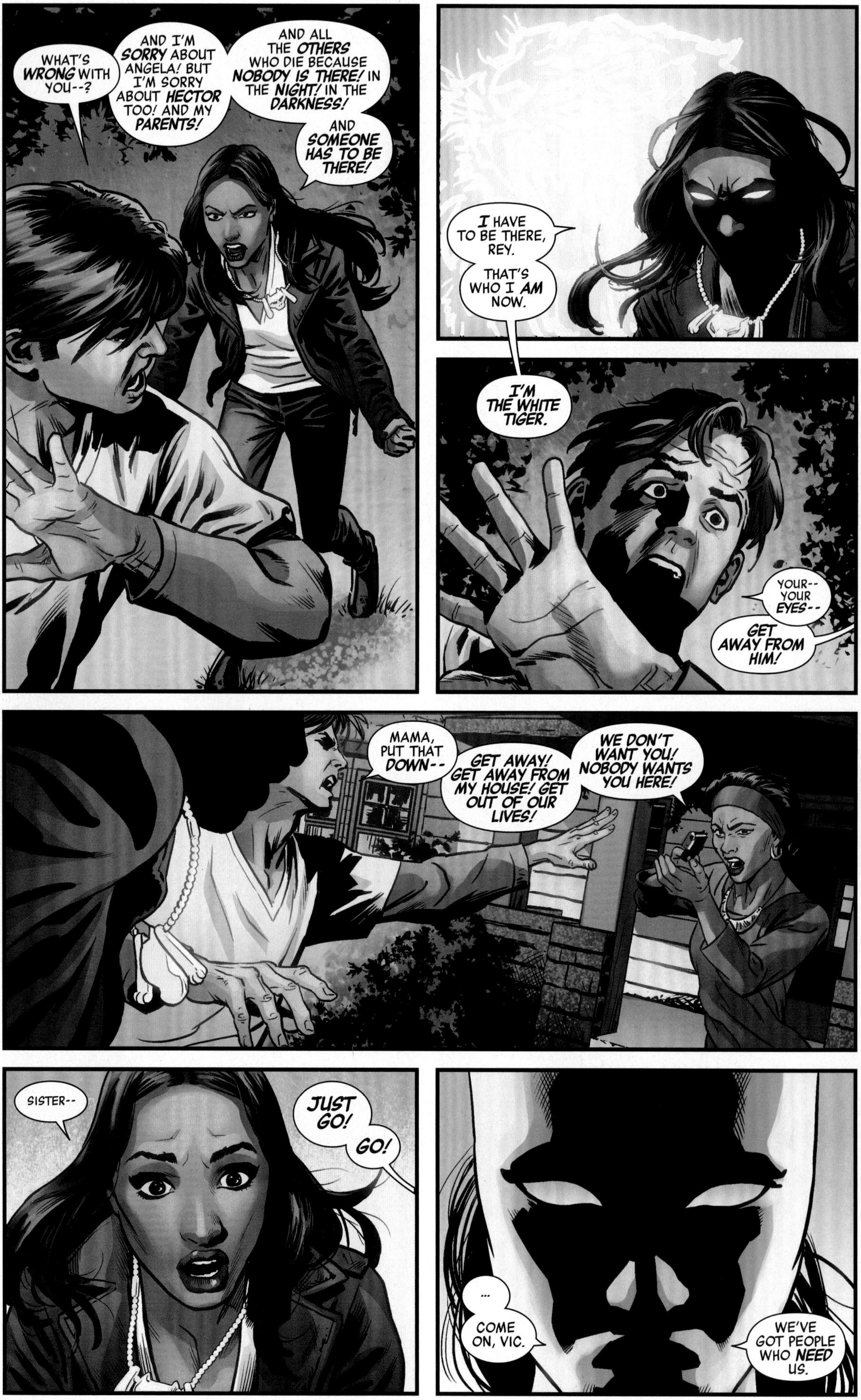
WHAT'S WRONG WITH YOU--?
AND I'M SORRY ABOUT ANGELA! BUT I'M SORRY ABOUT HECTOR TOO! AND MY PARENTS!
AND ALL THE OTHERS WHO DIE BECAUSE NOBODY IS THERE! IN THE NIGHT! IN THE DARKNESS!
AND SOMEONE HAS TO BE THERE!
I HAVE TO BE THERE, REY.
THAT'S WHO I AM NOW.
I'M THE WHITE TIGER.
YOUR-- YOUR EYES--
GET AWAY FROM HIM!
MAMA, PUT THAT DOWN--
GET AWAY! GET AWAY FROM MY HOUSE! GET OUT OF OUR LIVES!
WE DON'T WANT YOU! NOBODY WANTS YOU HERE!
SISTER--
JUST GO!
GO!
...
COME ON, VIC.
WE'VE GOT PEOPLE WHO NEED US.

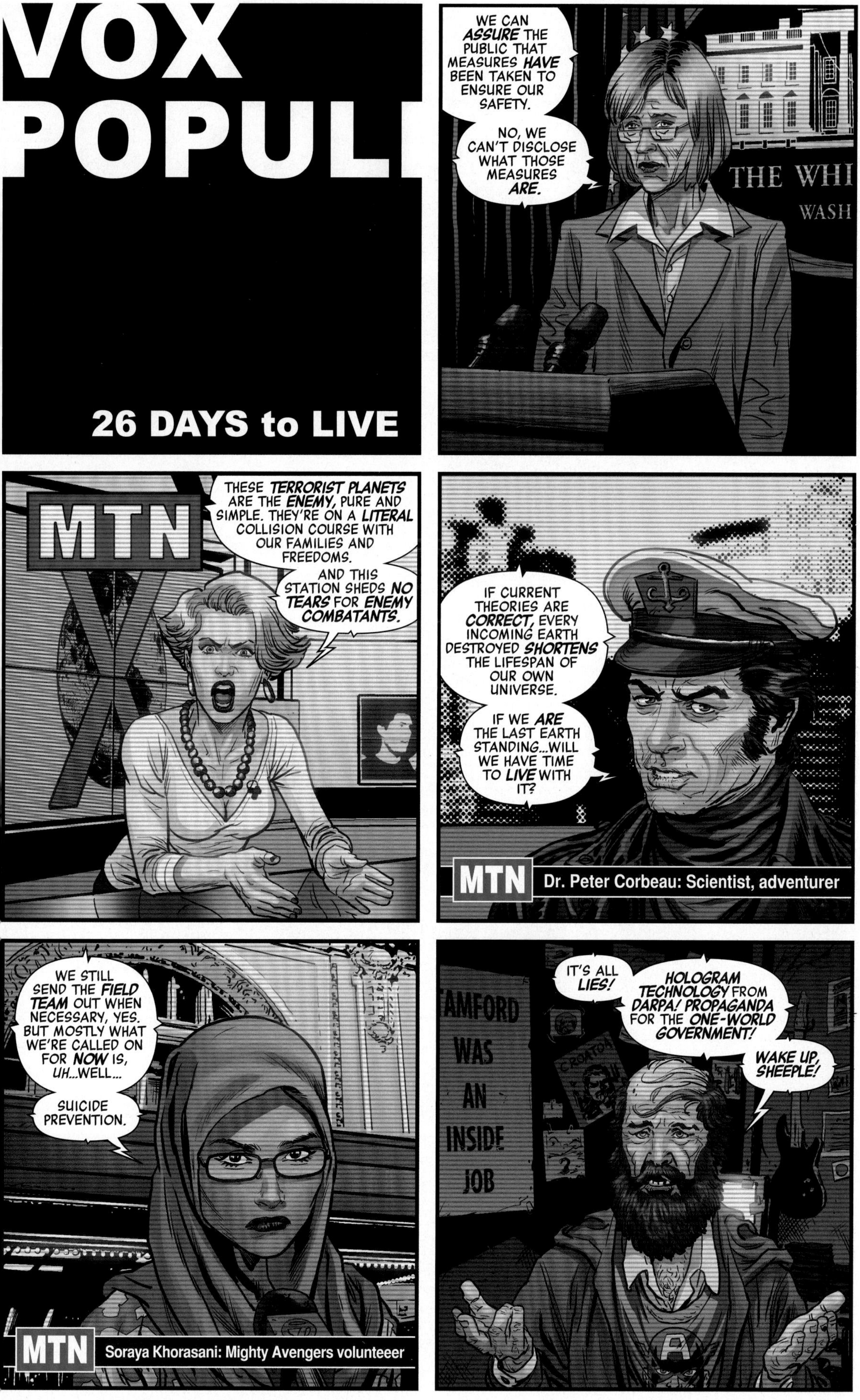
VOX POPULI
26 DAYS to LIVE
WE CAN ASSURE THE PUBLIC THAT MEASURES HAVE BEEN TAKEN TO ENSURE OUR SAFETY.
NO, WE CAN'T DISCLOSE WHAT THOSE MEASURES ARE.
THE WHI
WASH
MTN
THESE TERRORIST PLANETS ARE THE ENEMY, PURE AND SIMPLE. THEY'RE ON A LITERAL COLLISION COURSE WITH OUR FAMILIES AND FREEDOMS.
AND THIS STATION SHEDS NO TEARS FOR ENEMY COMBATANTS.
IF CURRENT THEORIES ARE CORRECT, EVERY INCOMING EARTH DESTROYED SHORTENS THE LIFESPAN OF OUR OWN UNIVERSE.
IF WE ARE THE LAST EARTH STANDING...WILL WE HAVE TIME TO LIVE WITH IT?
MTN
Dr. Peter Corbeau: Scientist, adventurer
WE STILL SEND THE FIELD TEAM OUT WHEN NECESSARY, YES. BUT MOSTLY WHAT WE'RE CALLED ON FOR NOW IS, UH...WELL...
SUICIDE PREVENTION.
MTN
Soraya Khorasani: Mighty Avengers volunteeer
IT'S ALL LIES!
HOLOGRAM TECHNOLOGY FROM DARPA! PROPAGANDA FOR THE ONE-WORLD GOVERNMENT!
WAKE UP, SHEEPLE!
STAMFORD WAS AN INSIDE JOB

WE, THE PEOPLE

19 DAYS to LIVE

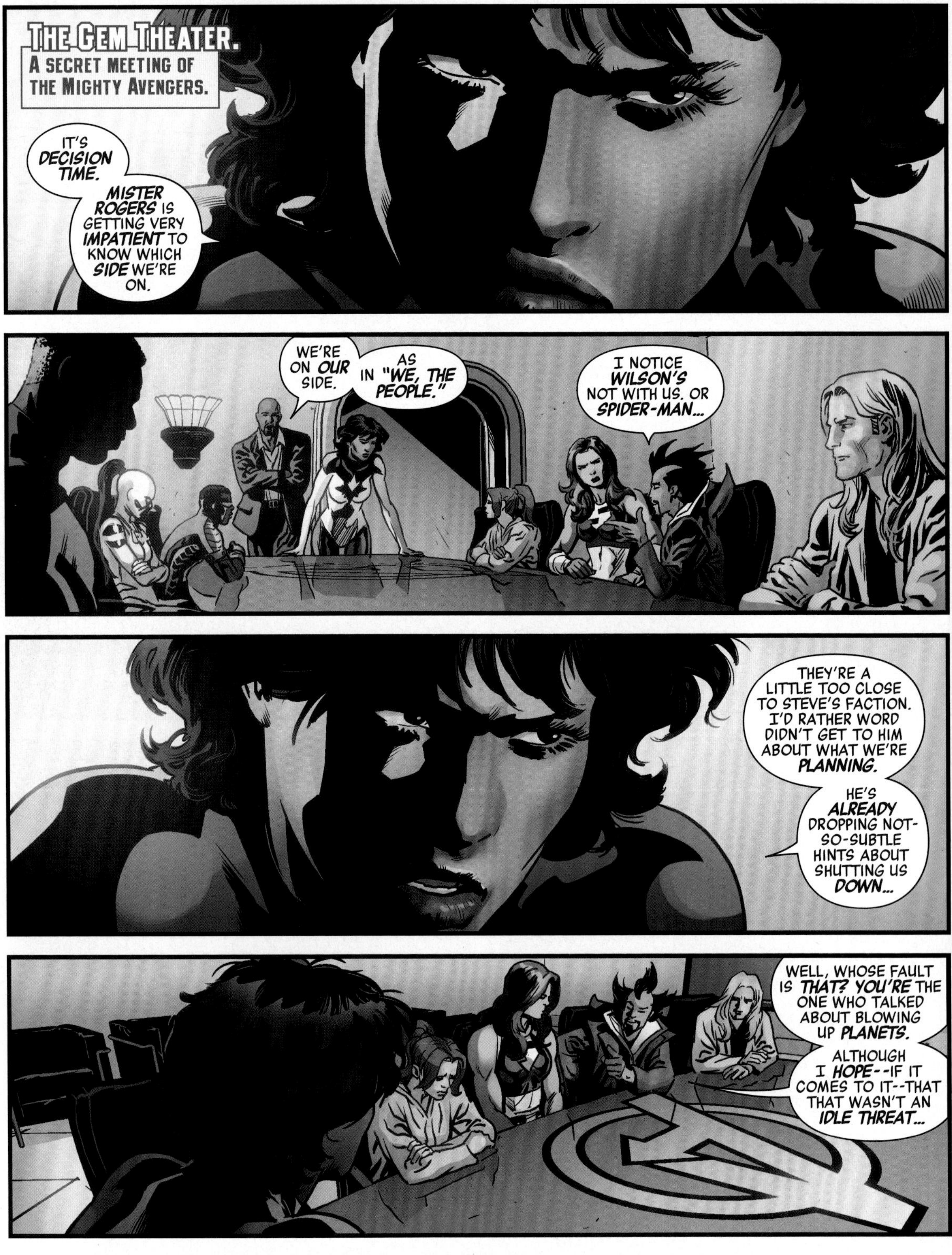
THE GEM THEATER.
A SECRET MEETING OF THE MIGHTY AVENGERS.
IT'S DECISION TIME.
MISTER ROGERS IS GETTING VERY IMPATIENT TO KNOW WHICH SIDE WE'RE ON.
WE'RE ON OUR SIDE.
AS IN "WE, THE PEOPLE."
I NOTICE WILSON'S NOT WITH US. OR SPIDER-MAN...
THEY'RE A LITTLE TOO CLOSE TO STEVE'S FACTION. I'D RATHER WORD DIDN'T GET TO HIM ABOUT WHAT WE'RE PLANNING.
HE'S ALREADY DROPPING NOT-SO-SUBTLE HINTS ABOUT SHUTTING US DOWN...
WELL, WHOSE FAULT IS THAT? YOU'RE THE ONE WHO TALKED ABOUT BLOWING UP PLANETS.
ALTHOUGH I HOPE--IF IT COMES TO IT--THAT THAT WASN'T AN IDLE THREAT...

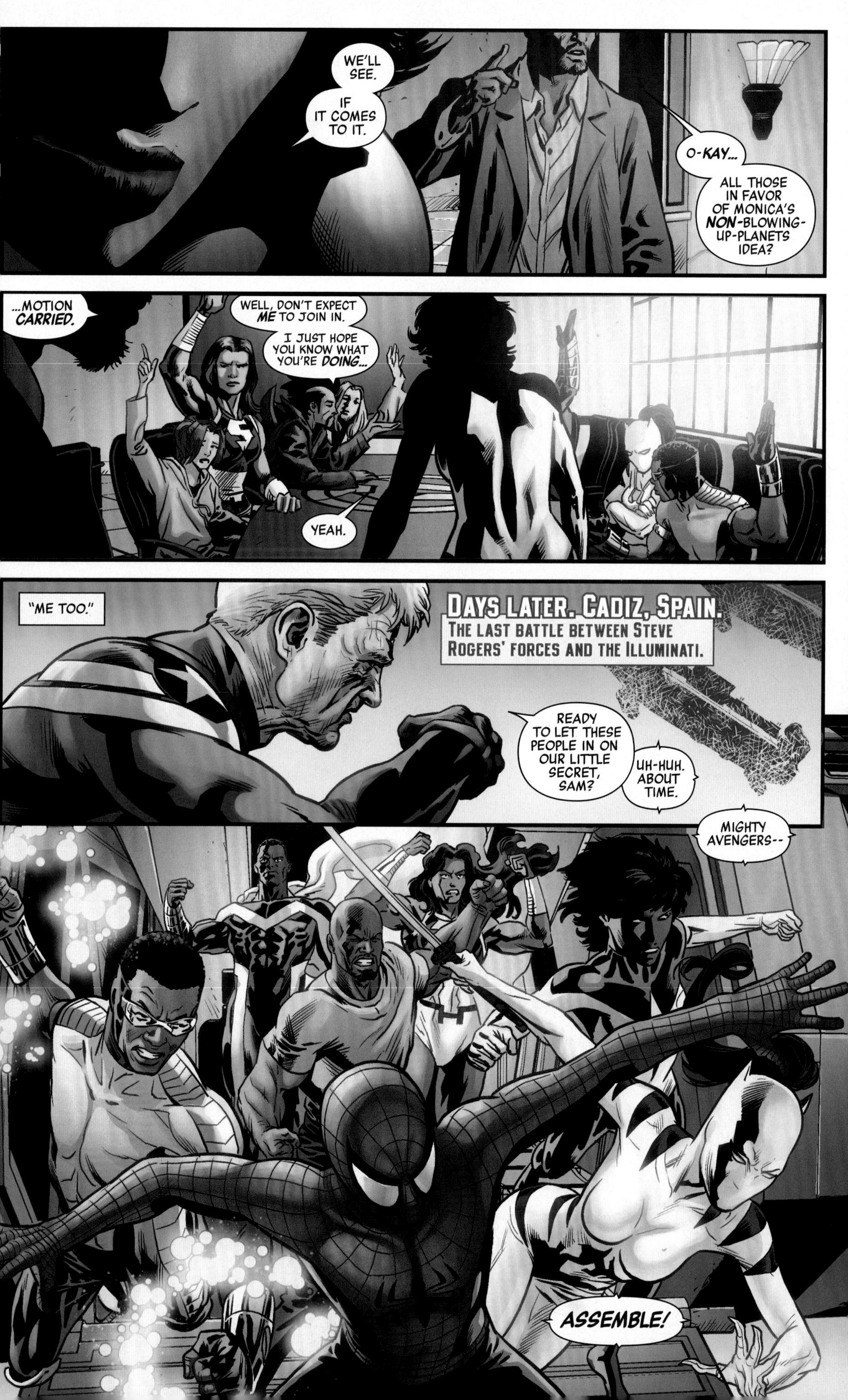
WE'LL SEE.
IF IT COMES TO IT.
O-KAY...
ALL THOSE IN FAVOR OF MONICA'S NON-BLOWING-UP-PLANETS IDEA?
...MOTION CARRIED.
WELL, DON'T EXPECT ME TO JOIN IN.
I JUST HOPE YOU KNOW WHAT YOU'RE DOING...
YEAH.
"ME TOO."
DAYS LATER. CADIZ, SPAIN.
THE LAST BATTLE BETWEEN STEVE ROGERS' FORCES AND THE ILLUMINATI.
READY TO LET THESE PEOPLE IN ON OUR LITTLE SECRET, SAM?
UH-HUH. ABOUT TIME.
MIGHTY AVENGERS--
ASSEMBLE!

KINGS and PRINCES

14 DAYS to LIVE

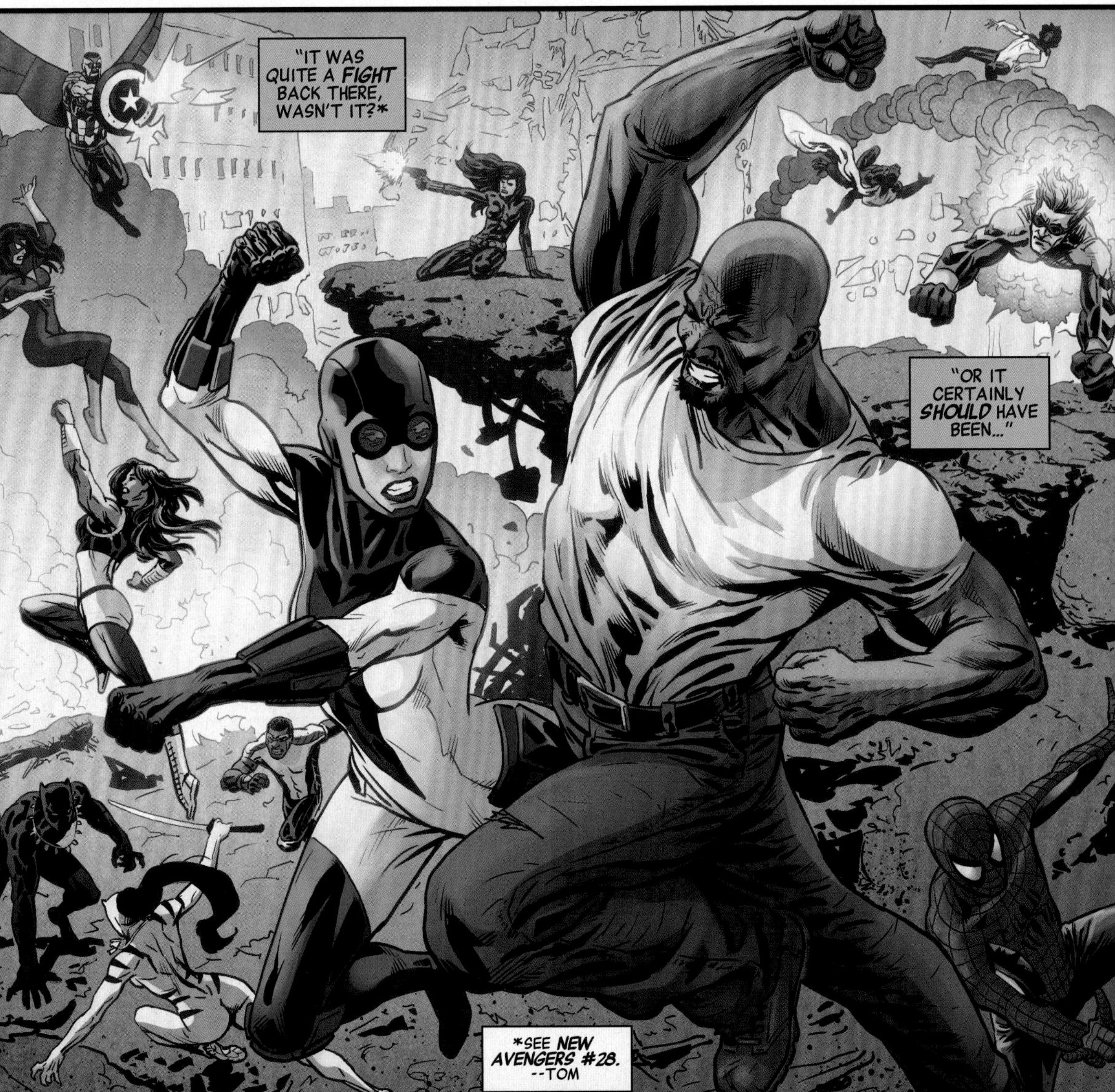
"IT WAS QUITE A FIGHT BACK THERE, WASN'T IT?*
"OR IT CERTAINLY SHOULD HAVE BEEN..."
*SEE NEW AVENGERS #28. --TOM

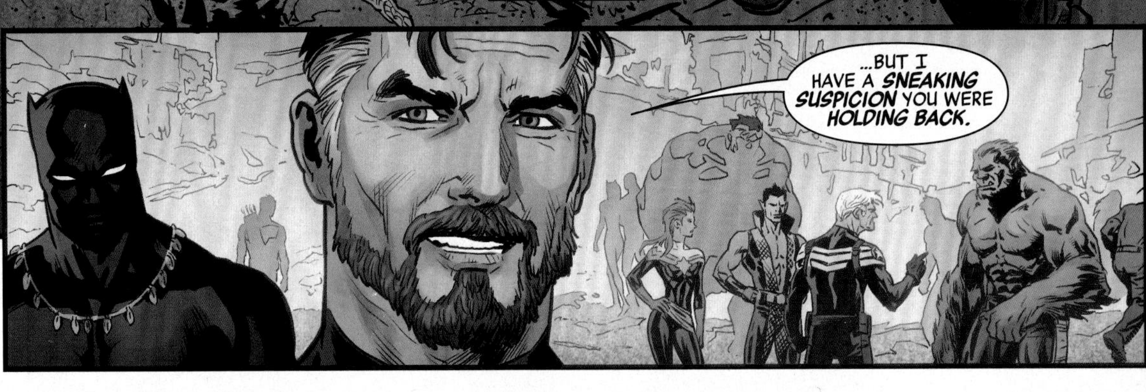
...BUT I HAVE A SNEAKING SUSPICION YOU WERE HOLDING BACK.

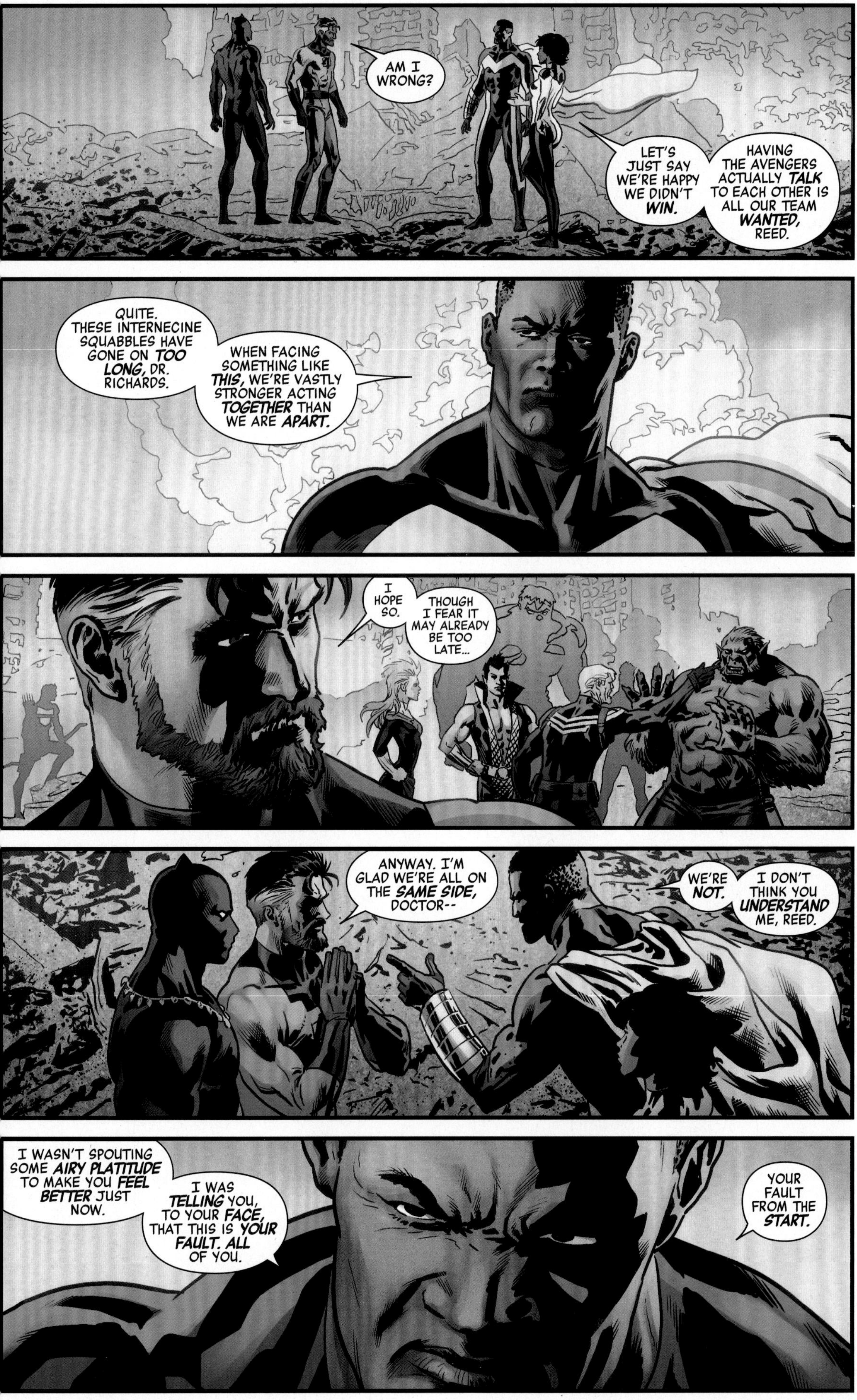
AM I WRONG?
LET'S JUST SAY WE'RE HAPPY WE DIDN'T WIN.
HAVING THE AVENGERS ACTUALLY TALK TO EACH OTHER IS ALL OUR TEAM WANTED, REED.
QUITE. THESE INTERNECINE SQUABBLES HAVE GONE ON TOO LONG, DR. RICHARDS.
WHEN FACING SOMETHING LIKE THIS, WE'RE VASTLY STRONGER ACTING TOGETHER THAN WE ARE APART.
I HOPE SO.
THOUGH I FEAR IT MAY ALREADY BE TOO LATE...
ANYWAY. I'M GLAD WE'RE ALL ON THE SAME SIDE, DOCTOR--
WE'RE NOT.
I DON'T THINK YOU UNDERSTAND ME, REED.
I WASN'T SPOUTING SOME AIRY PLATITUDE TO MAKE YOU FEEL BETTER JUST NOW.
I WAS TELLING YOU, TO YOUR FACE, THAT THIS IS YOUR FAULT. ALL OF YOU.
YOUR FAULT FROM THE START.

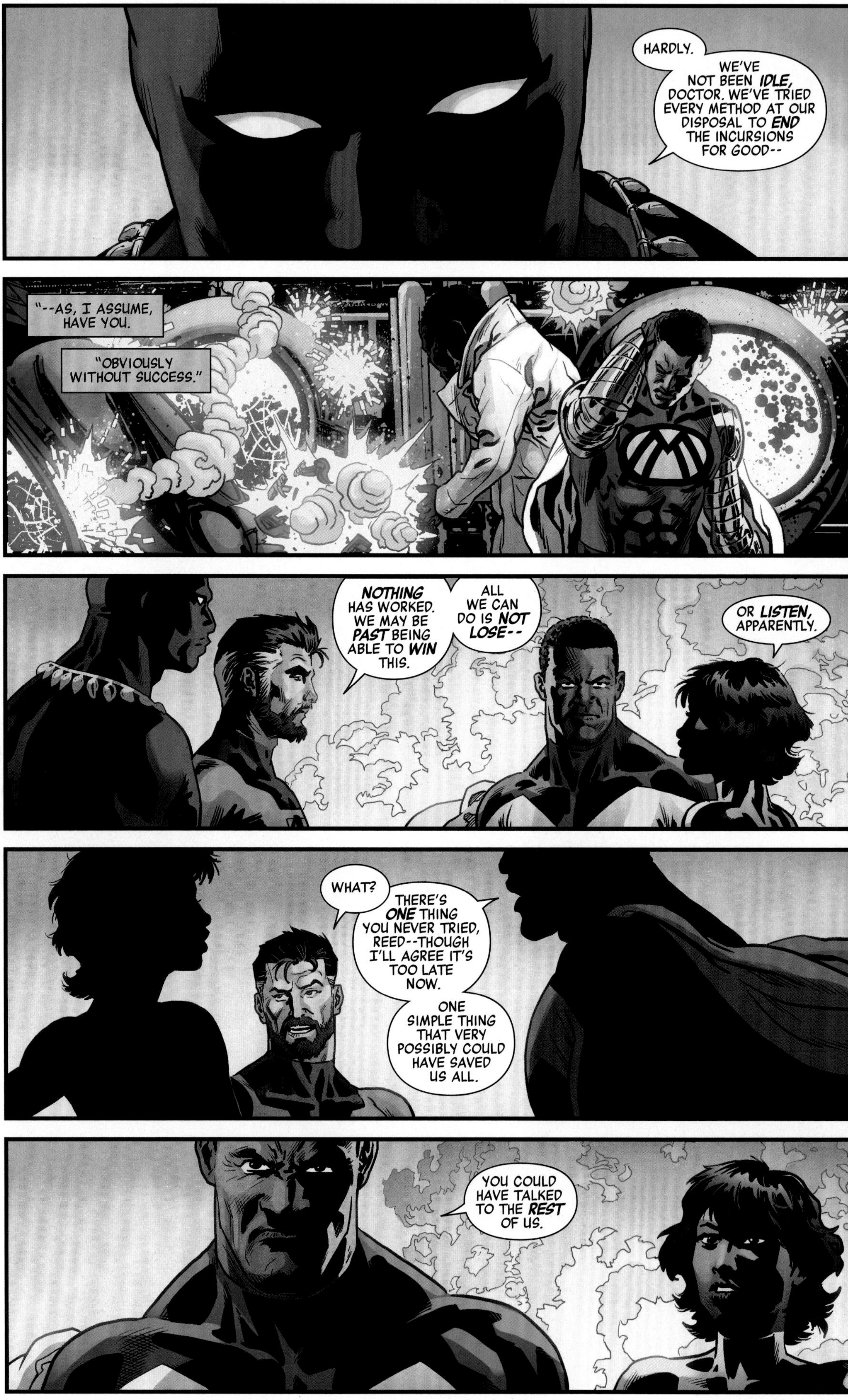
HARDLY.
WE'VE NOT BEEN IDLE, DOCTOR. WE'VE TRIED EVERY METHOD AT OUR DISPOSAL TO END THE INCURSIONS FOR GOOD--
"--AS, I ASSUME, HAVE YOU.
"OBVIOUSLY WITHOUT SUCCESS."
NOTHING HAS WORKED. WE MAY BE PAST BEING ABLE TO WIN THIS.
ALL WE CAN DO IS NOT LOSE--
OR LISTEN, APPARENTLY.
WHAT?
THERE'S ONE THING YOU NEVER TRIED, REED--THOUGH I'LL AGREE IT'S TOO LATE NOW.
ONE SIMPLE THING THAT VERY POSSIBLY COULD HAVE SAVED US ALL.
YOU COULD HAVE TALKED TO THE REST OF US.

DR. BRASHEAR-- WE COULD NOT INVITE JUST ANYBODY INTO--

SPARE ME. GOD KNOWS I'D RATHER NOT BE PART OF YOUR ILLUMINATI, OR WHATEVER YOU CALL YOURSELVES.

I'VE SEEN HOW YOU TREAT DISSENTING VOICES.

AND THAT'S THE ISSUE IN A NUTSHELL, T'CHALLA. A PLURALITY OF VOICES.

"WE, THE PEOPLE."

YOU COULD HAVE HAD FAITH IN YOUR PEERS. ALL OF US. WORKING TOGETHER, RIGHT FROM THE START, WE MIGHT HAVE STOOD A CHANCE.

OR NOT. WE'LL NEVER KNOW.

BECAUSE YEARS AGO, YOU FORMED AN ELITE GROUP ON THE BASIS THAT YOU KNEW BEST.

WELL, HOW'S THAT WORKING OUT, DOCTOR?

ADAM-- YOU'RE NOT BEING FAIR--

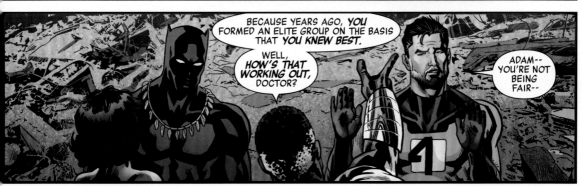

AND YOU.

YOU DISCOVERED A CRISIS THAT AFFECTS EVERY LIVING THING IN THE UNIVERSE--IN THE MULTIVERSE--

--AND YOU CHOSE TO SHARE IT WITH FIVE PEOPLE.

WITH THE RIGHT FIVE PEOPLE, DR. BRASHEAR.

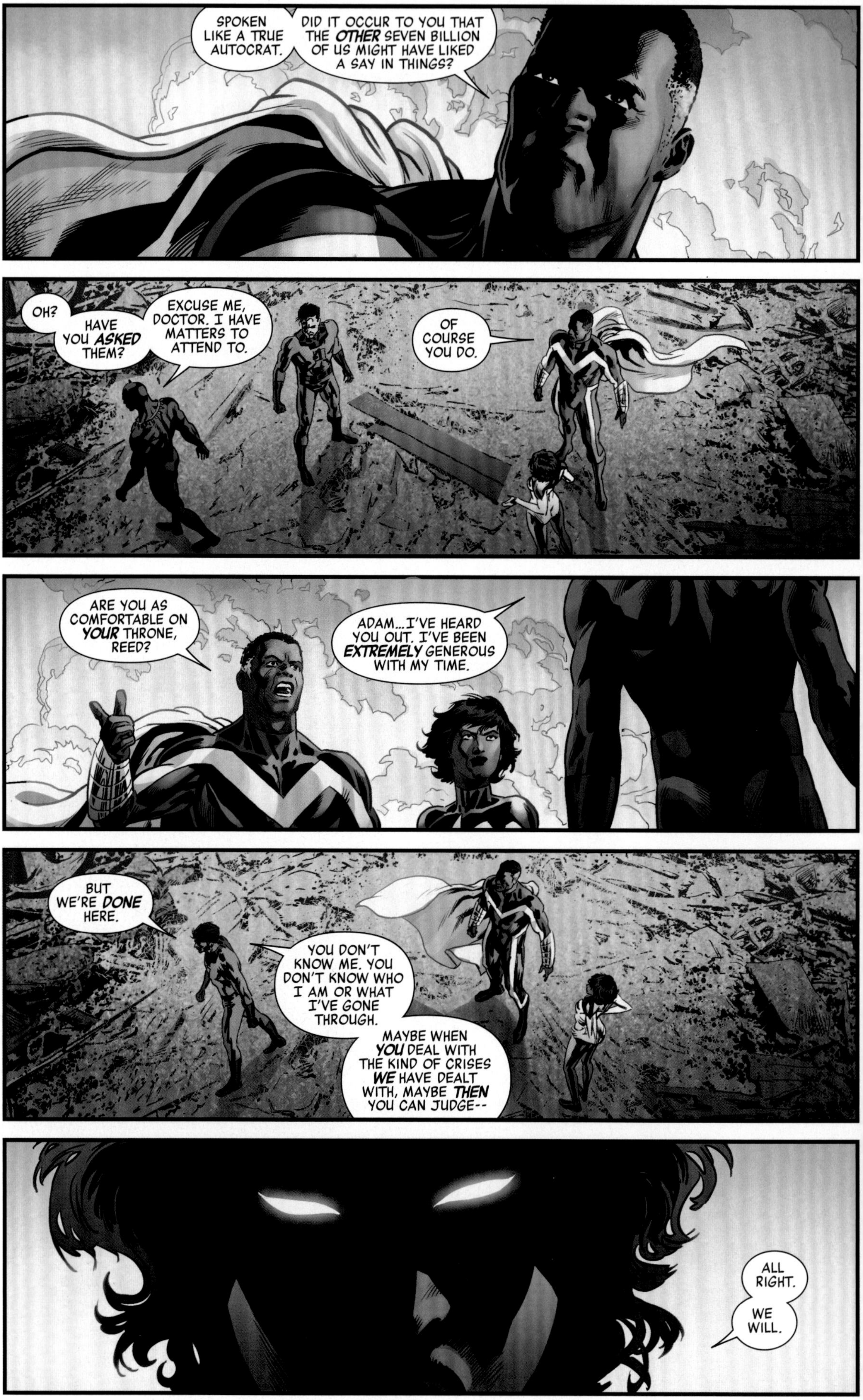
SPOKEN LIKE A TRUE AUTOCRAT.
DID IT OCCUR TO YOU THAT THE OTHER SEVEN BILLION OF US MIGHT HAVE LIKED A SAY IN THINGS?
OH?
HAVE YOU ASKED THEM?
EXCUSE ME, DOCTOR. I HAVE MATTERS TO ATTEND TO.
OF COURSE YOU DO.
ARE YOU AS COMFORTABLE ON YOUR THRONE, REED?
ADAM...I'VE HEARD YOU OUT. I'VE BEEN EXTREMELY GENEROUS WITH MY TIME.
BUT WE'RE DONE HERE.
YOU DON'T KNOW ME. YOU DON'T KNOW WHO I AM OR WHAT I'VE GONE THROUGH.
MAYBE WHEN YOU DEAL WITH THE KIND OF CRISES WE HAVE DEALT WITH, MAYBE THEN YOU CAN JUDGE--
ALL RIGHT.
WE WILL.

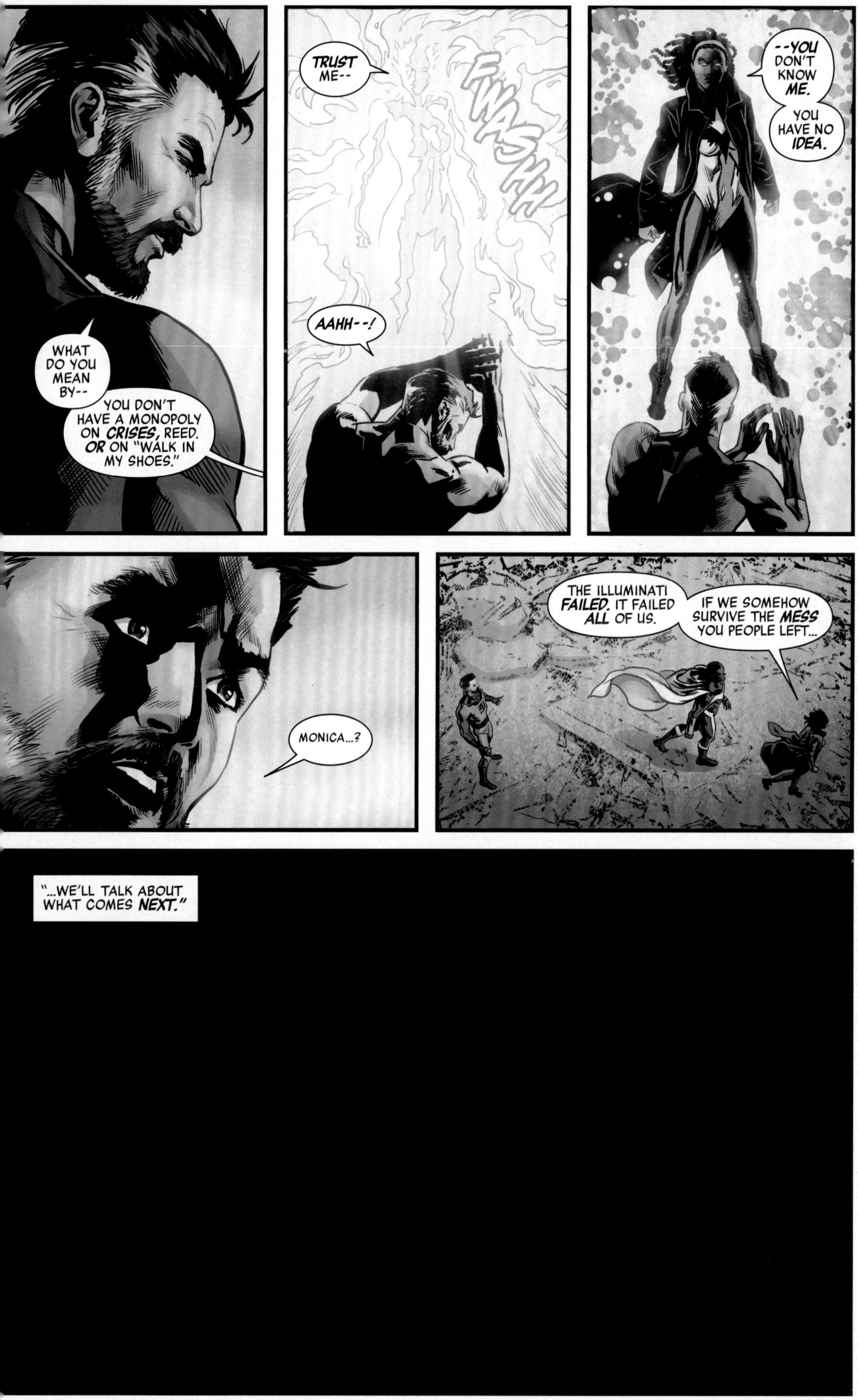
WHAT DO YOU MEAN BY--
YOU DON'T HAVE A MONOPOLY ON CRISES, REED. OR ON "WALK IN MY SHOES."
TRUST ME--
FWASHH
AAHH--!
--YOU DON'T KNOW ME.
YOU HAVE NO IDEA.
MONICA...?
THE ILLUMINATI FAILED. IT FAILED ALL OF US.
IF WE SOMEHOW SURVIVE THE MESS YOU PEOPLE LEFT...
"...WE'LL TALK ABOUT WHAT COMES NEXT."

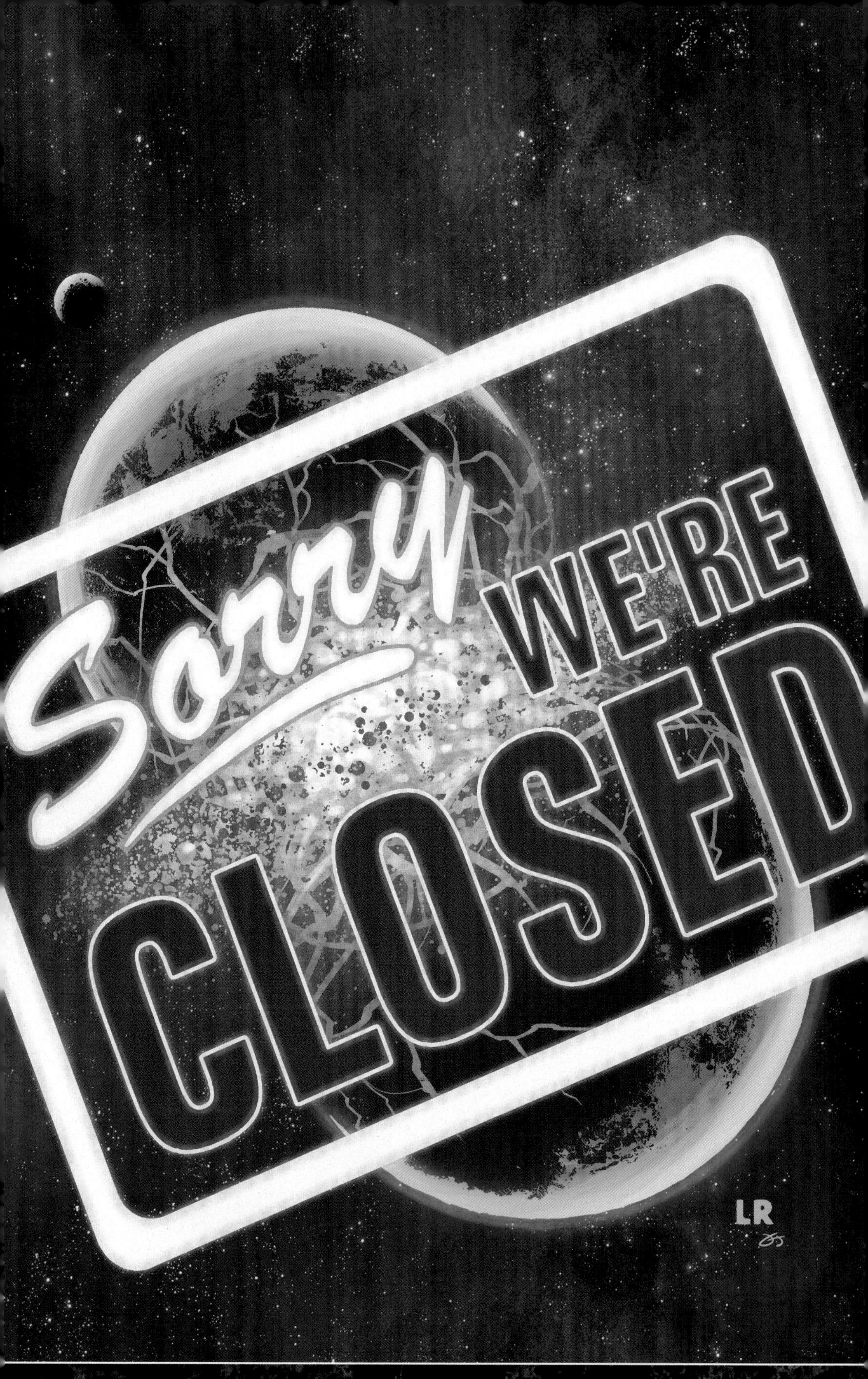
Sorry
WE'RE
CLOSED
LR

CAPTAIN AMERICA AND THE MIGHTY AVENGERS #9

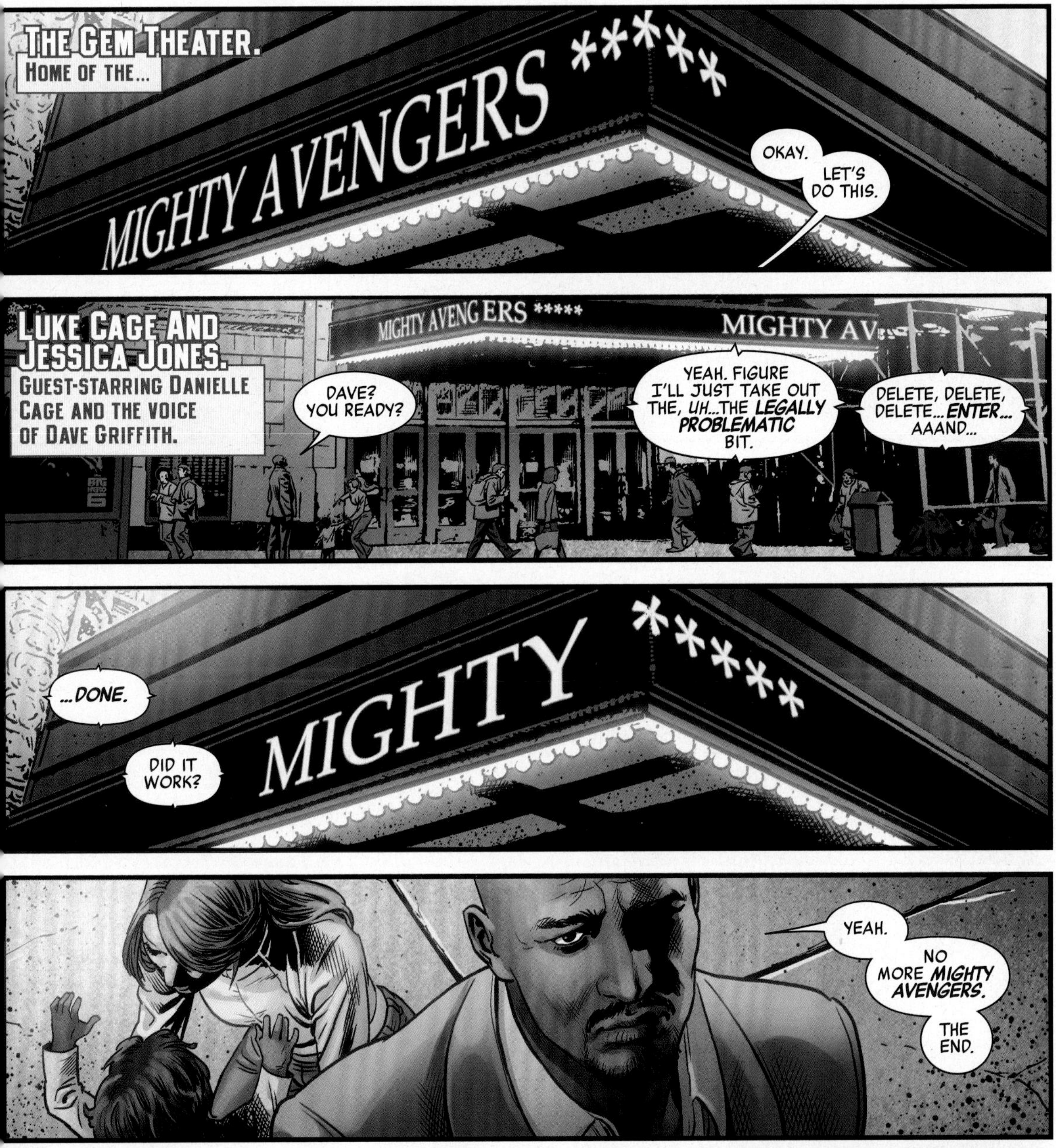
THE GEM THEATER.
HOME OF THE...
MIGHTY AVENGERS *****
OKAY.
LET'S DO THIS.
LUKE CAGE AND JESSICA JONES.
GUEST-STARRING DANIELLE CAGE AND THE VOICE OF DAVE GRIFFITH.
MIGHTY AVENGERS *****
MIGHTY AV
DAVE? YOU READY?
YEAH. FIGURE I'LL JUST TAKE OUT THE, UH...THE LEGALLY PROBLEMATIC BIT.
DELETE, DELETE, DELETE...ENTER... AAAND...
MIGHTY *****
...DONE.
DID IT WORK?
YEAH.
NO MORE MIGHTY AVENGERS.
THE END.

SORRY, WE'RE CLOSED

242 MINUTES TO LIVE

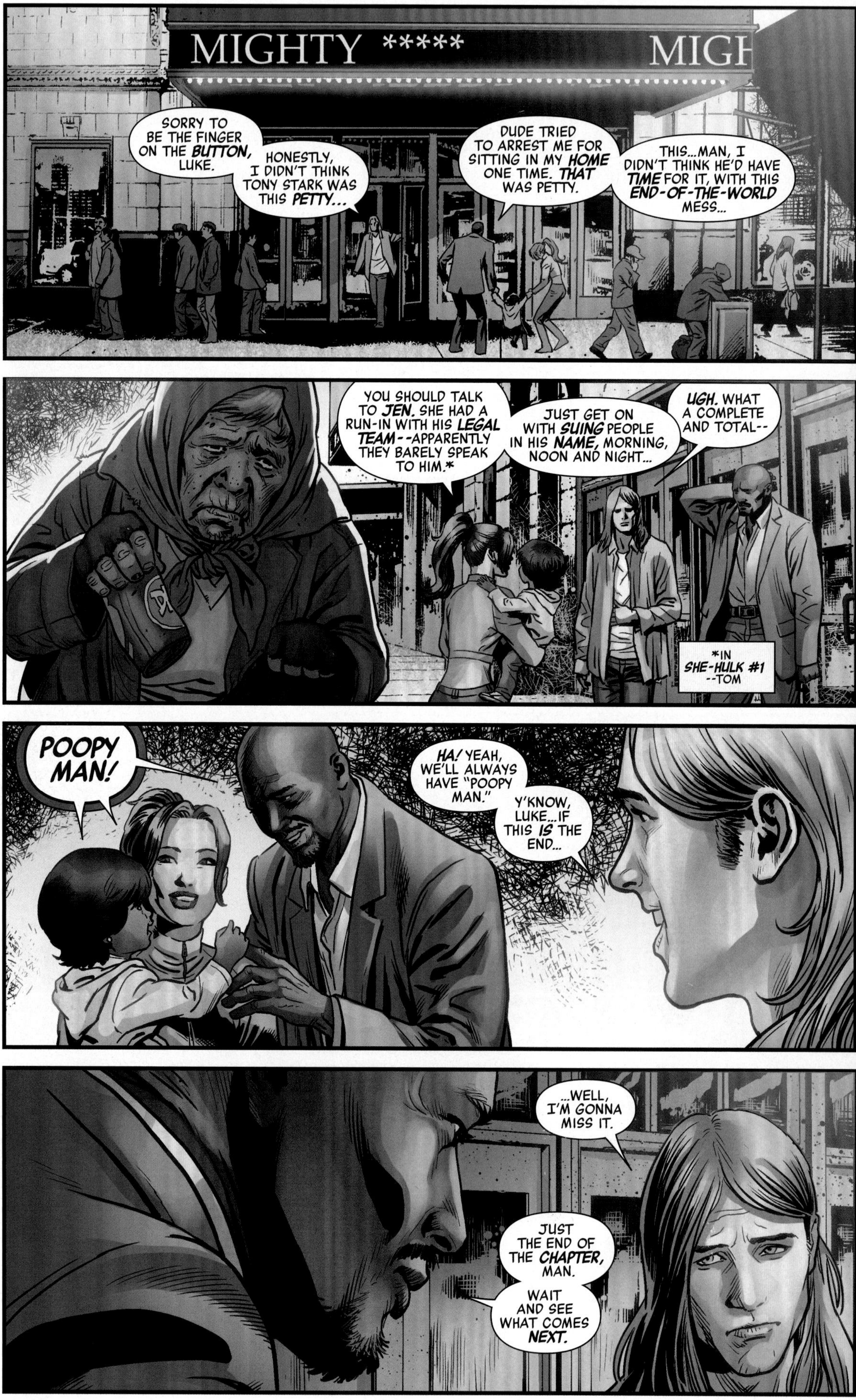
MIGHTY ***** MIGH
SORRY TO BE THE FINGER ON THE BUTTON, LUKE.
HONESTLY, I DIDN'T THINK TONY STARK WAS THIS PETTY...
DUDE TRIED TO ARREST ME FOR SITTING IN MY HOME ONE TIME. THAT WAS PETTY.
THIS...MAN, I DIDN'T THINK HE'D HAVE TIME FOR IT, WITH THIS END-OF-THE-WORLD MESS...
YOU SHOULD TALK TO JEN. SHE HAD A RUN-IN WITH HIS LEGAL TEAM--APPARENTLY THEY BARELY SPEAK TO HIM.*
JUST GET ON WITH SUING PEOPLE IN HIS NAME, MORNING, NOON AND NIGHT...
UGH. WHAT A COMPLETE AND TOTAL--
*IN SHE-HULK #1 --TOM
POOPY MAN!
HA! YEAH, WE'LL ALWAYS HAVE "POOPY MAN."
Y'KNOW, LUKE...IF THIS IS THE END...
...WELL, I'M GONNA MISS IT.
JUST THE END OF THE CHAPTER, MAN.
WAIT AND SEE WHAT COMES NEXT.

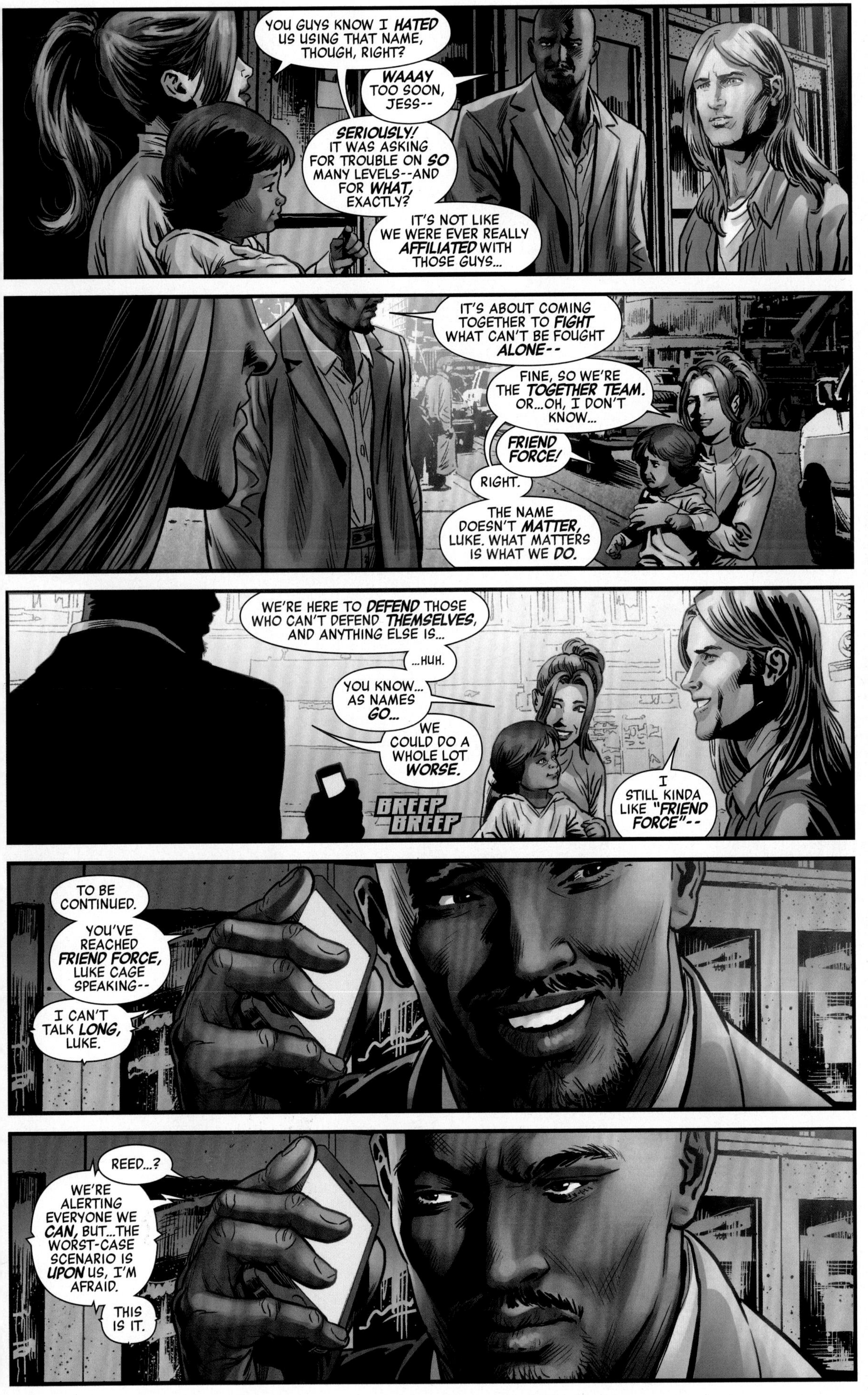
YOU GUYS KNOW I HATED US USING THAT NAME, THOUGH, RIGHT?
WAAAY TOO SOON, JESS--
SERIOUSLY! IT WAS ASKING FOR TROUBLE ON SO MANY LEVELS--AND FOR WHAT, EXACTLY?
IT'S NOT LIKE WE WERE EVER REALLY AFFILIATED WITH THOSE GUYS...
IT'S ABOUT COMING TOGETHER TO FIGHT WHAT CAN'T BE FOUGHT ALONE--
FINE, SO WE'RE THE TOGETHER TEAM. OR...OH, I DON'T KNOW...
FRIEND FORCE!
RIGHT.
THE NAME DOESN'T MATTER, LUKE. WHAT MATTERS IS WHAT WE DO.
WE'RE HERE TO DEFEND THOSE WHO CAN'T DEFEND THEMSELVES, AND ANYTHING ELSE IS...
...HUH.
YOU KNOW... AS NAMES GO...
WE COULD DO A WHOLE LOT WORSE.
BREEP BREEP
I STILL KINDA LIKE "FRIEND FORCE"--
TO BE CONTINUED.
YOU'VE REACHED FRIEND FORCE, LUKE CAGE SPEAKING--
I CAN'T TALK LONG, LUKE.
REED...?
WE'RE ALERTING EVERYONE WE CAN, BUT...THE WORST-CASE SCENARIO IS UPON US, I'M AFRAID.
THIS IS IT.

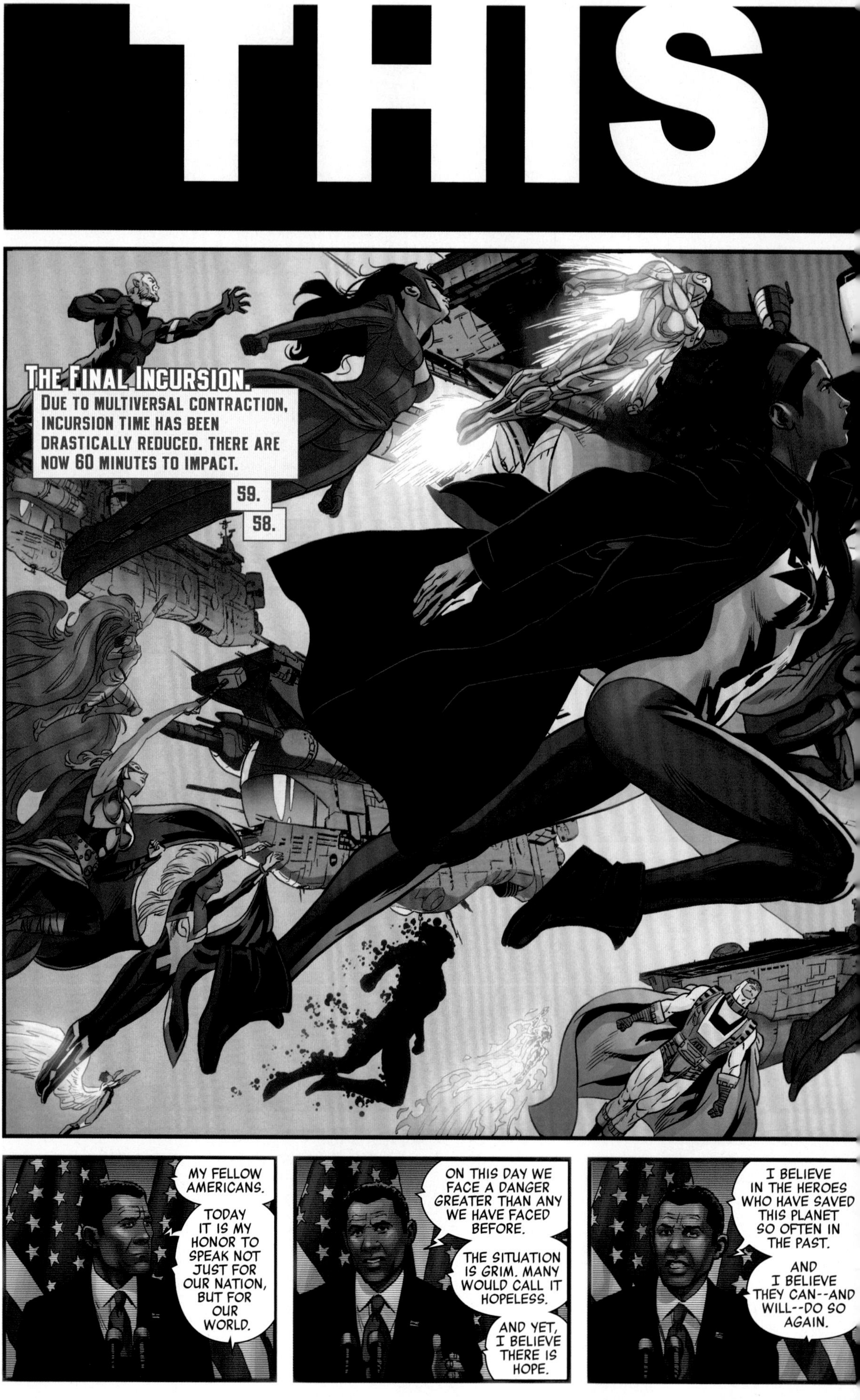
THIS
THE FINAL INCURSION.
DUE TO MULTIVERSAL CONTRACTION, INCURSION TIME HAS BEEN DRASTICALLY REDUCED. THERE ARE NOW 60 MINUTES TO IMPACT.
59.
58.
MY FELLOW AMERICANS.
TODAY IT IS MY HONOR TO SPEAK NOT JUST FOR OUR NATION, BUT FOR OUR WORLD.
ON THIS DAY WE FACE A DANGER GREATER THAN ANY WE HAVE FACED BEFORE.
THE SITUATION IS GRIM. MANY WOULD CALL IT HOPELESS.
AND YET, I BELIEVE THERE IS HOPE.
I BELIEVE IN THE HEROES WHO HAVE SAVED THIS PLANET SO OFTEN IN THE PAST.
AND I BELIEVE THEY CAN--AND WILL--DO SO AGAIN.

SIT

60 MINUTES TO LIVE

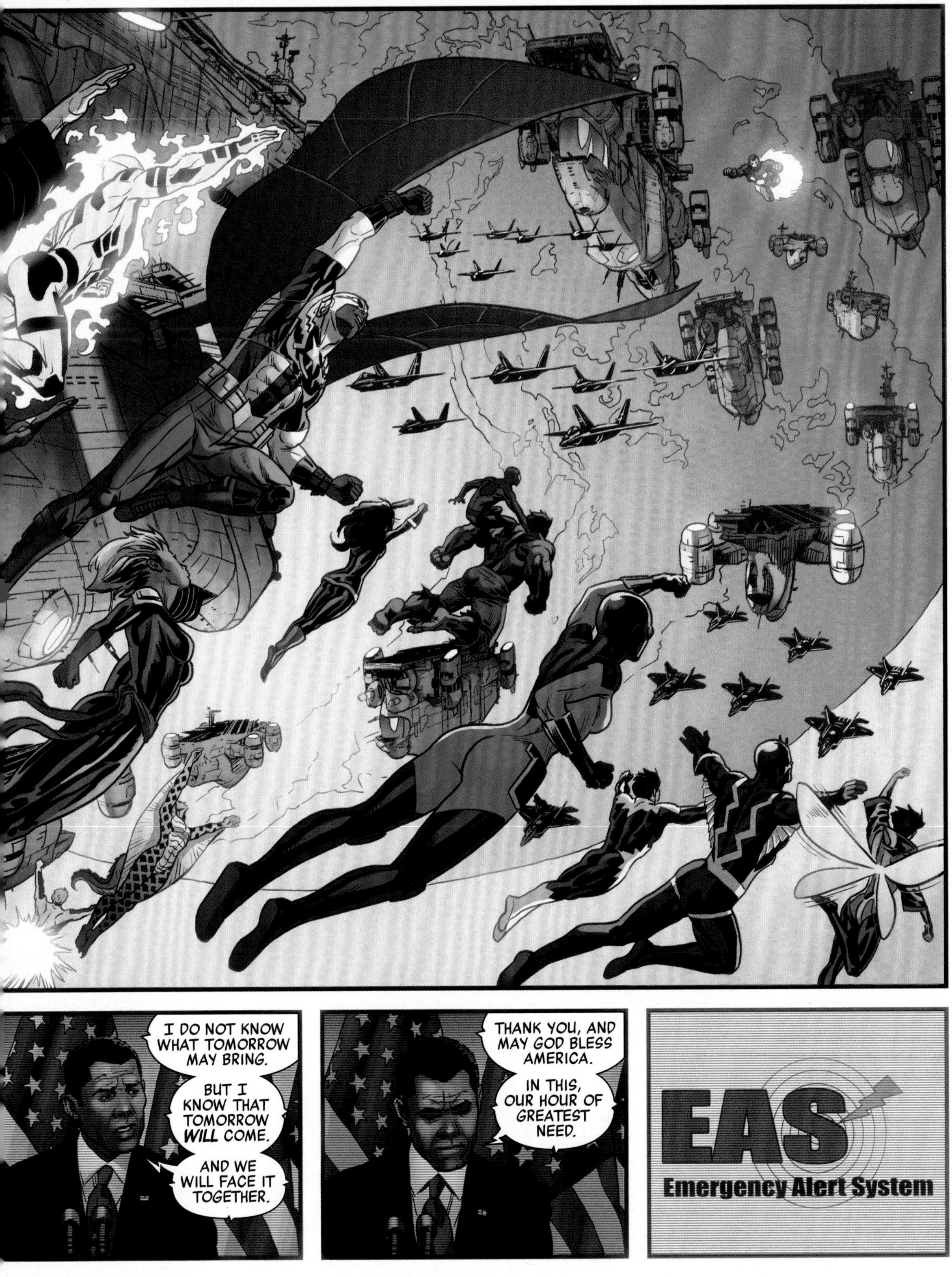

I DO NOT KNOW WHAT TOMORROW MAY BRING.
BUT I KNOW THAT TOMORROW *WILL* COME.
AND WE WILL FACE IT TOGETHER.
THANK YOU, AND MAY GOD BLESS AMERICA.
IN THIS, OUR HOUR OF GREATEST NEED.
EAS
Emergency Alert System

THE TERMS
57 MINUTES TO LIVE

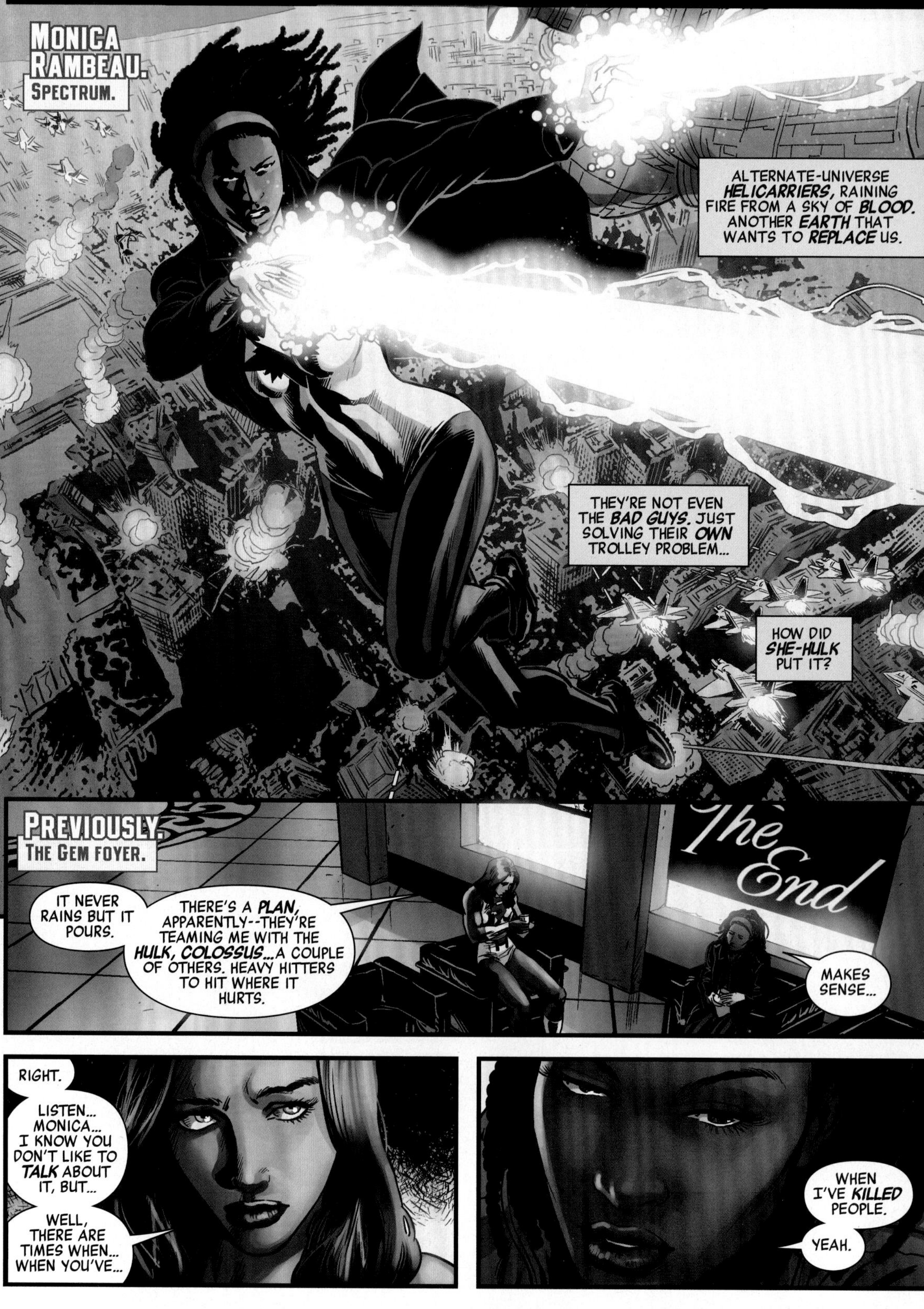

MONICA RAMBEAU.
SPECTRUM.
ALTERNATE-UNIVERSE HELICARRIERS, RAINING FIRE FROM A SKY OF BLOOD. ANOTHER EARTH THAT WANTS TO REPLACE US.
THEY'RE NOT EVEN THE BAD GUYS. JUST SOLVING THEIR OWN TROLLEY PROBLEM...
HOW DID SHE-HULK PUT IT?
PREVIOUSLY.
THE GEM FOYER.
The End
IT NEVER RAINS BUT IT POURS.
THERE'S A PLAN, APPARENTLY--THEY'RE TEAMING ME WITH THE HULK, COLOSSUS...A COUPLE OF OTHERS. HEAVY HITTERS TO HIT WHERE IT HURTS.
MAKES SENSE...
RIGHT.
LISTEN... MONICA... I KNOW YOU DON'T LIKE TO TALK ABOUT IT, BUT...
WELL, THERE ARE TIMES WHEN... WHEN YOU'VE...
WHEN I'VE KILLED PEOPLE.
YEAH.

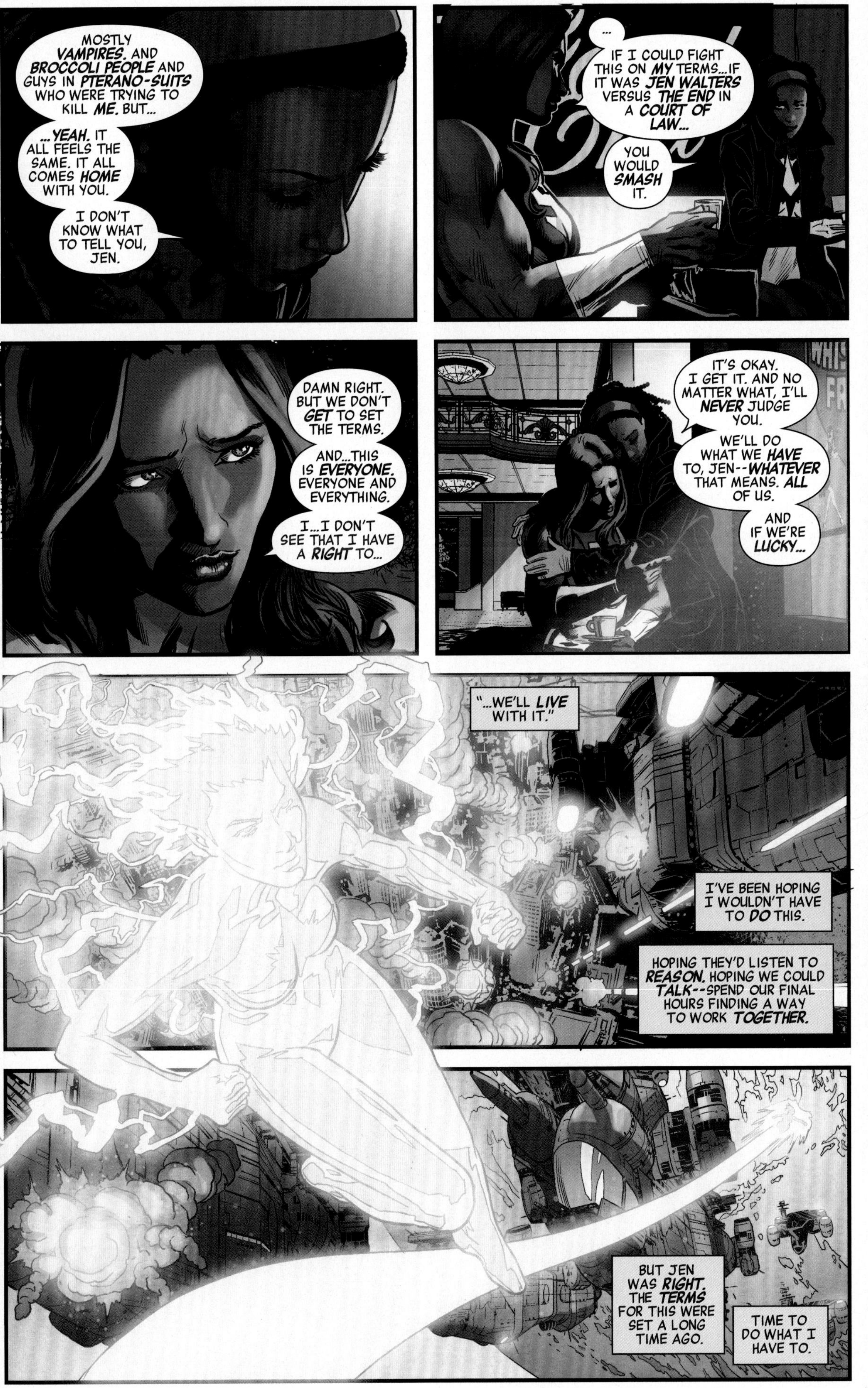
MOSTLY VAMPIRES. AND BROCCOLI PEOPLE AND GUYS IN PTERANO-SUITS WHO WERE TRYING TO KILL ME. BUT...
...YEAH. IT ALL FEELS THE SAME. IT ALL COMES HOME WITH YOU.
I DON'T KNOW WHAT TO TELL YOU, JEN.
...
IF I COULD FIGHT THIS ON MY TERMS...IF IT WAS JEN WALTERS VERSUS THE END IN A COURT OF LAW...
YOU WOULD SMASH IT.
DAMN RIGHT. BUT WE DON'T GET TO SET THE TERMS.
AND...THIS IS EVERYONE. EVERYONE AND EVERYTHING.
I...I DON'T SEE THAT I HAVE A RIGHT TO...
IT'S OKAY. I GET IT. AND NO MATTER WHAT, I'LL NEVER JUDGE YOU.
WE'LL DO WHAT WE HAVE TO, JEN--WHATEVER THAT MEANS. ALL OF US.
AND IF WE'RE LUCKY...
"...WE'LL LIVE WITH IT."
I'VE BEEN HOPING I WOULDN'T HAVE TO DO THIS.
HOPING THEY'D LISTEN TO REASON. HOPING WE COULD TALK--SPEND OUR FINAL HOURS FINDING A WAY TO WORK TOGETHER.
BUT JEN WAS RIGHT. THE TERMS FOR THIS WERE SET A LONG TIME AGO.
TIME TO DO WHAT I HAVE TO.

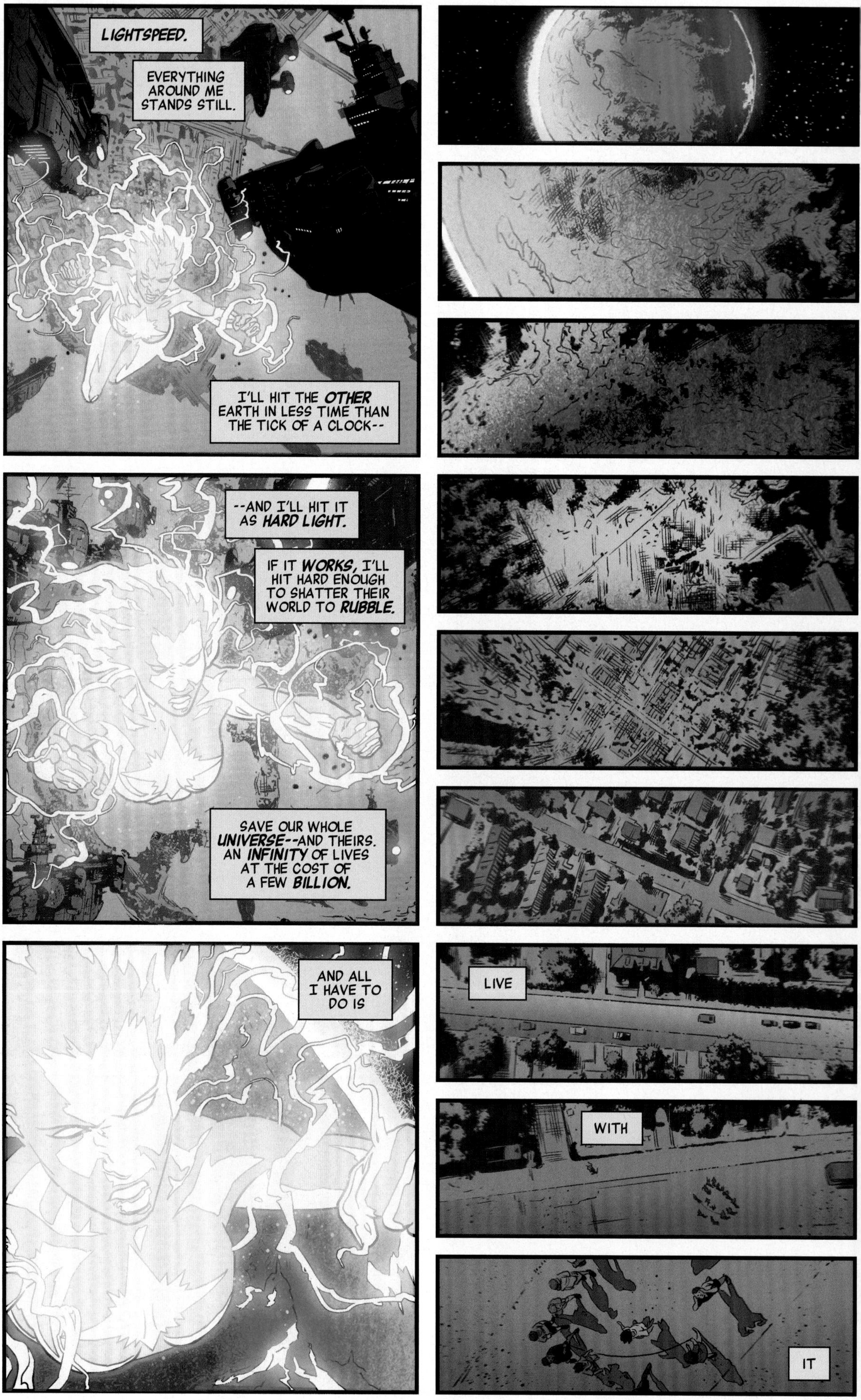
LIGHTSPEED.
EVERYTHING AROUND ME STANDS STILL.
I'LL HIT THE OTHER EARTH IN LESS TIME THAN THE TICK OF A CLOCK--
--AND I'LL HIT IT AS HARD LIGHT.
IF IT WORKS, I'LL HIT HARD ENOUGH TO SHATTER THEIR WORLD TO RUBBLE.
SAVE OUR WHOLE UNIVERSE--AND THEIRS. AN INFINITY OF LIVES AT THE COST OF A FEW BILLION.
AND ALL I HAVE TO DO IS
LIVE
WITH
IT

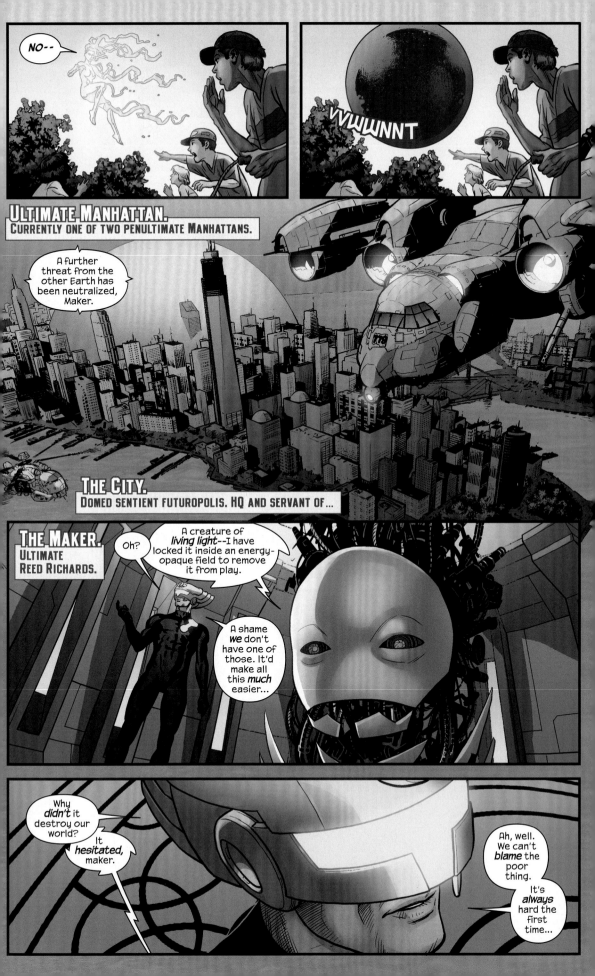

NO--

VWWNNT

ULTIMATE MANHATTAN.
CURRENTLY ONE OF TWO PENULTIMATE MANHATTANS.

A further threat from the other Earth has been neutralized, Maker.

THE CITY.
DOMED SENTIENT FUTUROPOLIS. HQ AND SERVANT OF...

THE MAKER.
ULTIMATE REED RICHARDS.

Oh?

A creature of *living light*--I have locked it inside an energy-opaque field to remove it from play.

A shame *we* don't have one of those. It'd make all this *much* easier...

Why *didn't* it destroy our world?

It *hesitated*, maker.

Ah, well. We can't *blame* the poor thing.

It's *always* hard the first time...

WHAT WE DO

53 MINUTES TO LIVE

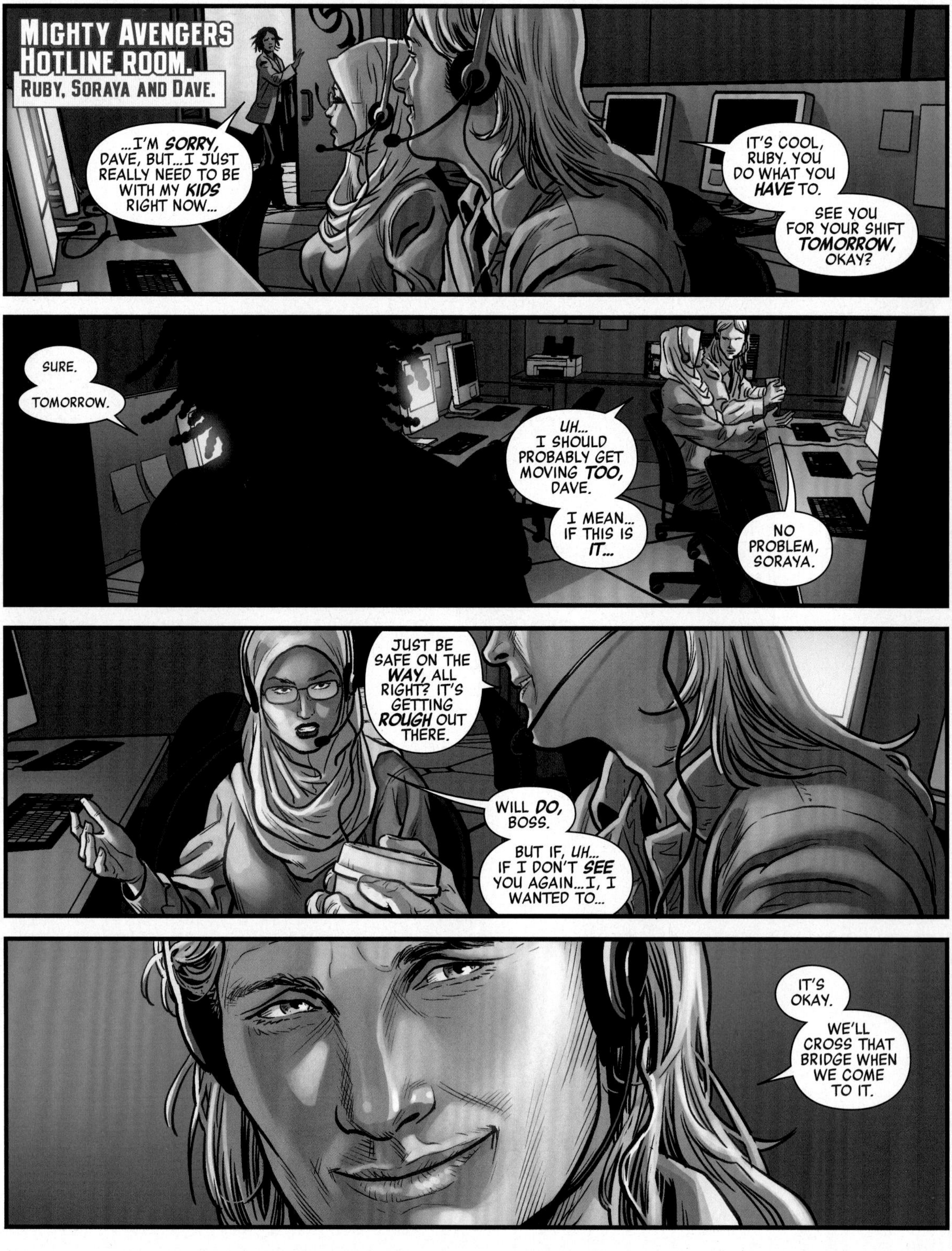
MIGHTY AVENGERS HOTLINE ROOM.
RUBY, SORAYA AND DAVE.
...I'M SORRY, DAVE, BUT...I JUST REALLY NEED TO BE WITH MY KIDS RIGHT NOW...
IT'S COOL, RUBY. YOU DO WHAT YOU HAVE TO.
SEE YOU FOR YOUR SHIFT TOMORROW, OKAY?
SURE.
TOMORROW.
UH... I SHOULD PROBABLY GET MOVING TOO, DAVE.
I MEAN... IF THIS IS IT...
NO PROBLEM, SORAYA.
JUST BE SAFE ON THE WAY, ALL RIGHT? IT'S GETTING ROUGH OUT THERE.
WILL DO, BOSS.
BUT IF, UH... IF I DON'T SEE YOU AGAIN...I, I WANTED TO...
IT'S OKAY.
WE'LL CROSS THAT BRIDGE WHEN WE COME TO IT.

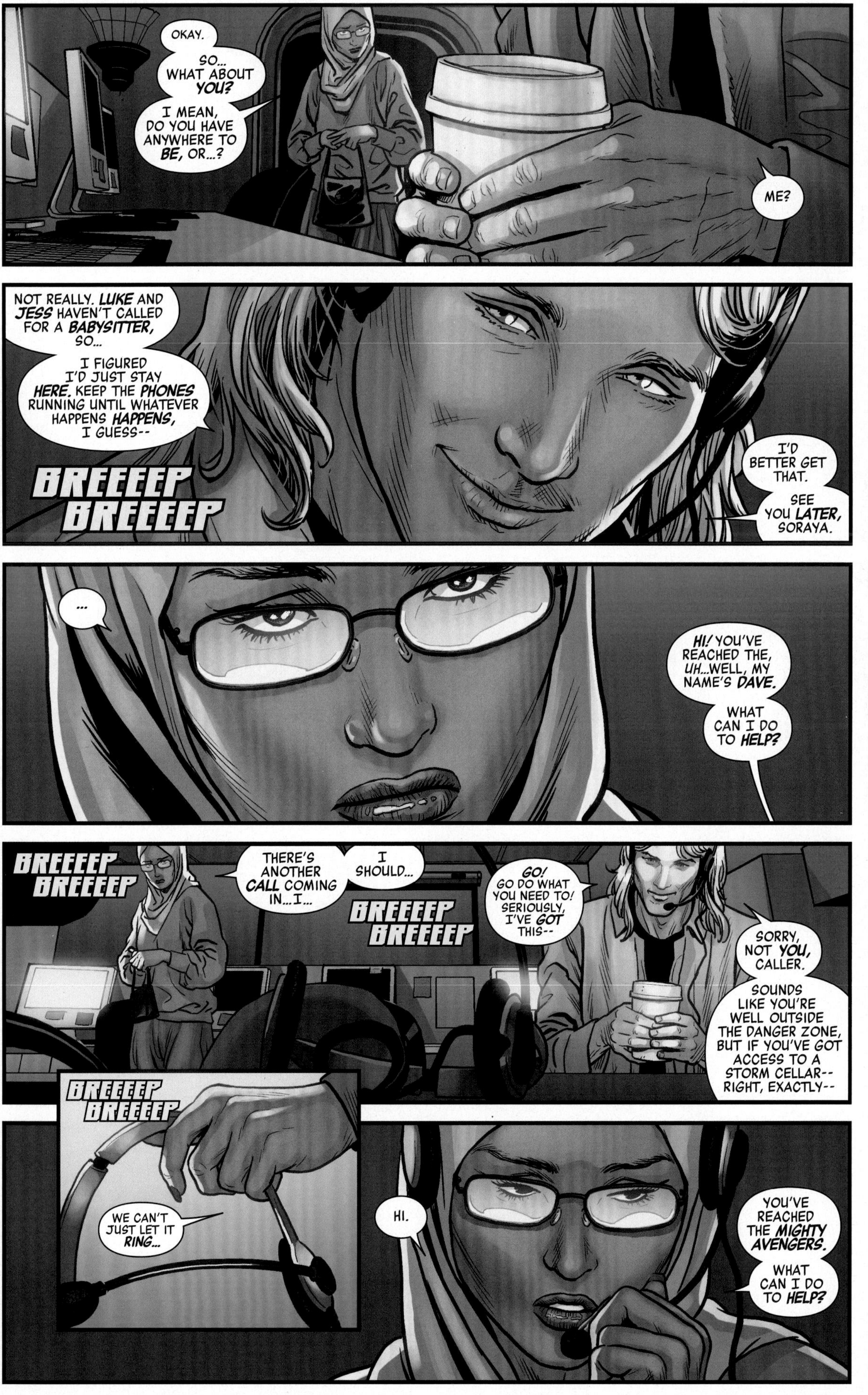

OKAY.
SO... WHAT ABOUT YOU?
I MEAN, DO YOU HAVE ANYWHERE TO BE, OR...?
ME?
NOT REALLY. LUKE AND JESS HAVEN'T CALLED FOR A BABYSITTER, SO...
I FIGURED I'D JUST STAY HERE. KEEP THE PHONES RUNNING UNTIL WHATEVER HAPPENS HAPPENS, I GUESS--
BREEEEP BREEEEP
I'D BETTER GET THAT.
SEE YOU LATER, SORAYA.
...
HI! YOU'VE REACHED THE, UH...WELL, MY NAME'S DAVE.
WHAT CAN I DO TO HELP?
BREEEEP BREEEEP
THERE'S ANOTHER CALL COMING IN...I...
I SHOULD...
BREEEEP BREEEEP
GO! GO DO WHAT YOU NEED TO! SERIOUSLY, I'VE GOT THIS--
SORRY, NOT YOU, CALLER.
SOUNDS LIKE YOU'RE WELL OUTSIDE THE DANGER ZONE, BUT IF YOU'VE GOT ACCESS TO A STORM CELLAR-- RIGHT, EXACTLY--
BREEEEP BREEEEP
WE CAN'T JUST LET IT RING...
HI.
YOU'VE REACHED THE MIGHTY AVENGERS.
WHAT CAN I DO TO HELP?

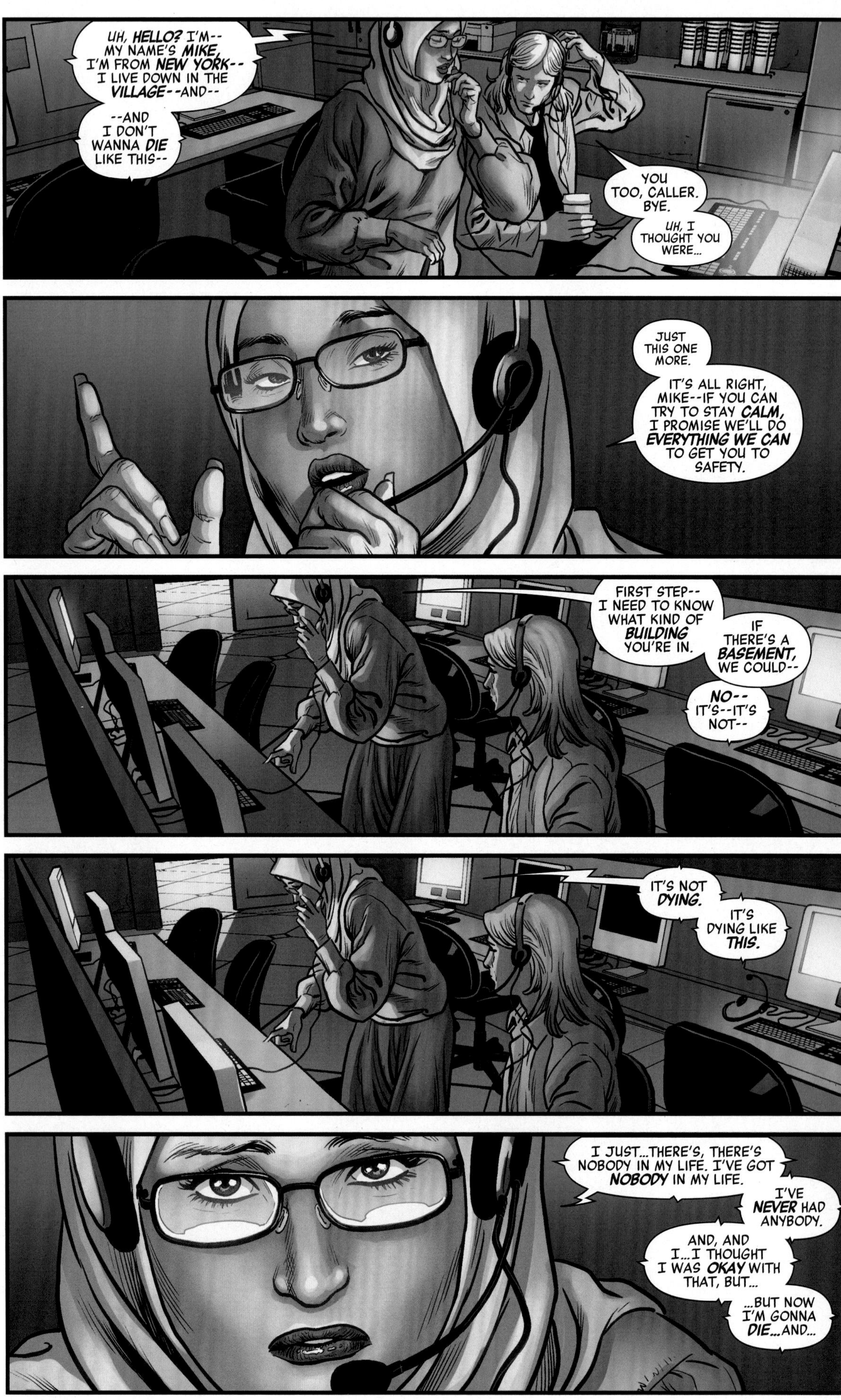
UH, HELLO? I'M-- MY NAME'S MIKE, I'M FROM NEW YORK-- I LIVE DOWN IN THE VILLAGE--AND--
--AND I DON'T WANNA DIE LIKE THIS--
YOU TOO, CALLER. BYE.
UH, I THOUGHT YOU WERE...
JUST THIS ONE MORE.
IT'S ALL RIGHT, MIKE--IF YOU CAN TRY TO STAY CALM, I PROMISE WE'LL DO EVERYTHING WE CAN TO GET YOU TO SAFETY.
FIRST STEP-- I NEED TO KNOW WHAT KIND OF BUILDING YOU'RE IN.
IF THERE'S A BASEMENT, WE COULD--
NO-- IT'S--IT'S NOT--
IT'S NOT DYING.
IT'S DYING LIKE THIS.
I JUST...THERE'S, THERE'S NOBODY IN MY LIFE. I'VE GOT NOBODY IN MY LIFE.
I'VE NEVER HAD ANYBODY.
AND, AND I...I THOUGHT I WAS OKAY WITH THAT, BUT...
...BUT NOW I'M GONNA DIE...AND...

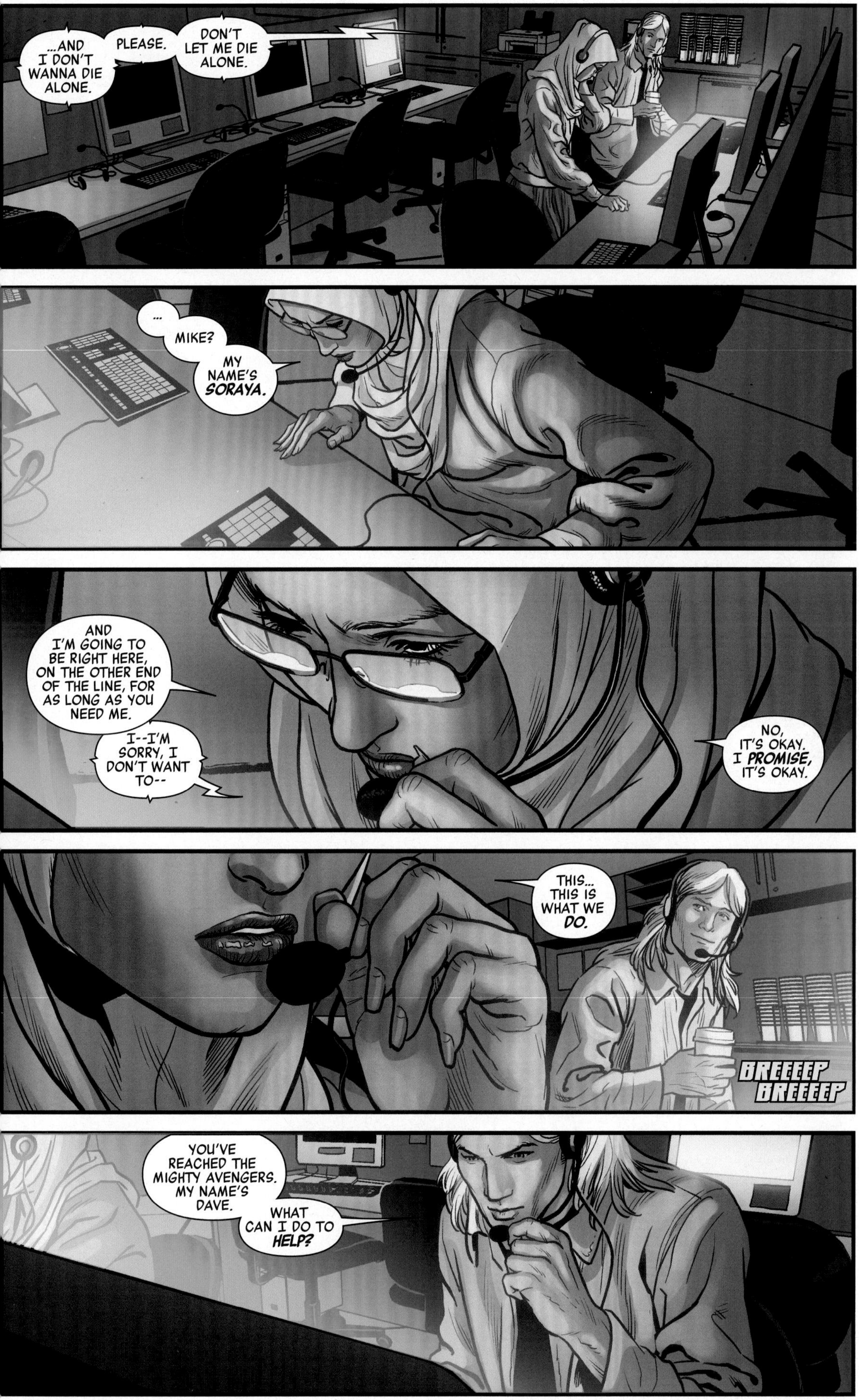

...AND I DON'T WANNA DIE ALONE.
PLEASE.
DON'T LET ME DIE ALONE.
...
MIKE?
MY NAME'S SORAYA.
AND I'M GOING TO BE RIGHT HERE, ON THE OTHER END OF THE LINE, FOR AS LONG AS YOU NEED ME.
I--I'M SORRY, I DON'T WANT TO--
NO, IT'S OKAY. I PROMISE, IT'S OKAY.
THIS... THIS IS WHAT WE DO.
BREEEEP BREEEEP
YOU'VE REACHED THE MIGHTY AVENGERS. MY NAME'S DAVE.
WHAT CAN I DO TO HELP?

MIGHTY

49 MINUTES TO LIVE

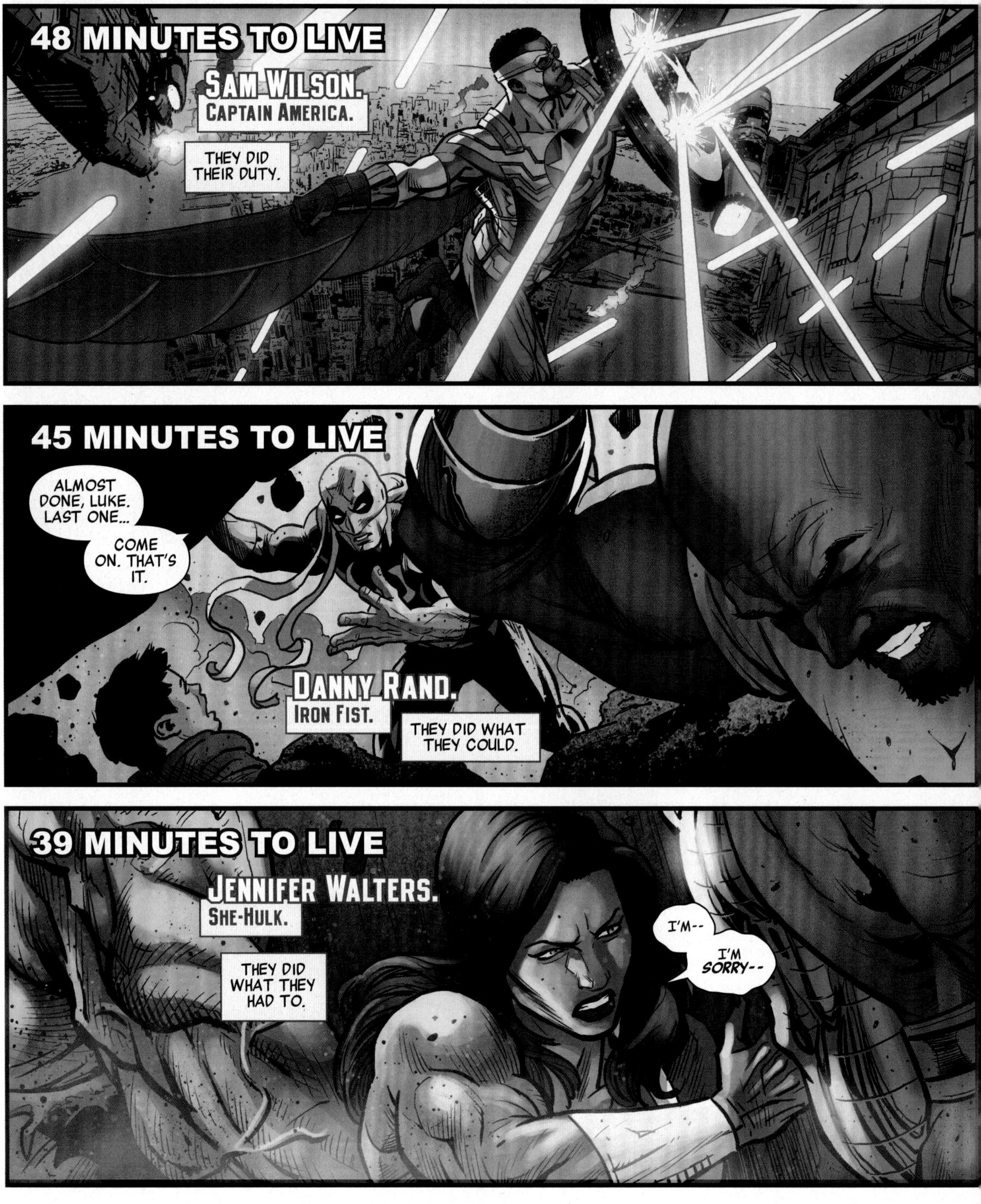
48 MINUTES TO LIVE
SAM WILSON.
CAPTAIN AMERICA.
THEY DID THEIR DUTY.
45 MINUTES TO LIVE
ALMOST DONE, LUKE. LAST ONE...
COME ON. THAT'S IT.
DANNY RAND.
IRON FIST.
THEY DID WHAT THEY COULD.
39 MINUTES TO LIVE
JENNIFER WALTERS.
SHE-HULK.
THEY DID WHAT THEY HAD TO.
I'M--
I'M *SORRY*--

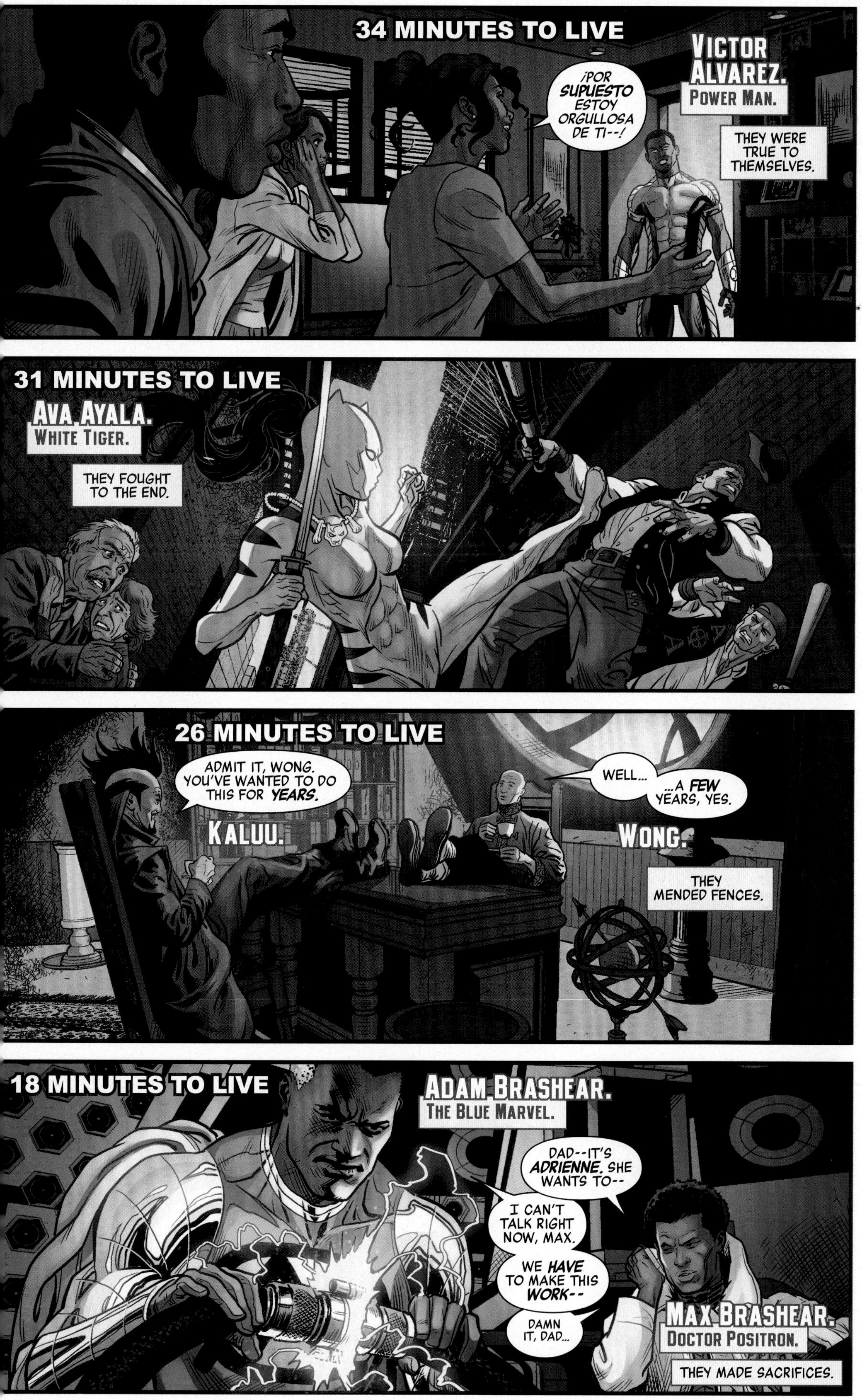
34 MINUTES TO LIVE
¡POR SUPUESTO ESTOY ORGULLOSA DE TI--!
VICTOR ALVAREZ.
POWER MAN.
THEY WERE TRUE TO THEMSELVES.
31 MINUTES TO LIVE
AVA AYALA.
WHITE TIGER.
THEY FOUGHT TO THE END.
26 MINUTES TO LIVE
ADMIT IT, WONG. YOU'VE WANTED TO DO THIS FOR YEARS.
KALUU.
WELL...
...A FEW YEARS, YES.
WONG.
THEY MENDED FENCES.
18 MINUTES TO LIVE
ADAM BRASHEAR.
THE BLUE MARVEL.
DAD--IT'S ADRIENNE. SHE WANTS TO--
I CAN'T TALK RIGHT NOW, MAX.
WE HAVE TO MAKE THIS WORK--
DAMN IT, DAD...
MAX BRASHEAR.
DOCTOR POSITRON.
THEY MADE SACRIFICES.

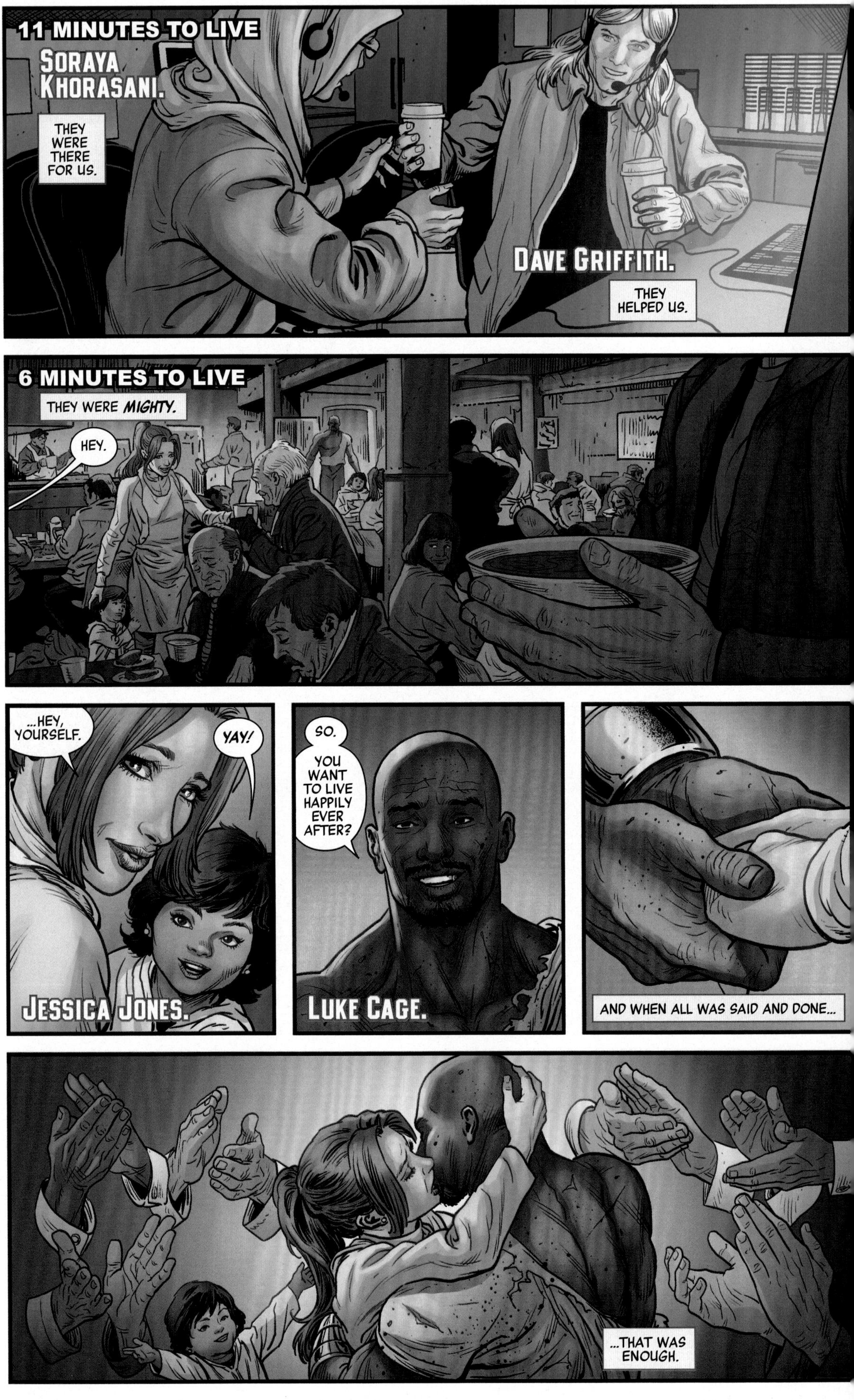
11 MINUTES TO LIVE
SORAYA KHORASANI.
THEY WERE THERE FOR US.
DAVE GRIFFITH.
THEY HELPED US.
6 MINUTES TO LIVE
THEY WERE MIGHTY.
HEY.
...HEY, YOURSELF.
YAY!
JESSICA JONES.
SO.
YOU WANT TO LIVE HAPPILY EVER AFTER?
LUKE CAGE.
AND WHEN ALL WAS SAID AND DONE...
...THAT WAS ENOUGH.

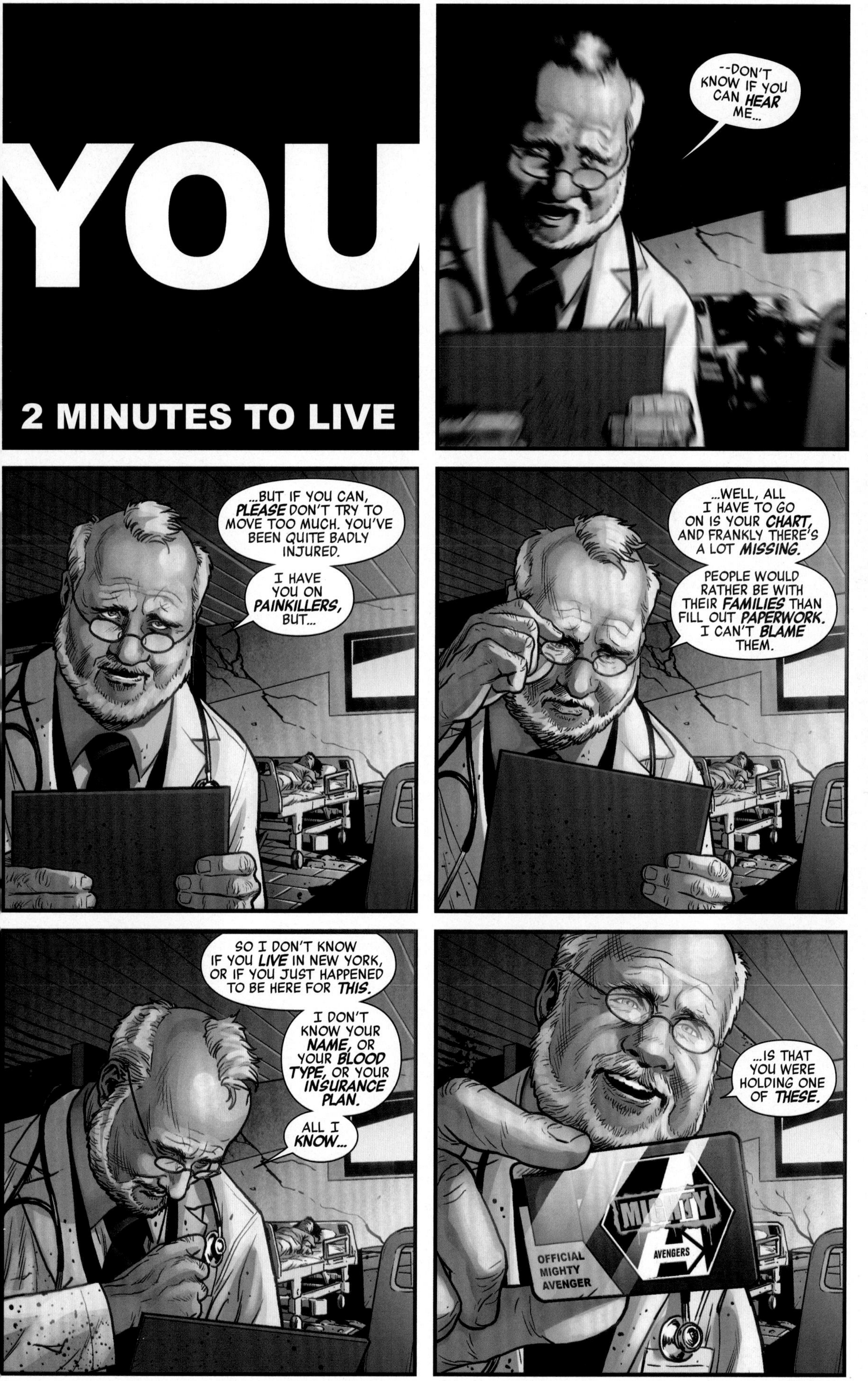
YOU
2 MINUTES TO LIVE
--DON'T KNOW IF YOU CAN HEAR ME...
...BUT IF YOU CAN, PLEASE DON'T TRY TO MOVE TOO MUCH. YOU'VE BEEN QUITE BADLY INJURED.
I HAVE YOU ON PAINKILLERS, BUT...
...WELL, ALL I HAVE TO GO ON IS YOUR CHART, AND FRANKLY THERE'S A LOT MISSING.
PEOPLE WOULD RATHER BE WITH THEIR FAMILIES THAN FILL OUT PAPERWORK. I CAN'T BLAME THEM.
SO I DON'T KNOW IF YOU LIVE IN NEW YORK, OR IF YOU JUST HAPPENED TO BE HERE FOR THIS.
I DON'T KNOW YOUR NAME, OR YOUR BLOOD TYPE, OR YOUR INSURANCE PLAN.
ALL I KNOW...
...IS THAT YOU WERE HOLDING ONE OF THESE.
OFFICIAL MIGHTY AVENGER
MIGHTY
AVENGERS

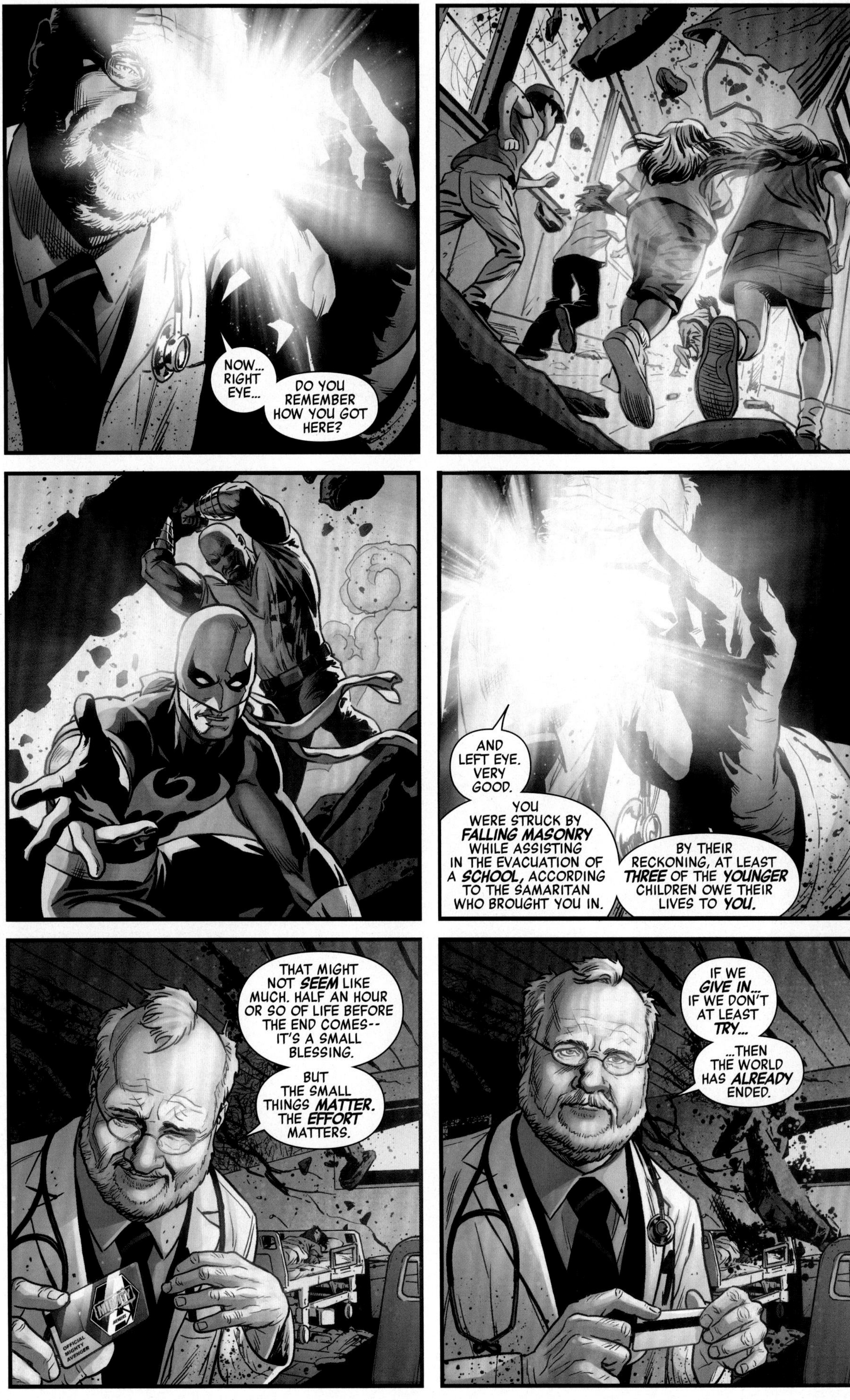
NOW... RIGHT EYE...
DO YOU REMEMBER HOW YOU GOT HERE?
AND LEFT EYE. VERY GOOD.
YOU WERE STRUCK BY FALLING MASONRY WHILE ASSISTING IN THE EVACUATION OF A SCHOOL, ACCORDING TO THE SAMARITAN WHO BROUGHT YOU IN.
BY THEIR RECKONING, AT LEAST THREE OF THE YOUNGER CHILDREN OWE THEIR LIVES TO YOU.
THAT MIGHT NOT SEEM LIKE MUCH. HALF AN HOUR OR SO OF LIFE BEFORE THE END COMES--IT'S A SMALL BLESSING.
BUT THE SMALL THINGS MATTER. THE EFFORT MATTERS.
OFFICIAL MIGHTY AVENGER
IF WE GIVE IN... IF WE DON'T AT LEAST TRY...
...THEN THE WORLD HAS ALREADY ENDED.

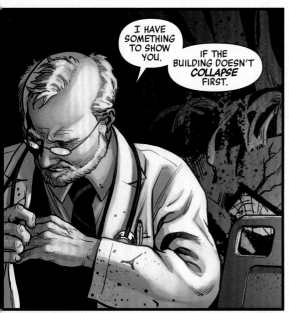

I HAVE SOMETHING TO SHOW YOU.

IF THE BUILDING DOESN'T COLLAPSE FIRST.

THERE. MY CARD. WE WERE AVENGERS, YOU AND I. THE MIGHTIEST OF AVENGERS.

OFFICIAL MIGHTY AVENGER

MIGHTY AVENGERS

AT THE END OF THE WORLD, WE ALL MEANT SOMETHING.

WE ALL COUNTED.

AND I AM VERY PROUD TO DIE ALONGSIDE YOU, MY FRIEND.

CAN YOU TURN YOUR HEAD?

IT REALLY IS QUITE A VIEW.

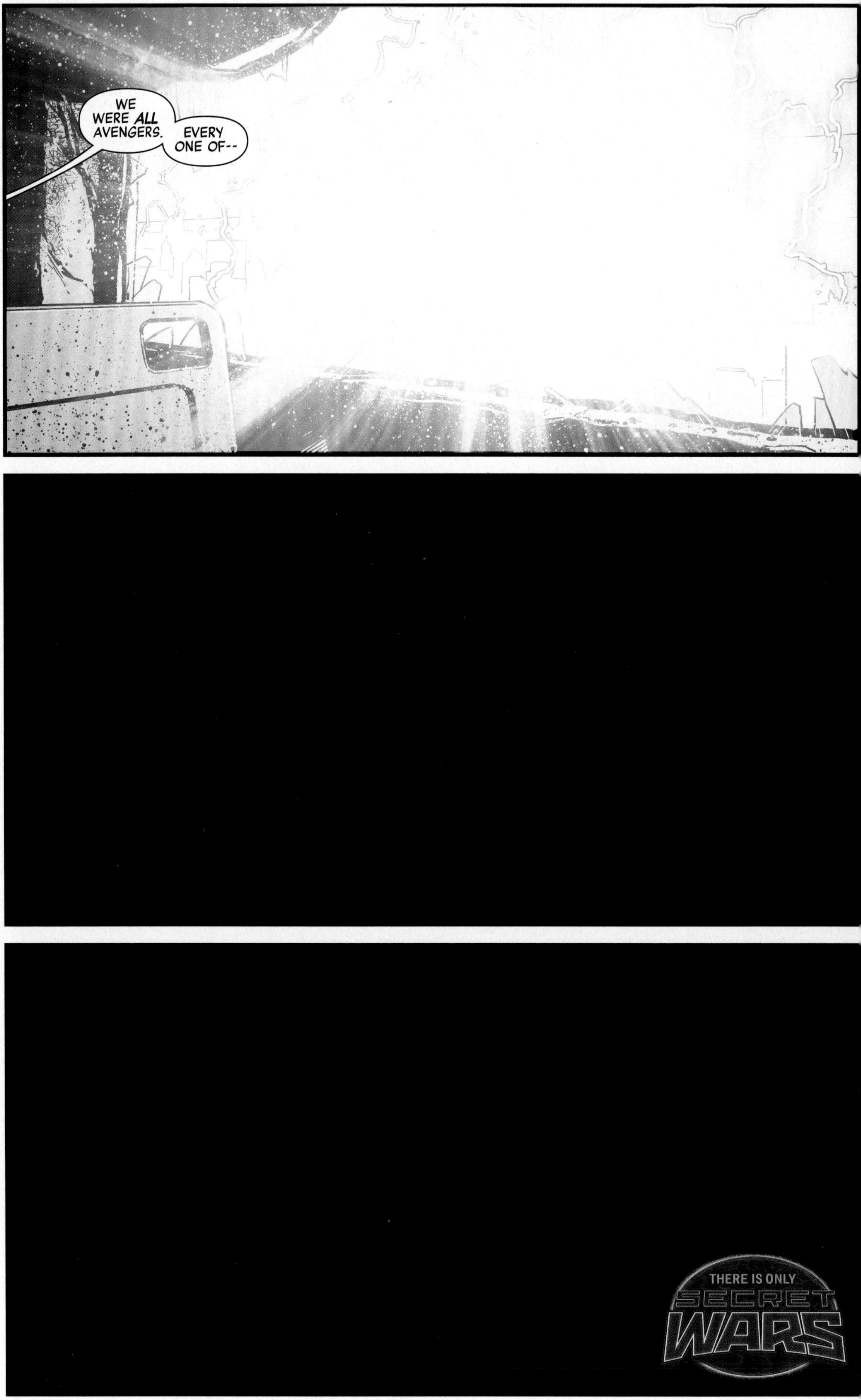
WE WERE ALL AVENGERS.
EVERY ONE OF--
THERE IS ONLY SECRET WARS

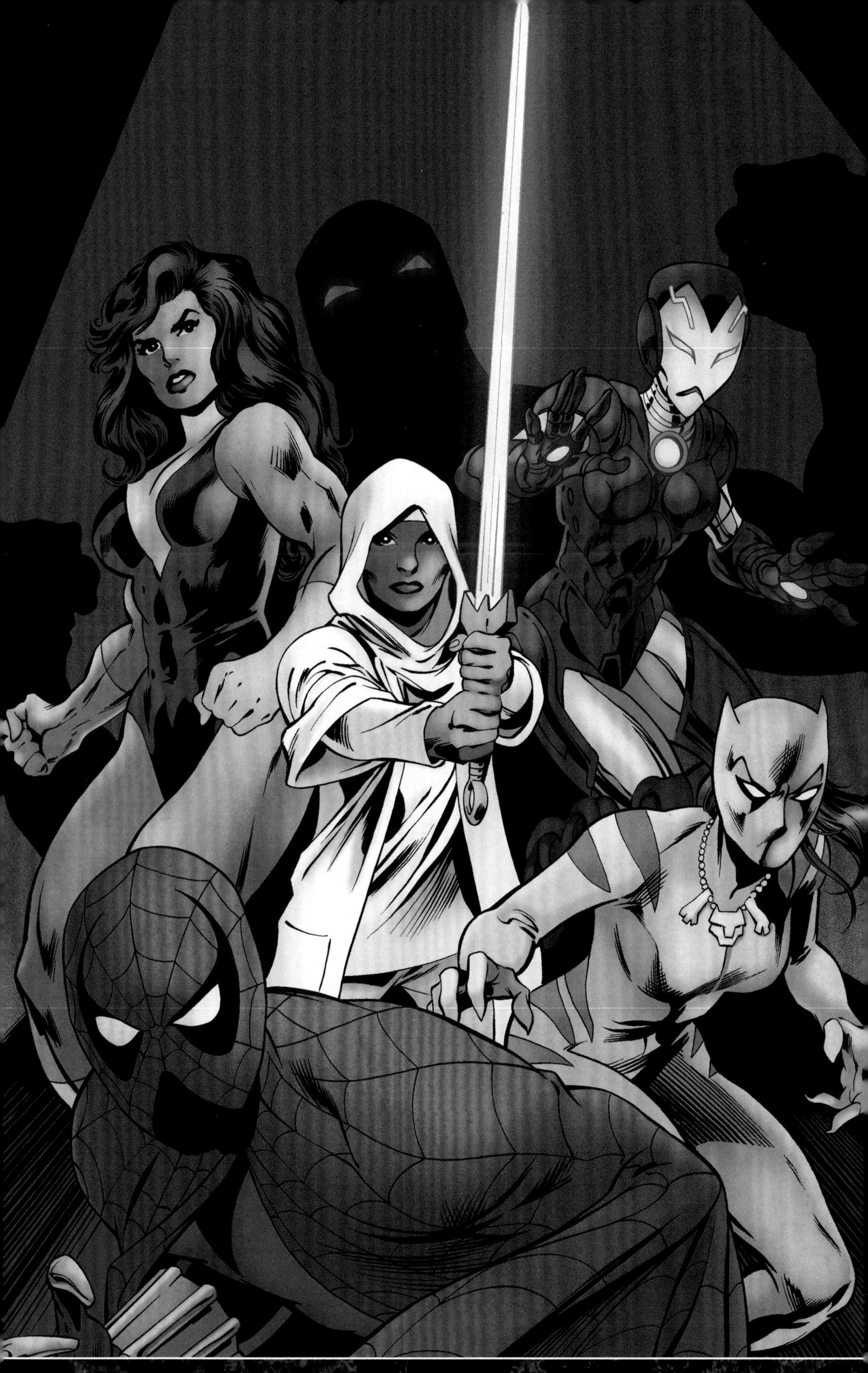

CAPTAIN BRITAIN AND THE MIGHTY DEFENDERS #1

SECRET WARS

THE MULTIVERSE WAS DESTROYED!

·

THE HEROES OF EARTH-616 AND EARTH-1610
WERE POWERLESS TO SAVE IT!

·

NOW, ALL THAT REMAINS...IS **BATTLEWORLD**!

·

A MASSIVE, PATCHWORK PLANET COMPOSED OF THE FRAGMENTS OF
WORLDS THAT NO LONGER EXIST, MAINTAINED BY THE IRON WILL OF ITS
GOD AND MASTER, VICTOR VON DOOM!

·

EACH REGION IS A DOMAIN UNTO ITSELF!

CAPTAIN BRITAIN AND THE MIGHTY DEFENDERS

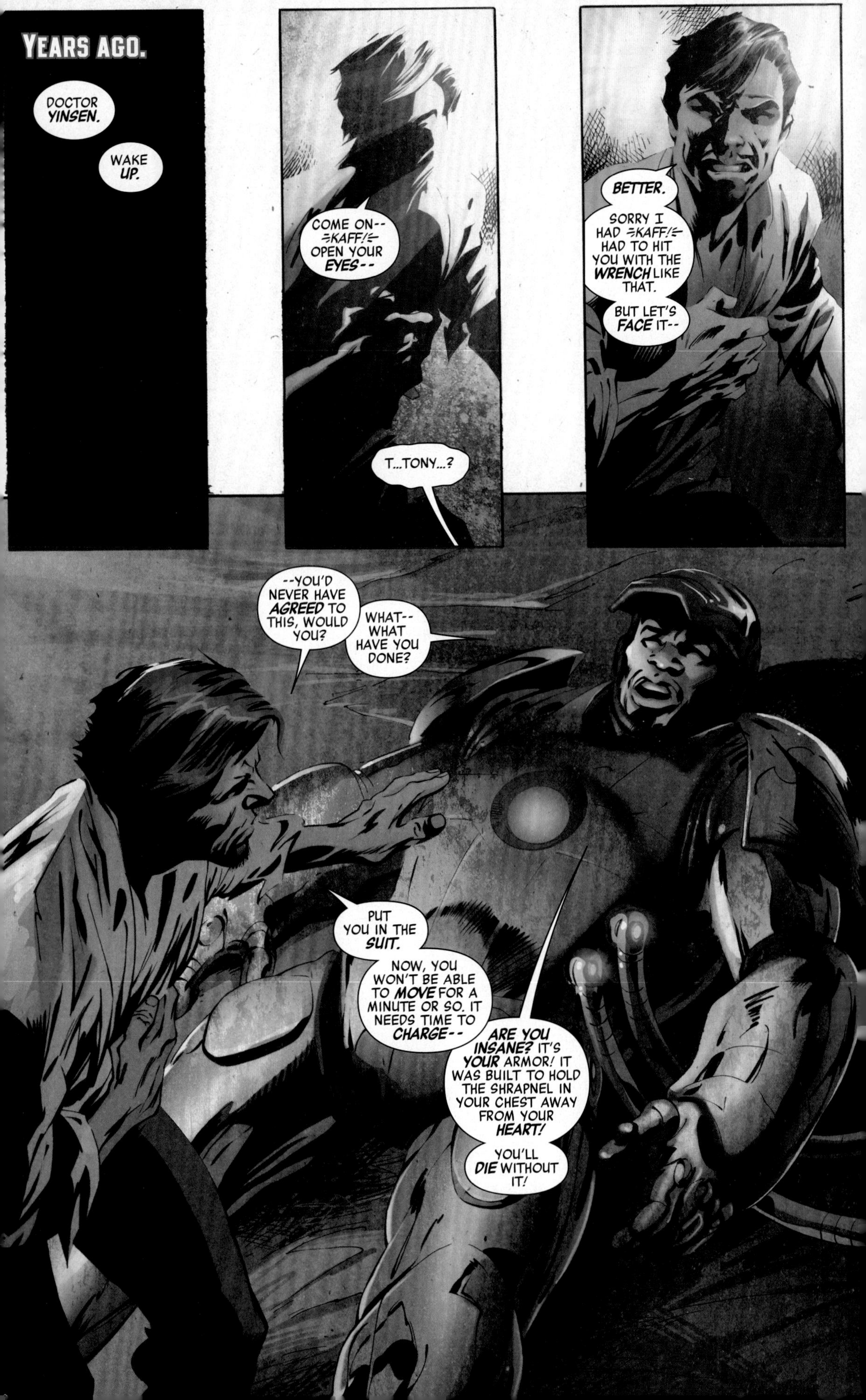
YEARS AGO.
DOCTOR YINSEN.
WAKE UP.
COME ON-- =KAFF!= OPEN YOUR EYES--
T...TONY...?
BETTER.
SORRY I HAD =KAFF!= HAD TO HIT YOU WITH THE WRENCH LIKE THAT.
BUT LET'S FACE IT--
--YOU'D NEVER HAVE AGREED TO THIS, WOULD YOU?
WHAT-- WHAT HAVE YOU DONE?
PUT YOU IN THE SUIT.
NOW, YOU WON'T BE ABLE TO MOVE FOR A MINUTE OR SO. IT NEEDS TIME TO CHARGE--
ARE YOU INSANE? IT'S YOUR ARMOR! IT WAS BUILT TO HOLD THE SHRAPNEL IN YOUR CHEST AWAY FROM YOUR HEART!
YOU'LL DIE WITHOUT IT!

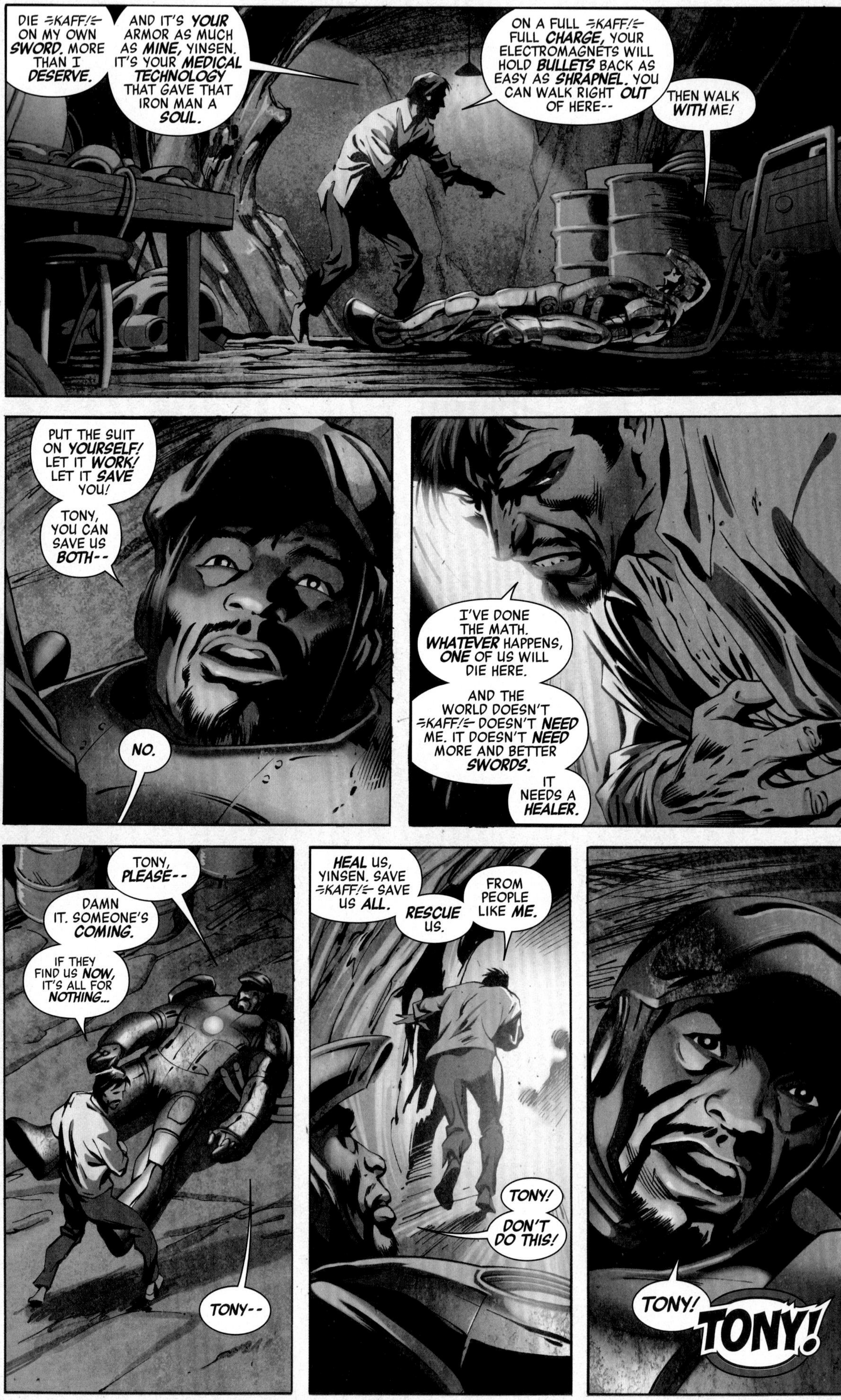
DIE =KAFF!= ON MY OWN SWORD. MORE THAN I DESERVE.
AND IT'S YOUR ARMOR AS MUCH AS MINE, YINSEN. IT'S YOUR MEDICAL TECHNOLOGY THAT GAVE THAT IRON MAN A SOUL.
ON A FULL =KAFF!= FULL CHARGE, YOUR ELECTROMAGNETS WILL HOLD BULLETS BACK AS EASY AS SHRAPNEL. YOU CAN WALK RIGHT OUT OF HERE--
THEN WALK WITH ME!
PUT THE SUIT ON YOURSELF! LET IT WORK! LET IT SAVE YOU!
TONY, YOU CAN SAVE US BOTH--
NO.
I'VE DONE THE MATH. WHATEVER HAPPENS, ONE OF US WILL DIE HERE.
AND THE WORLD DOESN'T =KAFF!= DOESN'T NEED ME. IT DOESN'T NEED MORE AND BETTER SWORDS.
IT NEEDS A HEALER.
TONY, PLEASE--
DAMN IT. SOMEONE'S COMING.
IF THEY FIND US NOW, IT'S ALL FOR NOTHING...
TONY--
HEAL US, YINSEN. SAVE =KAFF!= SAVE US ALL.
RESCUE US.
FROM PEOPLE LIKE ME.
TONY!
DON'T DO THIS!
TONY!
TONY!

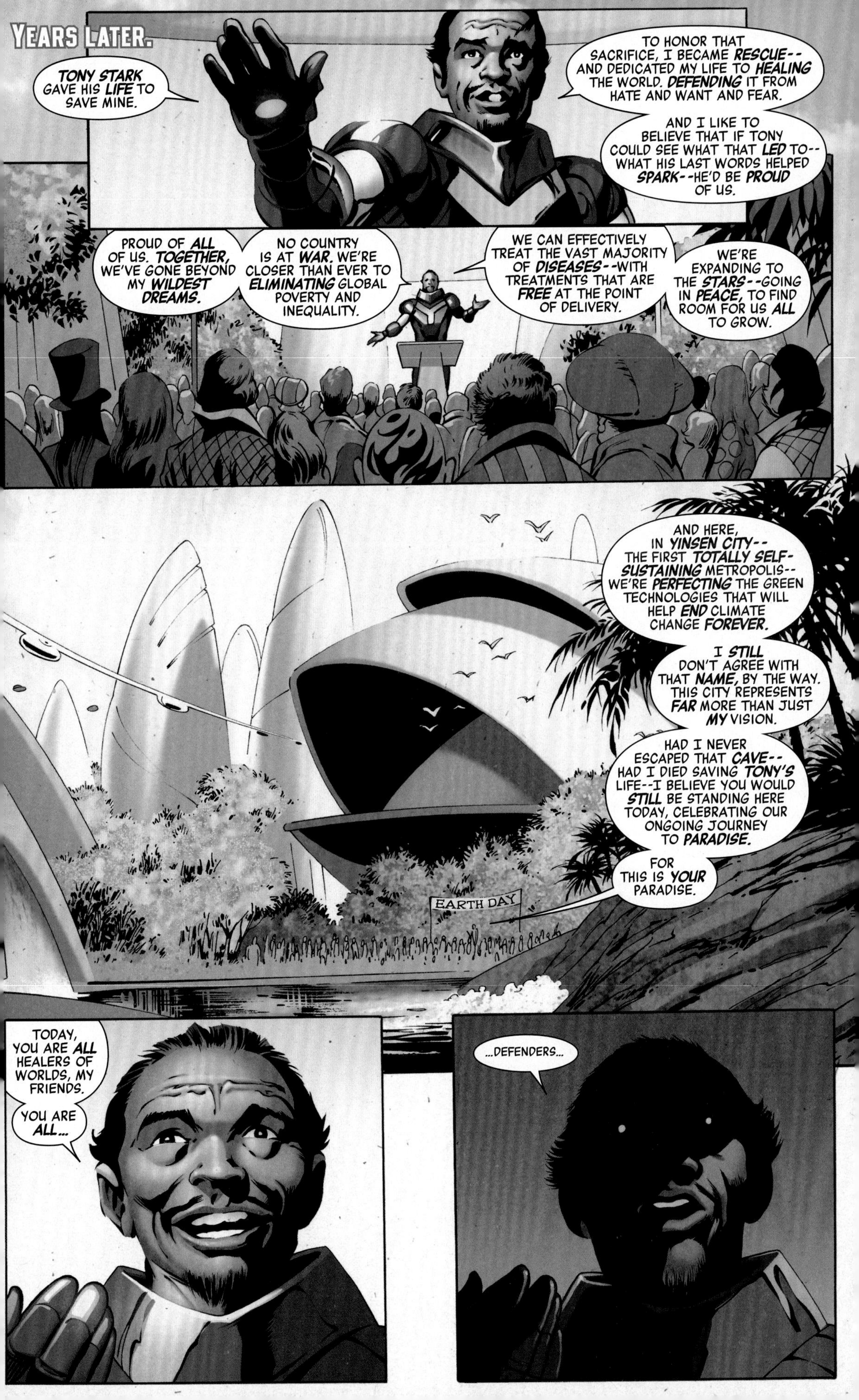
YEARS LATER.
TONY STARK GAVE HIS LIFE TO SAVE MINE.
TO HONOR THAT SACRIFICE, I BECAME RESCUE-- AND DEDICATED MY LIFE TO HEALING THE WORLD. DEFENDING IT FROM HATE AND WANT AND FEAR.
AND I LIKE TO BELIEVE THAT IF TONY COULD SEE WHAT THAT LED TO-- WHAT HIS LAST WORDS HELPED SPARK--HE'D BE PROUD OF US.
PROUD OF ALL OF US. TOGETHER, WE'VE GONE BEYOND MY WILDEST DREAMS.
NO COUNTRY IS AT WAR. WE'RE CLOSER THAN EVER TO ELIMINATING GLOBAL POVERTY AND INEQUALITY.
WE CAN EFFECTIVELY TREAT THE VAST MAJORITY OF DISEASES--WITH TREATMENTS THAT ARE FREE AT THE POINT OF DELIVERY.
WE'RE EXPANDING TO THE STARS--GOING IN PEACE, TO FIND ROOM FOR US ALL TO GROW.
AND HERE, IN YINSEN CITY-- THE FIRST TOTALLY SELF-SUSTAINING METROPOLIS-- WE'RE PERFECTING THE GREEN TECHNOLOGIES THAT WILL HELP END CLIMATE CHANGE FOREVER.
I STILL DON'T AGREE WITH THAT NAME, BY THE WAY. THIS CITY REPRESENTS FAR MORE THAN JUST MY VISION.
HAD I NEVER ESCAPED THAT CAVE-- HAD I DIED SAVING TONY'S LIFE--I BELIEVE YOU WOULD STILL BE STANDING HERE TODAY, CELEBRATING OUR ONGOING JOURNEY TO PARADISE.
FOR THIS IS YOUR PARADISE.
EARTH DAY
TODAY, YOU ARE ALL HEALERS OF WORLDS, MY FRIENDS.
YOU ARE ALL...
...DEFENDERS...

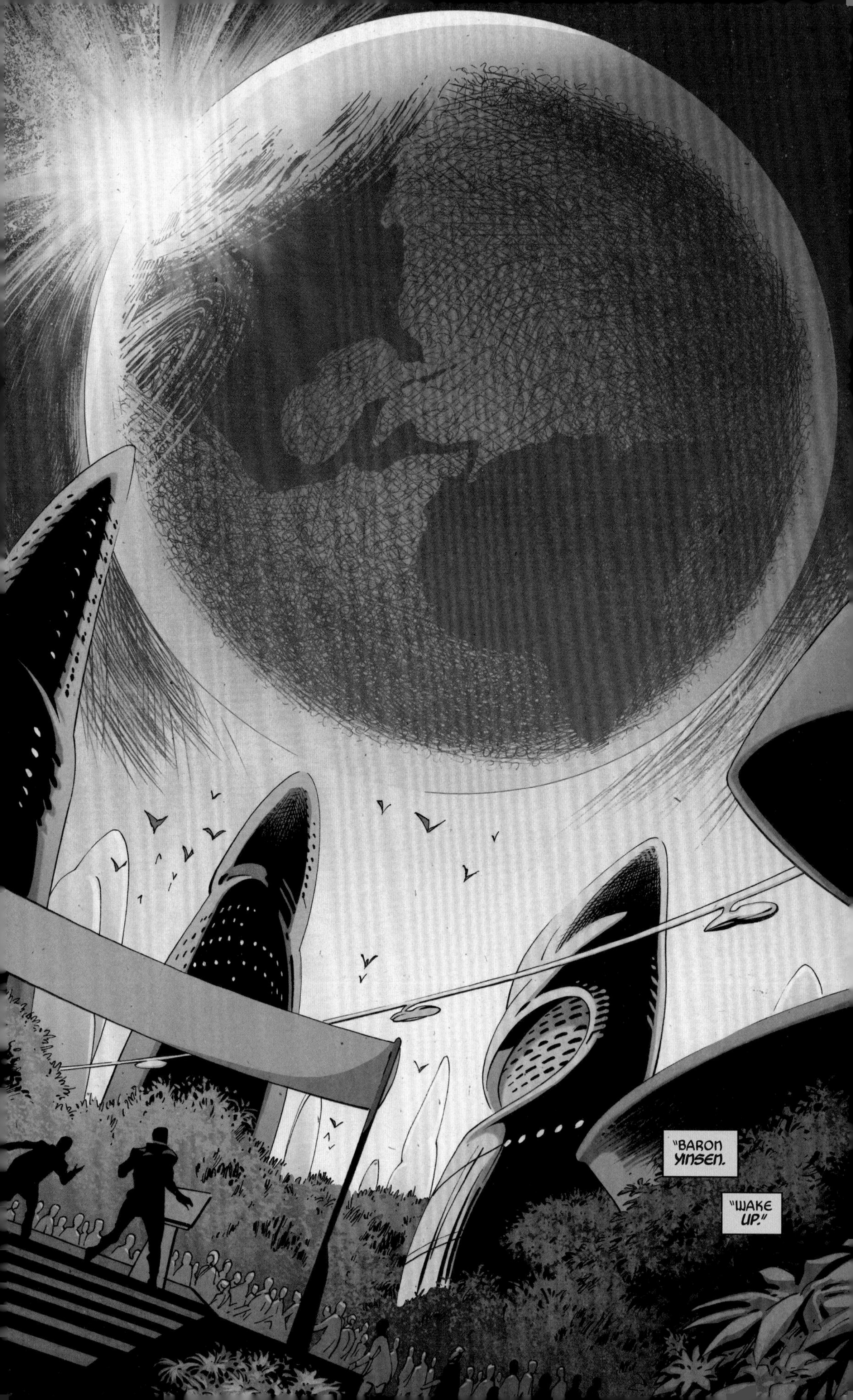
"BARON YINSEN.
"WAKE UP."

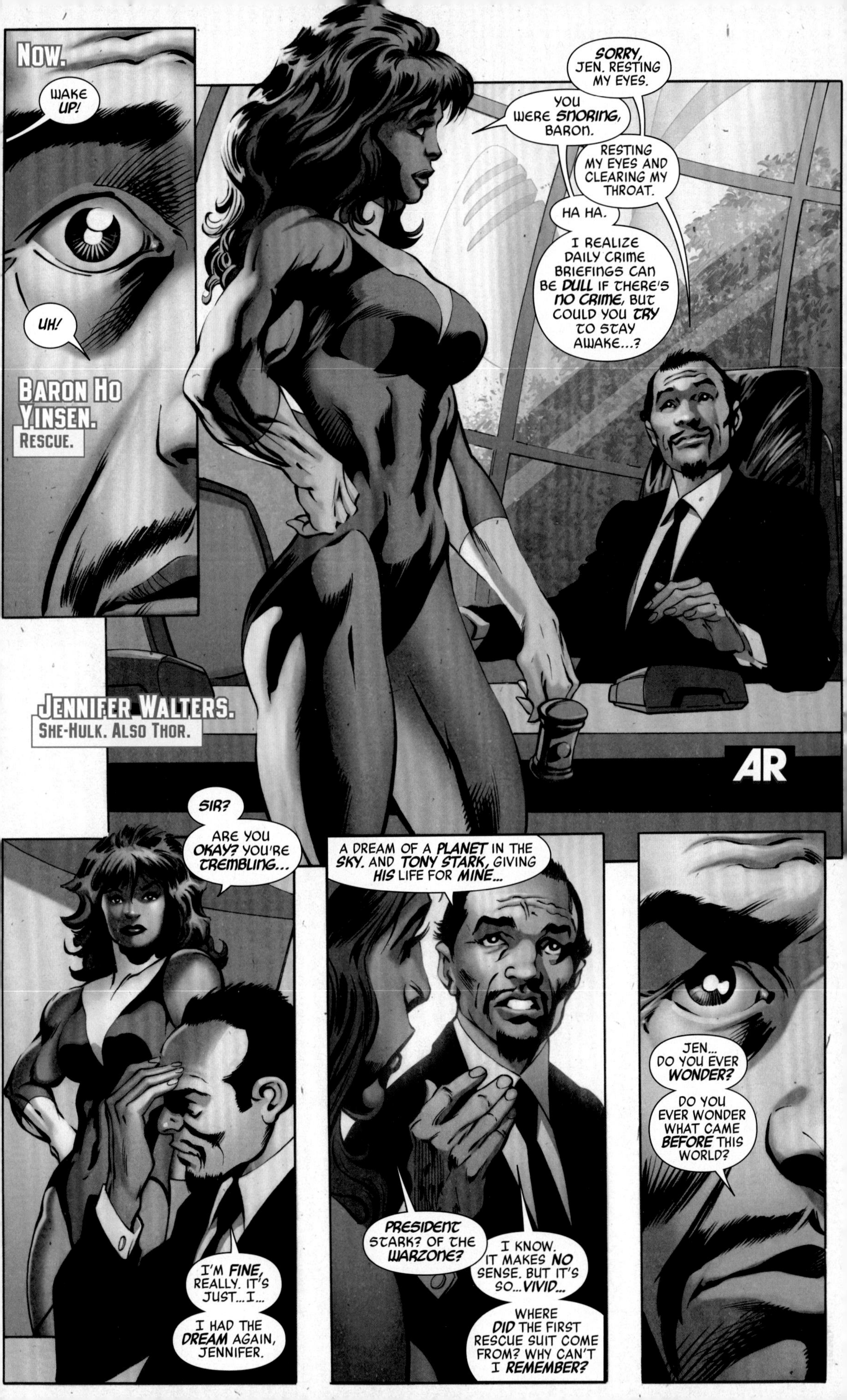
NOW.
WAKE UP!
UH!
BARON HO YINSEN.
RESCUE.
YOU WERE SNORING, BARON.
SORRY, JEN. RESTING MY EYES.
RESTING MY EYES AND CLEARING MY THROAT.
HA HA.
I REALIZE DAILY CRIME BRIEFINGS CAN BE DULL IF THERE'S NO CRIME, BUT COULD YOU TRY TO STAY AWAKE...?
JENNIFER WALTERS.
SHE-HULK. ALSO THOR.
AR
SIR?
ARE YOU OKAY? YOU'RE TREMBLING...
I'M FINE, REALLY. IT'S JUST...I...
I HAD THE DREAM AGAIN, JENNIFER.
A DREAM OF A PLANET IN THE SKY. AND TONY STARK, GIVING HIS LIFE FOR MINE...
PRESIDENT STARK? OF THE WARZONE?
I KNOW. IT MAKES NO SENSE. BUT IT'S SO...VIVID...
WHERE DID THE FIRST RESCUE SUIT COME FROM? WHY CAN'T I REMEMBER?
JEN... DO YOU EVER WONDER?
DO YOU EVER WONDER WHAT CAME BEFORE THIS WORLD?

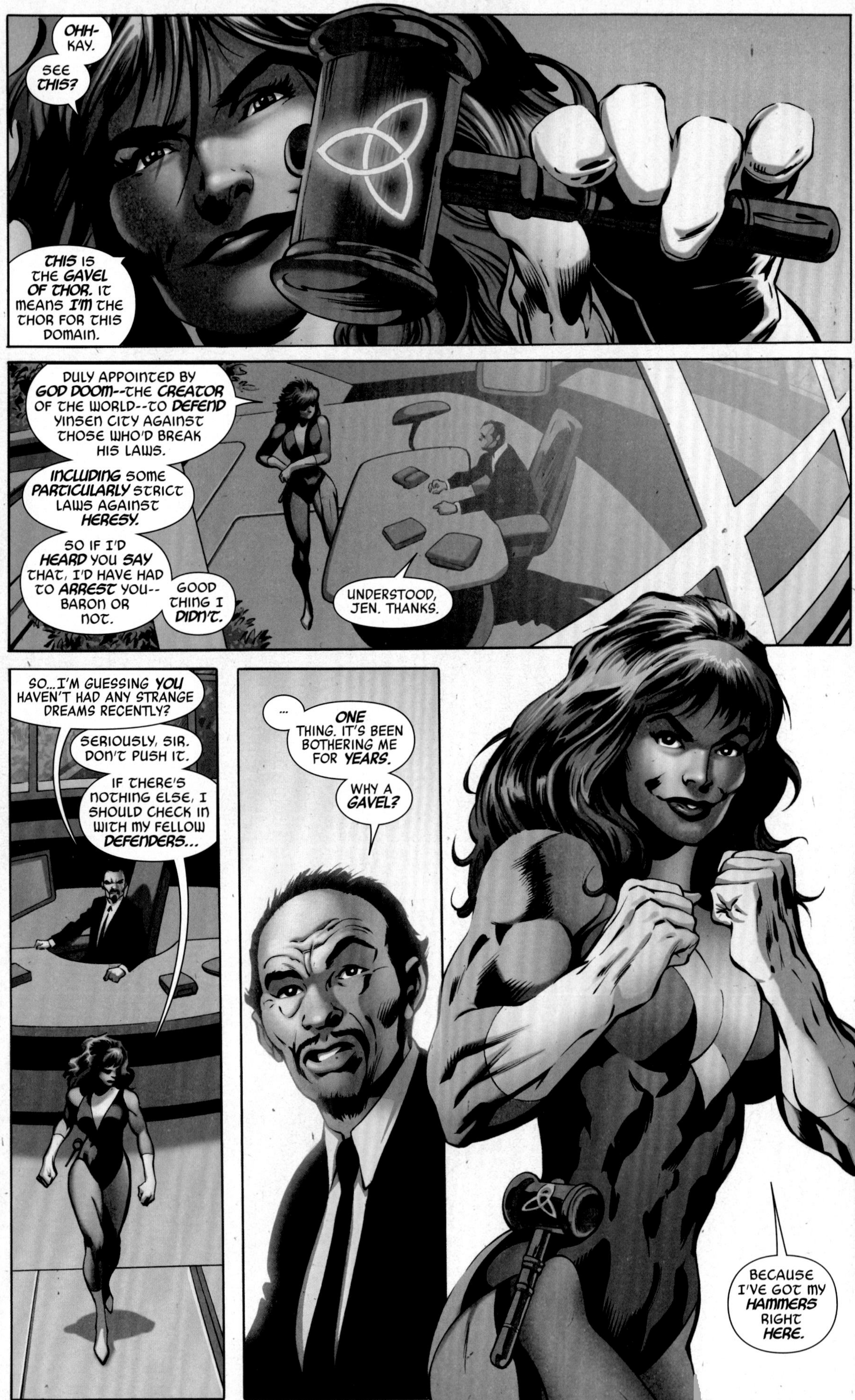
OHH-KAY.
SEE THIS?
THIS IS THE GAVEL OF THOR. IT MEANS I'M THE THOR FOR THIS DOMAIN.
DULY APPOINTED BY GOD DOOM--THE CREATOR OF THE WORLD--TO DEFEND YINSEN CITY AGAINST THOSE WHO'D BREAK HIS LAWS.
INCLUDING SOME PARTICULARLY STRICT LAWS AGAINST HERESY.
SO IF I'D HEARD YOU SAY THAT, I'D HAVE HAD TO ARREST YOU-- BARON OR NOT.
GOOD THING I DIDN'T.
UNDERSTOOD, JEN. THANKS.
SO...I'M GUESSING YOU HAVEN'T HAD ANY STRANGE DREAMS RECENTLY?
SERIOUSLY, SIR. DON'T PUSH IT.
IF THERE'S NOTHING ELSE, I SHOULD CHECK IN WITH MY FELLOW DEFENDERS...
... ONE THING. IT'S BEEN BOTHERING ME FOR YEARS.
WHY A GAVEL?
BECAUSE I'VE GOT MY HAMMERS RIGHT HERE.

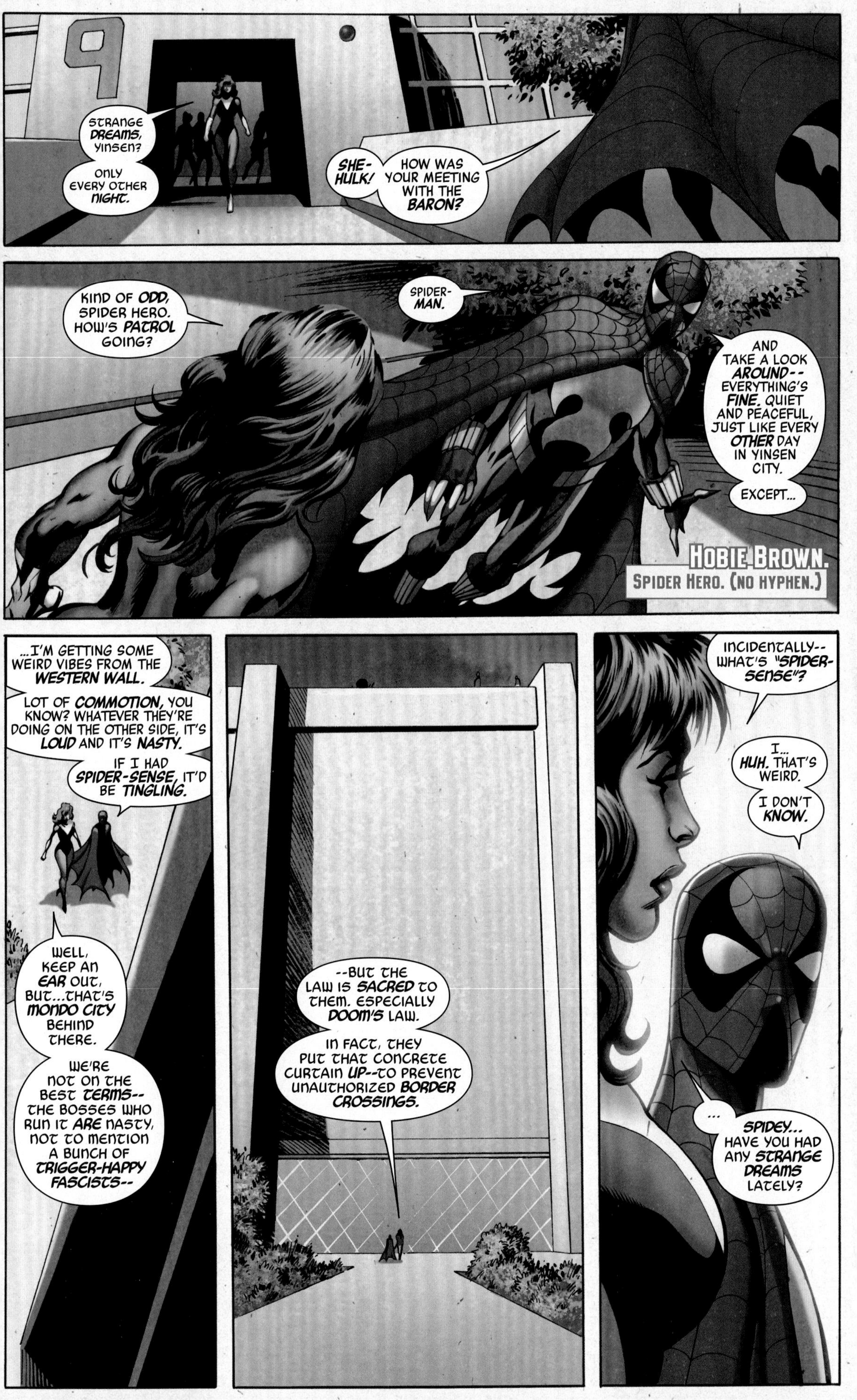

STRANGE DREAMS, YINSEN?
ONLY EVERY OTHER NIGHT.
SHE-HULK!
HOW WAS YOUR MEETING WITH THE BARON?
KIND OF ODD, SPIDER HERO. HOW'S PATROL GOING?
SPIDER-MAN.
AND TAKE A LOOK AROUND--EVERYTHING'S FINE. QUIET AND PEACEFUL, JUST LIKE EVERY OTHER DAY IN YINSEN CITY.
EXCEPT...
HOBIE BROWN.
SPIDER HERO. (NO HYPHEN.)
...I'M GETTING SOME WEIRD VIBES FROM THE WESTERN WALL.
LOT OF COMMOTION, YOU KNOW? WHATEVER THEY'RE DOING ON THE OTHER SIDE, IT'S LOUD AND IT'S NASTY.
IF I HAD SPIDER-SENSE, IT'D BE TINGLING.
WELL, KEEP AN EAR OUT, BUT...THAT'S MONDO CITY BEHIND THERE.
WE'RE NOT ON THE BEST TERMS--THE BOSSES WHO RUN IT ARE NASTY, NOT TO MENTION A BUNCH OF TRIGGER-HAPPY FASCISTS--
--BUT THE LAW IS SACRED TO THEM. ESPECIALLY DOOM'S LAW.
IN FACT, THEY PUT THAT CONCRETE CURTAIN UP--TO PREVENT UNAUTHORIZED BORDER CROSSINGS.
INCIDENTALLY--WHAT'S "SPIDER-SENSE"?
I... HUH. THAT'S WEIRD.
I DON'T KNOW.
...
SPIDEY... HAVE YOU HAD ANY STRANGE DREAMS LATELY?

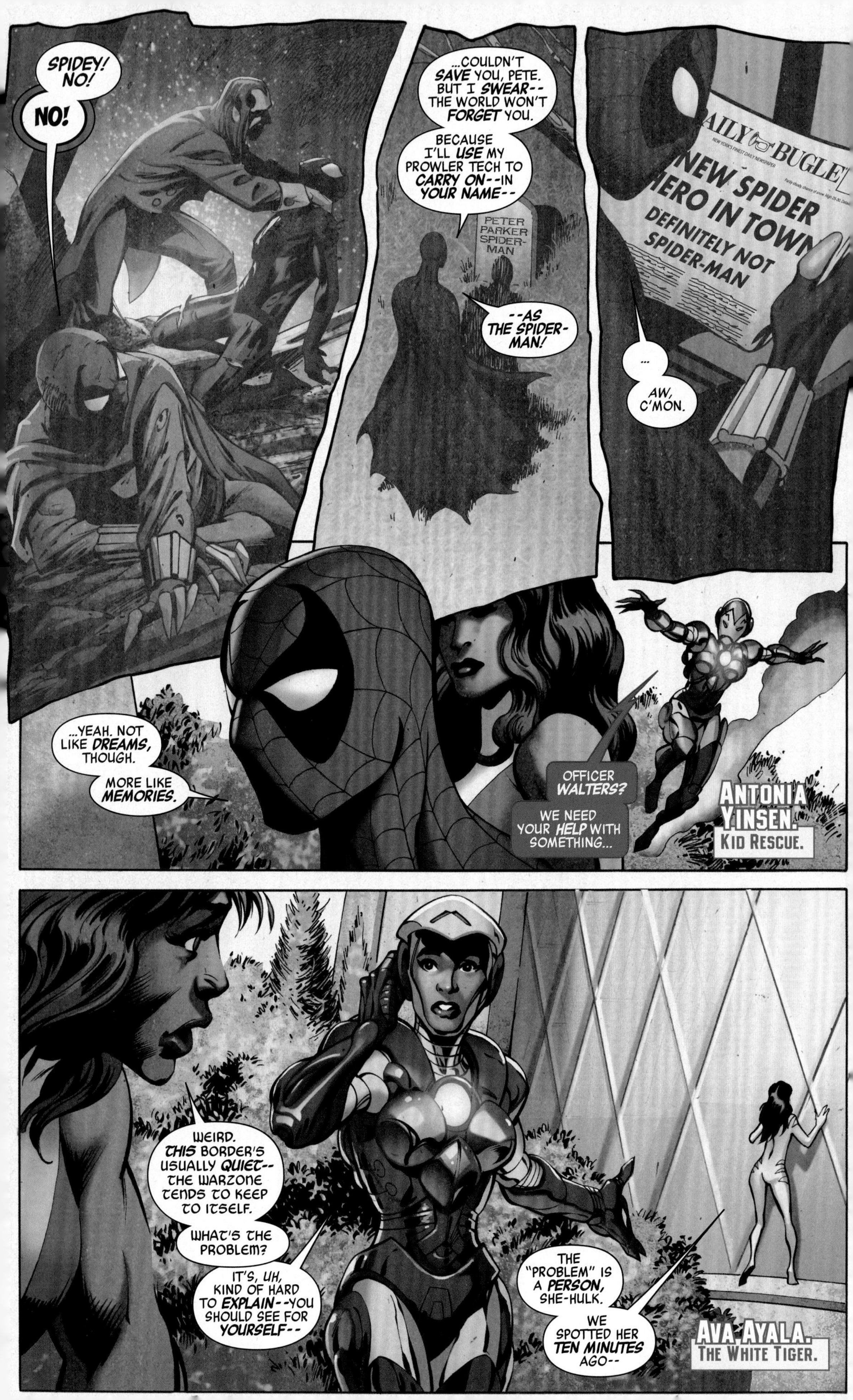

SPIDEY! NO!
NO!
...COULDN'T SAVE YOU, PETE. BUT I SWEAR-- THE WORLD WON'T FORGET YOU.
BECAUSE I'LL USE MY PROWLER TECH TO CARRY ON--IN YOUR NAME--
PETER PARKER SPIDER-MAN
--AS THE SPIDER-MAN!
DAILY BUGLE
NEW YORK'S FINEST DAILY NEWSPAPER
NEW SPIDER HERO IN TOWN
DEFINITELY NOT SPIDER-MAN
...
AW, C'MON.
...YEAH. NOT LIKE DREAMS, THOUGH.
MORE LIKE MEMORIES.
OFFICER WALTERS?
WE NEED YOUR HELP WITH SOMETHING...
ANTONIA YINSEN. KID RESCUE.
WEIRD. THIS BORDER'S USUALLY QUIET--THE WARZONE TENDS TO KEEP TO ITSELF.
WHAT'S THE PROBLEM?
IT'S, UH, KIND OF HARD TO EXPLAIN--YOU SHOULD SEE FOR YOURSELF--
THE "PROBLEM" IS A PERSON, SHE-HULK.
WE SPOTTED HER TEN MINUTES AGO--
AVA AYALA. THE WHITE TIGER.

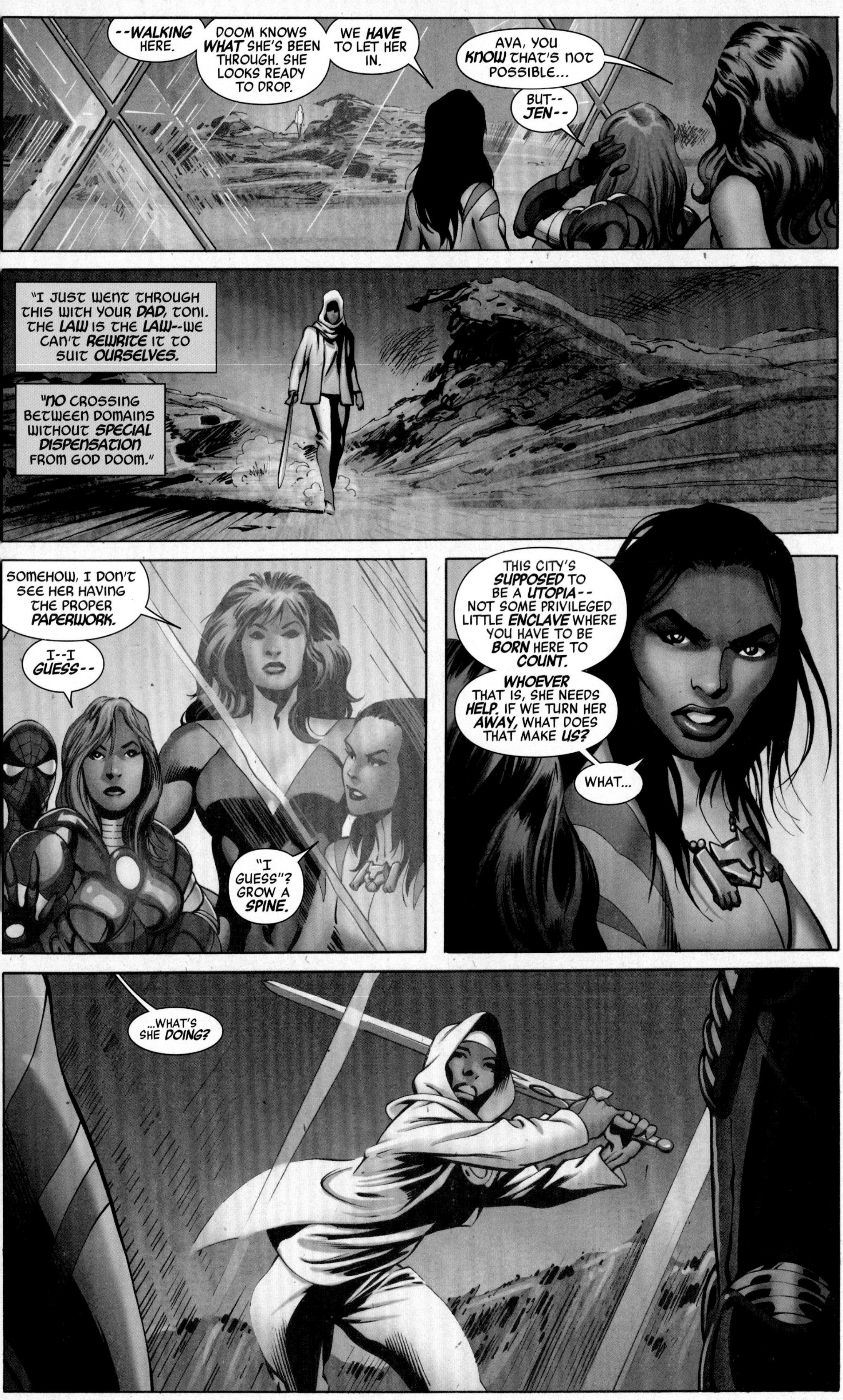
--WALKING HERE.
DOOM KNOWS WHAT SHE'S BEEN THROUGH. SHE LOOKS READY TO DROP.
WE HAVE TO LET HER IN.
AVA, YOU KNOW THAT'S NOT POSSIBLE...
BUT-- JEN--
"I JUST WENT THROUGH THIS WITH YOUR DAD, TONI. THE LAW IS THE LAW--WE CAN'T REWRITE IT TO SUIT OURSELVES.
"NO CROSSING BETWEEN DOMAINS WITHOUT SPECIAL DISPENSATION FROM GOD DOOM."
SOMEHOW, I DON'T SEE HER HAVING THE PROPER PAPERWORK.
I--I GUESS--
"I GUESS"? GROW A SPINE.
THIS CITY'S SUPPOSED TO BE A UTOPIA-- NOT SOME PRIVILEGED LITTLE ENCLAVE WHERE YOU HAVE TO BE BORN HERE TO COUNT.
WHOEVER THAT IS, SHE NEEDS HELP. IF WE TURN HER AWAY, WHAT DOES THAT MAKE US?
WHAT...
...WHAT'S SHE DOING?

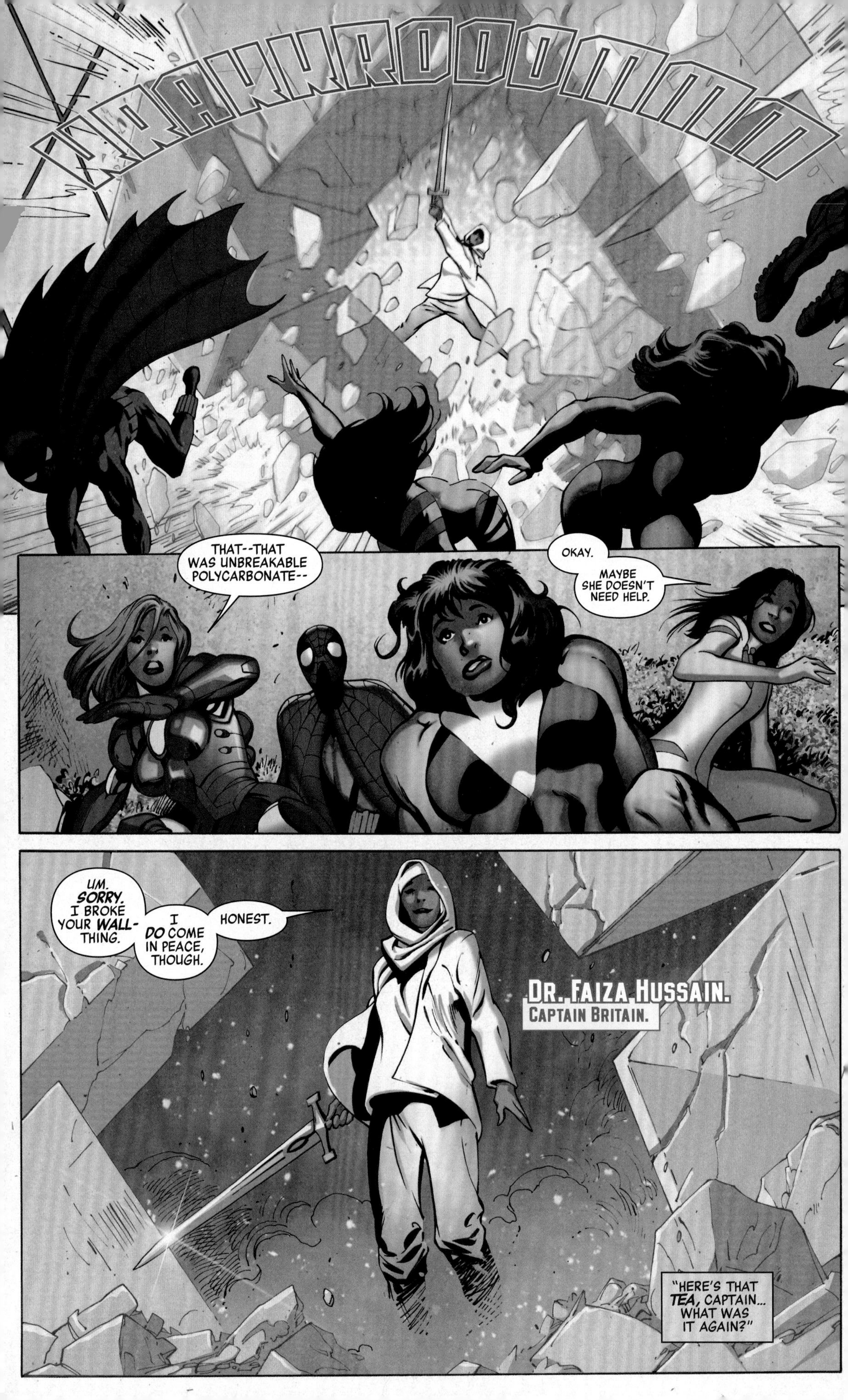

THAT--THAT WAS UNBREAKABLE POLYCARBONATE--
OKAY.
MAYBE SHE DOESN'T NEED HELP.
UM. SORRY. I BROKE YOUR WALL-THING.
I DO COME IN PEACE, THOUGH.
HONEST.
DR. FAIZA HUSSAIN.
CAPTAIN BRITAIN.
"HERE'S THAT TEA, CAPTAIN... WHAT WAS IT AGAIN?"

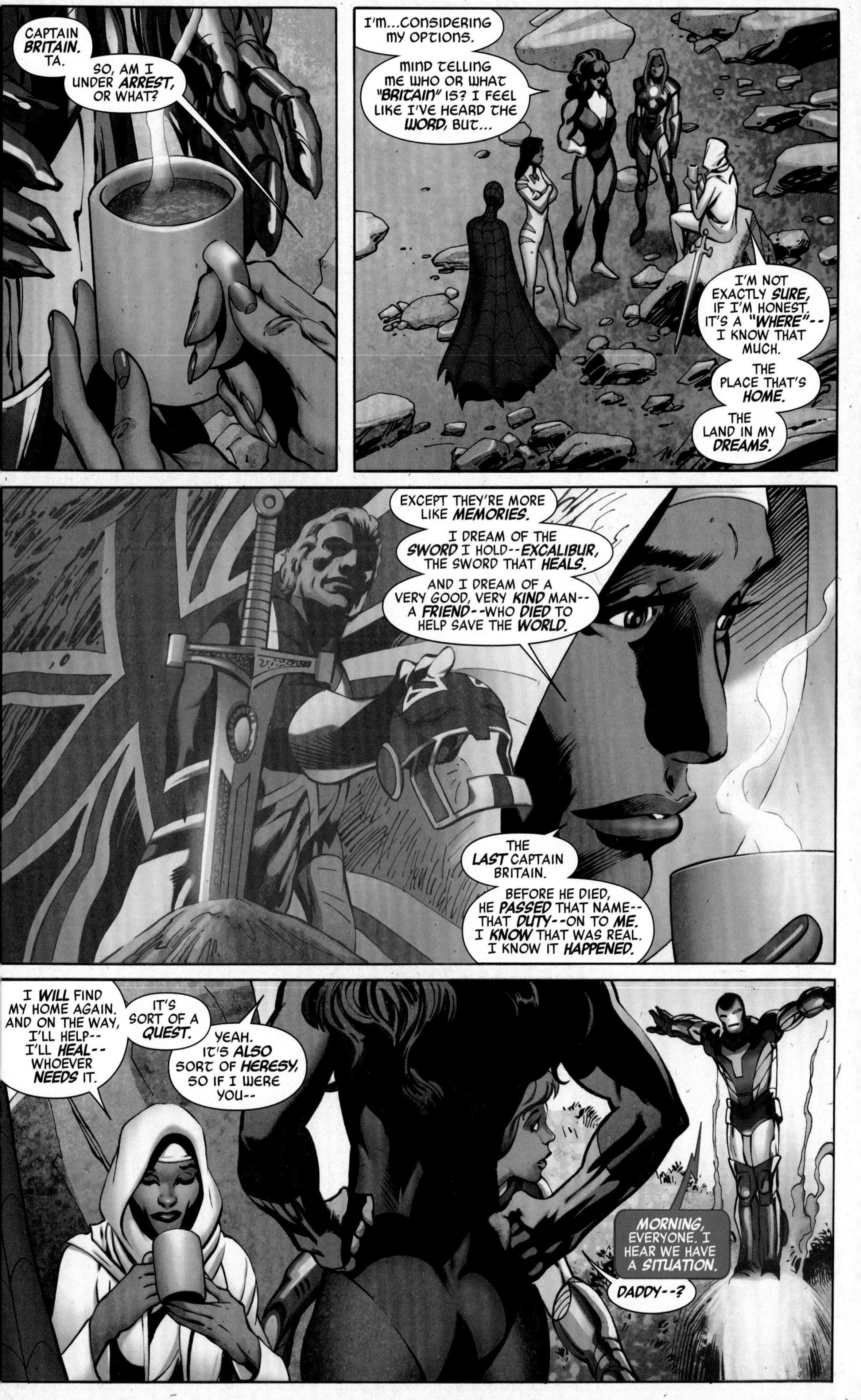
CAPTAIN BRITAIN. TA.
SO, AM I UNDER ARREST, OR WHAT?
I'M...CONSIDERING MY OPTIONS.
MIND TELLING ME WHO OR WHAT "BRITAIN" IS? I FEEL LIKE I'VE HEARD THE WORD, BUT...
I'M NOT EXACTLY SURE, IF I'M HONEST. IT'S A "WHERE"-- I KNOW THAT MUCH.
THE PLACE THAT'S HOME.
THE LAND IN MY DREAMS.
EXCEPT THEY'RE MORE LIKE MEMORIES.
I DREAM OF THE SWORD I HOLD--EXCALIBUR, THE SWORD THAT HEALS.
AND I DREAM OF A VERY GOOD, VERY KIND MAN-- A FRIEND--WHO DIED TO HELP SAVE THE WORLD.
THE LAST CAPTAIN BRITAIN.
BEFORE HE DIED, HE PASSED THAT NAME-- THAT DUTY--ON TO ME. I KNOW THAT WAS REAL. I KNOW IT HAPPENED.
I WILL FIND MY HOME AGAIN. AND ON THE WAY, I'LL HELP-- I'LL HEAL-- WHOEVER NEEDS IT.
IT'S SORT OF A QUEST.
YEAH. IT'S ALSO SORT OF HERESY, SO IF I WERE YOU--
MORNING, EVERYONE. I HEAR WE HAVE A SITUATION.
DADDY--?

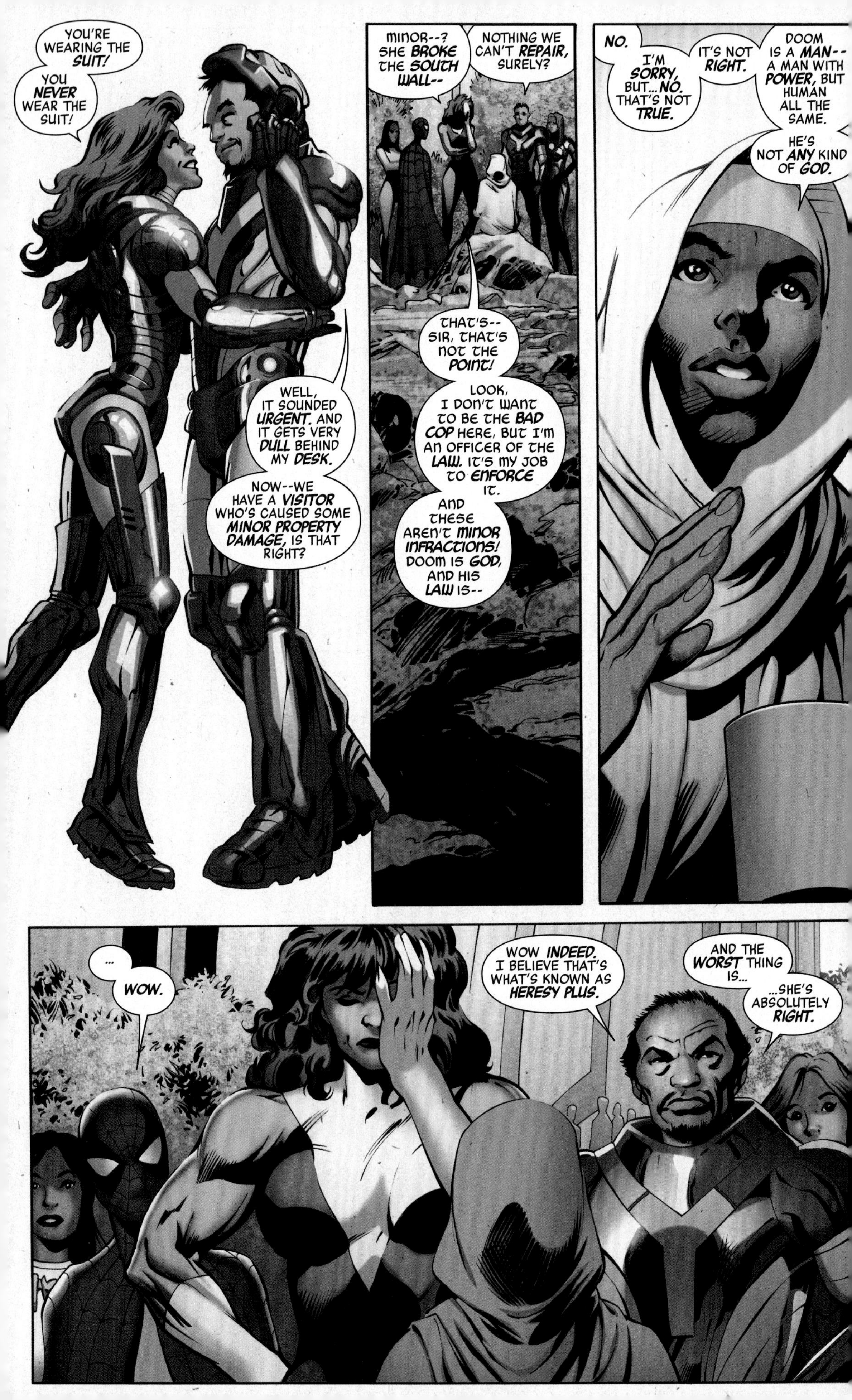
YOU'RE WEARING THE SUIT!
YOU NEVER WEAR THE SUIT!
WELL, IT SOUNDED URGENT. AND IT GETS VERY DULL BEHIND MY DESK.
NOW--WE HAVE A VISITOR WHO'S CAUSED SOME MINOR PROPERTY DAMAGE, IS THAT RIGHT?
MINOR--? SHE BROKE THE SOUTH WALL--
NOTHING WE CAN'T REPAIR, SURELY?
THAT'S-- SIR, THAT'S NOT THE POINT!
LOOK, I DON'T WANT TO BE THE BAD COP HERE, BUT I'M AN OFFICER OF THE LAW. IT'S MY JOB TO ENFORCE IT.
AND THESE AREN'T MINOR INFRACTIONS! DOOM IS GOD, AND HIS LAW IS--
NO.
I'M SORRY, BUT...NO. THAT'S NOT TRUE.
IT'S NOT RIGHT.
DOOM IS A MAN-- A MAN WITH POWER, BUT HUMAN ALL THE SAME.
HE'S NOT ANY KIND OF GOD.
...
WOW.
WOW INDEED. I BELIEVE THAT'S WHAT'S KNOWN AS HERESY PLUS.
AND THE WORST THING IS...
...SHE'S ABSOLUTELY RIGHT.

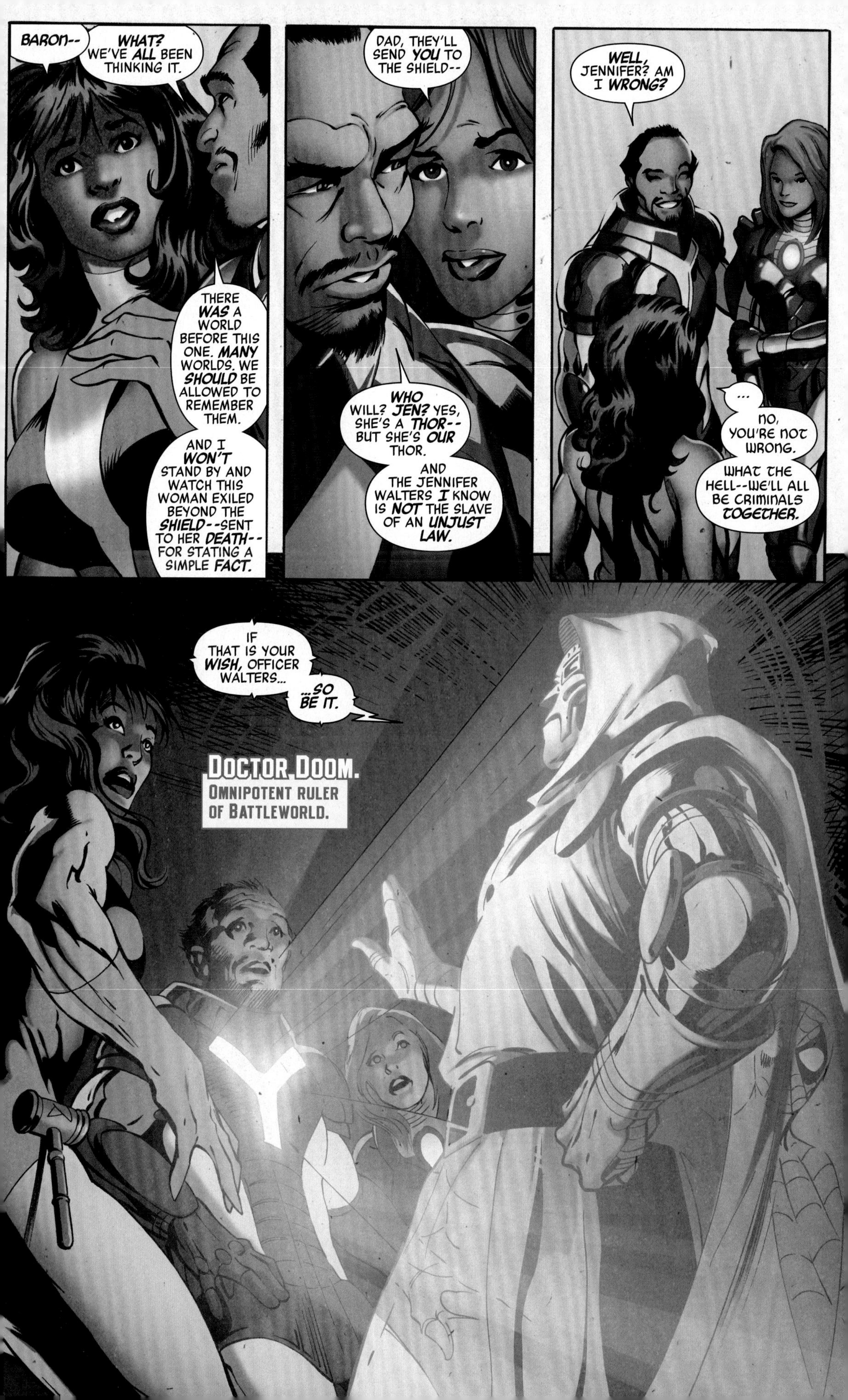

BARON--
WHAT? WE'VE ALL BEEN THINKING IT.
THERE WAS A WORLD BEFORE THIS ONE. MANY WORLDS. WE SHOULD BE ALLOWED TO REMEMBER THEM.
AND I WON'T STAND BY AND WATCH THIS WOMAN EXILED BEYOND THE SHIELD--SENT TO HER DEATH--FOR STATING A SIMPLE FACT.
DAD, THEY'LL SEND YOU TO THE SHIELD--
WHO WILL? JEN? YES, SHE'S A THOR--BUT SHE'S OUR THOR.
AND THE JENNIFER WALTERS I KNOW IS NOT THE SLAVE OF AN UNJUST LAW.
WELL, JENNIFER? AM I WRONG?
...
NO, YOU'RE NOT WRONG.
WHAT THE HELL--WE'LL ALL BE CRIMINALS TOGETHER.
IF THAT IS YOUR WISH, OFFICER WALTERS...
...SO BE IT.
DOCTOR DOOM.
OMNIPOTENT RULER OF BATTLEWORLD.

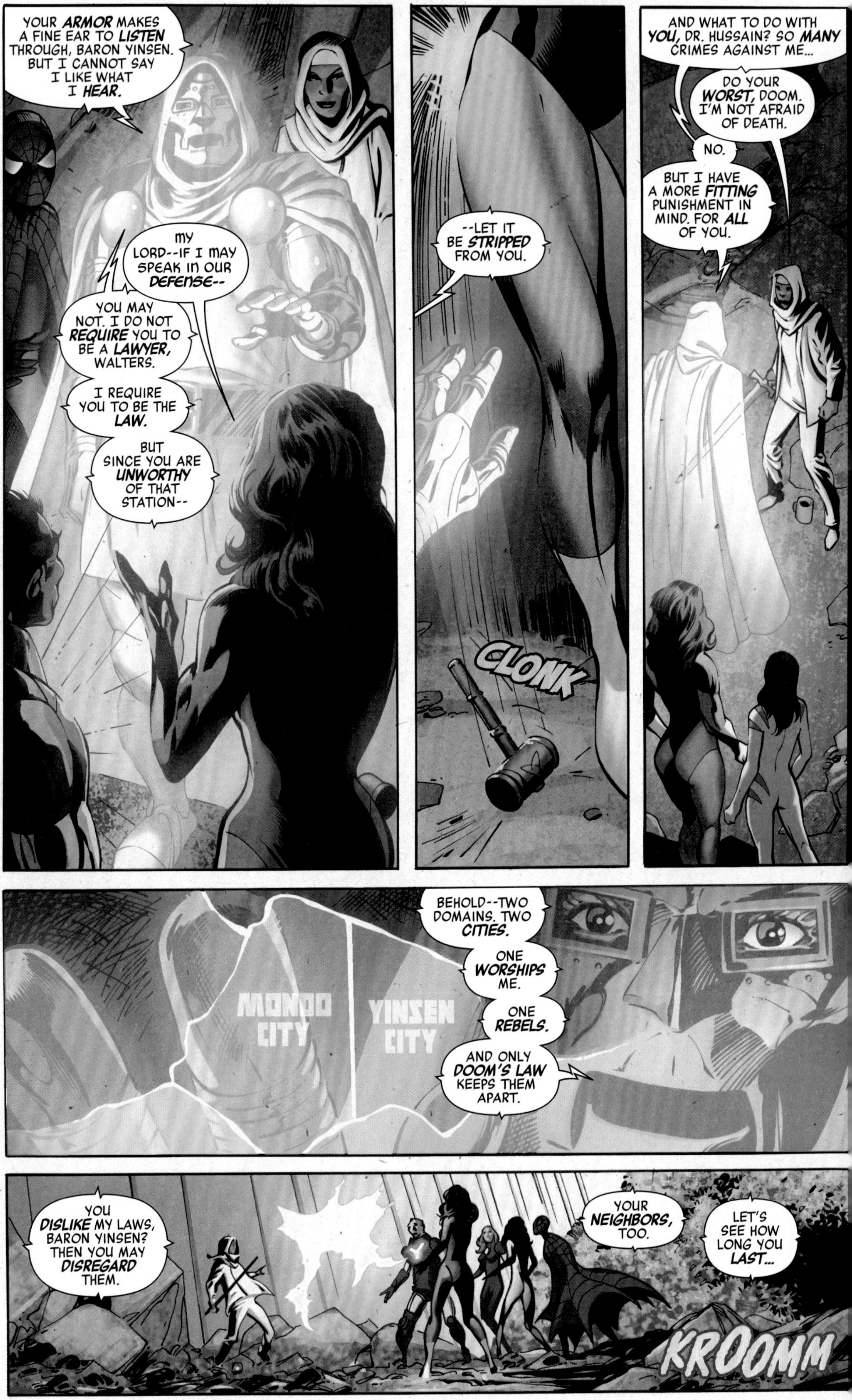
YOUR ARMOR MAKES A FINE EAR TO LISTEN THROUGH, BARON YINSEN. BUT I CANNOT SAY I LIKE WHAT I HEAR.
MY LORD--IF I MAY SPEAK IN OUR DEFENSE--
YOU MAY NOT. I DO NOT REQUIRE YOU TO BE A LAWYER, WALTERS.
I REQUIRE YOU TO BE THE LAW.
BUT SINCE YOU ARE UNWORTHY OF THAT STATION--
--LET IT BE STRIPPED FROM YOU.
CLONK
AND WHAT TO DO WITH YOU, DR. HUSSAIN? SO MANY CRIMES AGAINST ME...
DO YOUR WORST, DOOM. I'M NOT AFRAID OF DEATH.
NO.
BUT I HAVE A MORE FITTING PUNISHMENT IN MIND. FOR ALL OF YOU.
BEHOLD--TWO DOMAINS. TWO CITIES.
ONE WORSHIPS ME.
ONE REBELS.
AND ONLY DOOM'S LAW KEEPS THEM APART.
MONDO CITY
YINSEN CITY
YOU DISLIKE MY LAWS, BARON YINSEN? THEN YOU MAY DISREGARD THEM.
YOUR NEIGHBORS, TOO.
LET'S SEE HOW LONG YOU LAST...
KROOMM

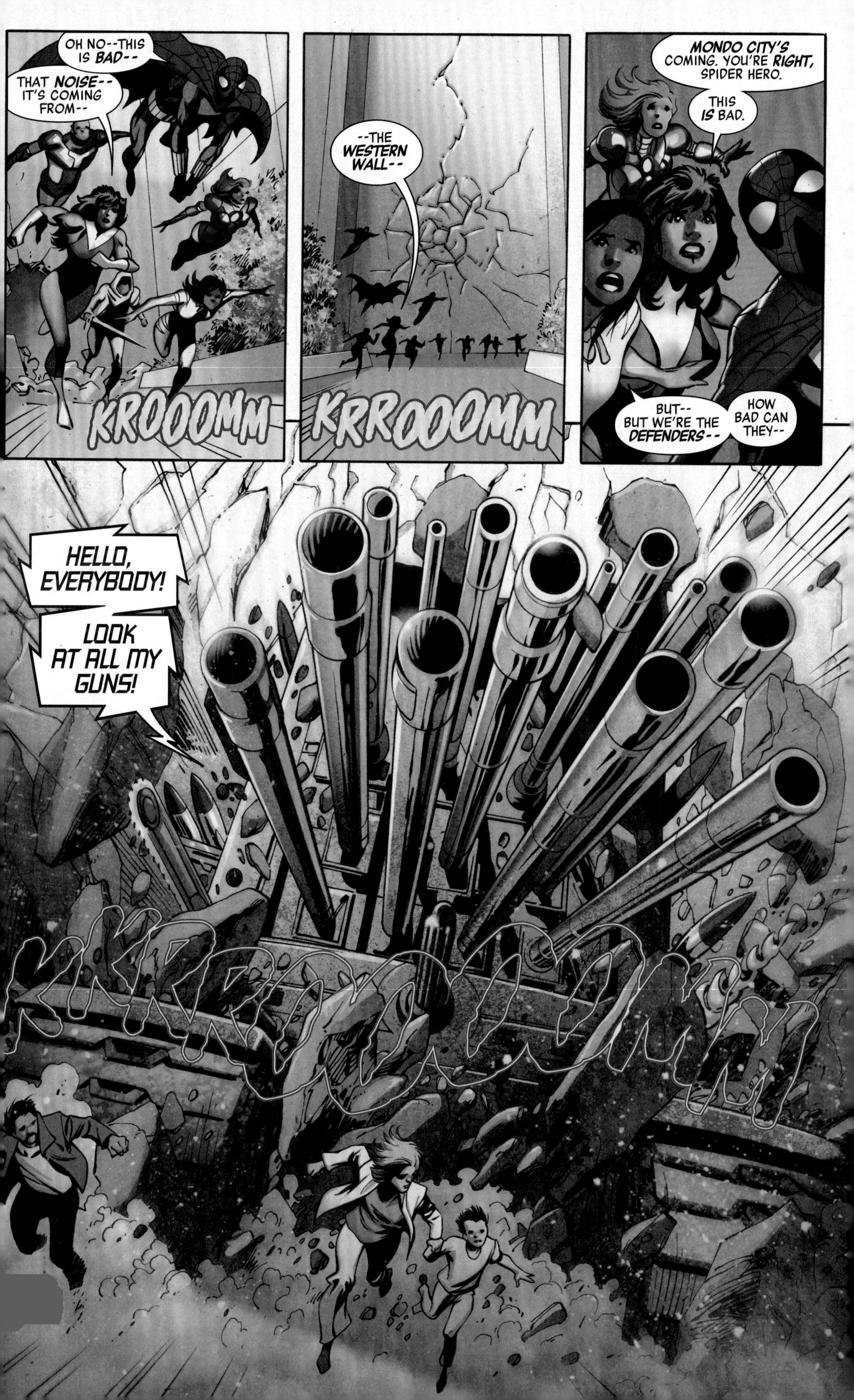
OH NO--THIS IS BAD--
THAT NOISE-- IT'S COMING FROM--
KROOOMM
--THE WESTERN WALL--
KRROOOMM
MONDO CITY'S COMING. YOU'RE RIGHT, SPIDER HERO.
THIS IS BAD.
BUT-- BUT WE'RE THE DEFENDERS--
HOW BAD CAN THEY--
HELLO, EVERYBODY!
LOOK AT ALL MY GUNS!
KKRROOOOMM

DEFENDERS! GET THE CIVILIANS OUT OF HERE!

I'LL HOLD THEM BACK--

DON'T *WORRY*, FOLKS--WE'VE *GOT* THIS--

BARON--

RELAX. I'M FINE.

WANT ME TO *SQUOOSH* HIM, BOSS?

NO THANKS, WAR MACHINE.

BOSS FROST-- MIND-SCAN. TELL ME WHAT KIND OF *FORCE SCREEN* THIS CREEP'S GOT.

BASIC *ELECTROMAGNETIC*, BOSS MAGNICONTE.

THEN IT'S *VULNERABLE*--

From the *Boss Cadet's Manual:*

The Boss's standard-use *"Overseer"* firearm fires *six* different types of bullets, chosen by voice command.

BOAM

--TO A *PHASER ROUND!*

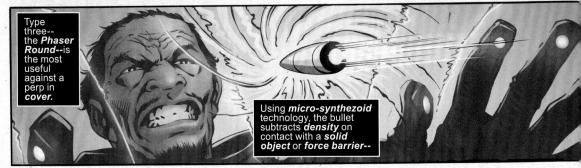

Type three-- the *Phaser Round*--is the most useful against a perp in *cover.*

Using *micro-synthezoid* technology, the bullet subtracts *density* on contact with a *solid object* or *force barrier*--

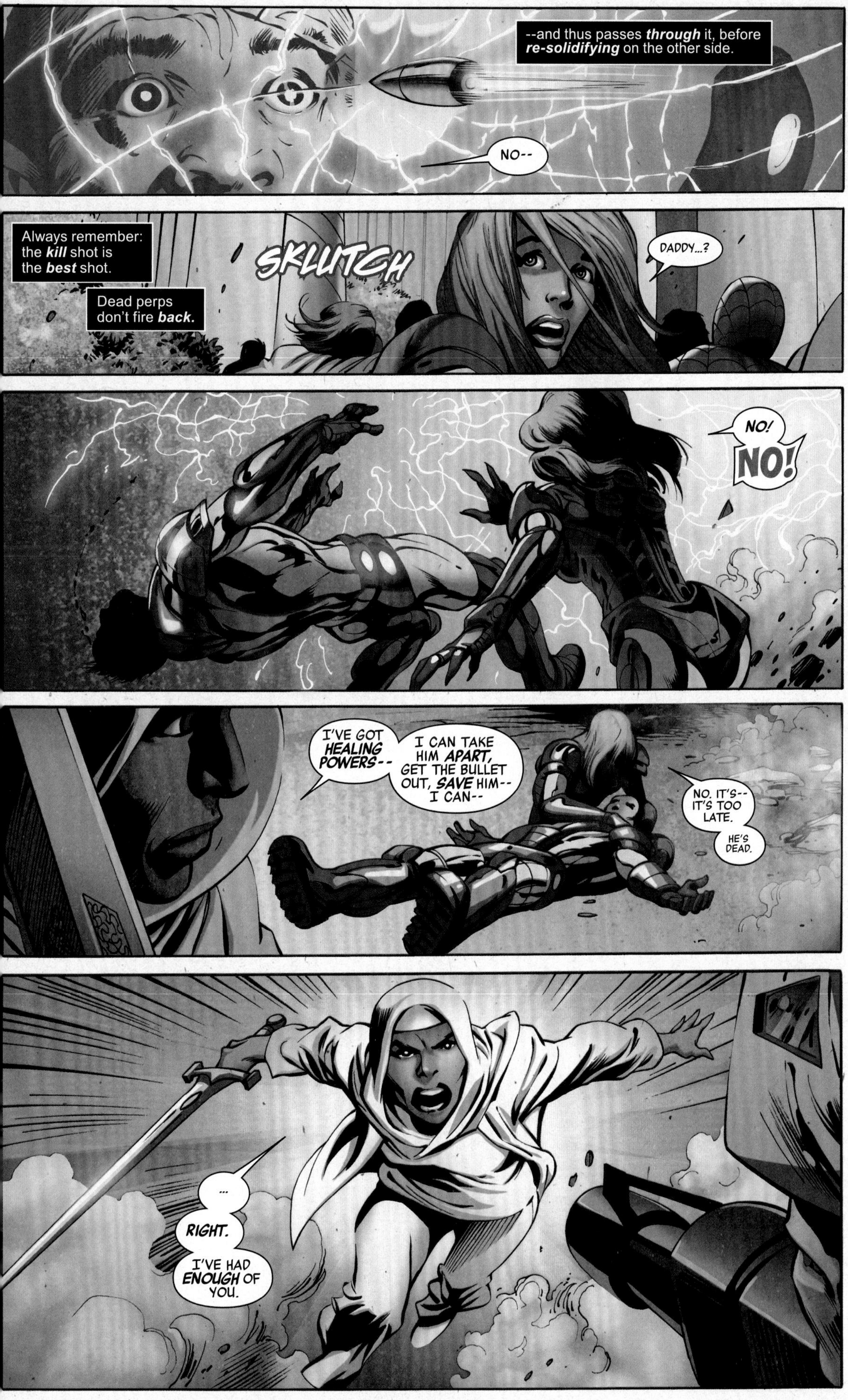

--and thus passes **through** it, before **re-solidifying** on the other side.
NO--
Always remember: the **kill** shot is the **best** shot.
SKLUTCH
Dead perps don't fire **back.**
DADDY...?
NO!
NO!
I'VE GOT **HEALING POWERS**--
I CAN TAKE HIM **APART,** GET THE BULLET OUT, **SAVE** HIM-- I CAN--
NO. IT'S-- IT'S TOO LATE.
HE'S DEAD.
...
RIGHT.
I'VE HAD **ENOUGH** OF YOU.

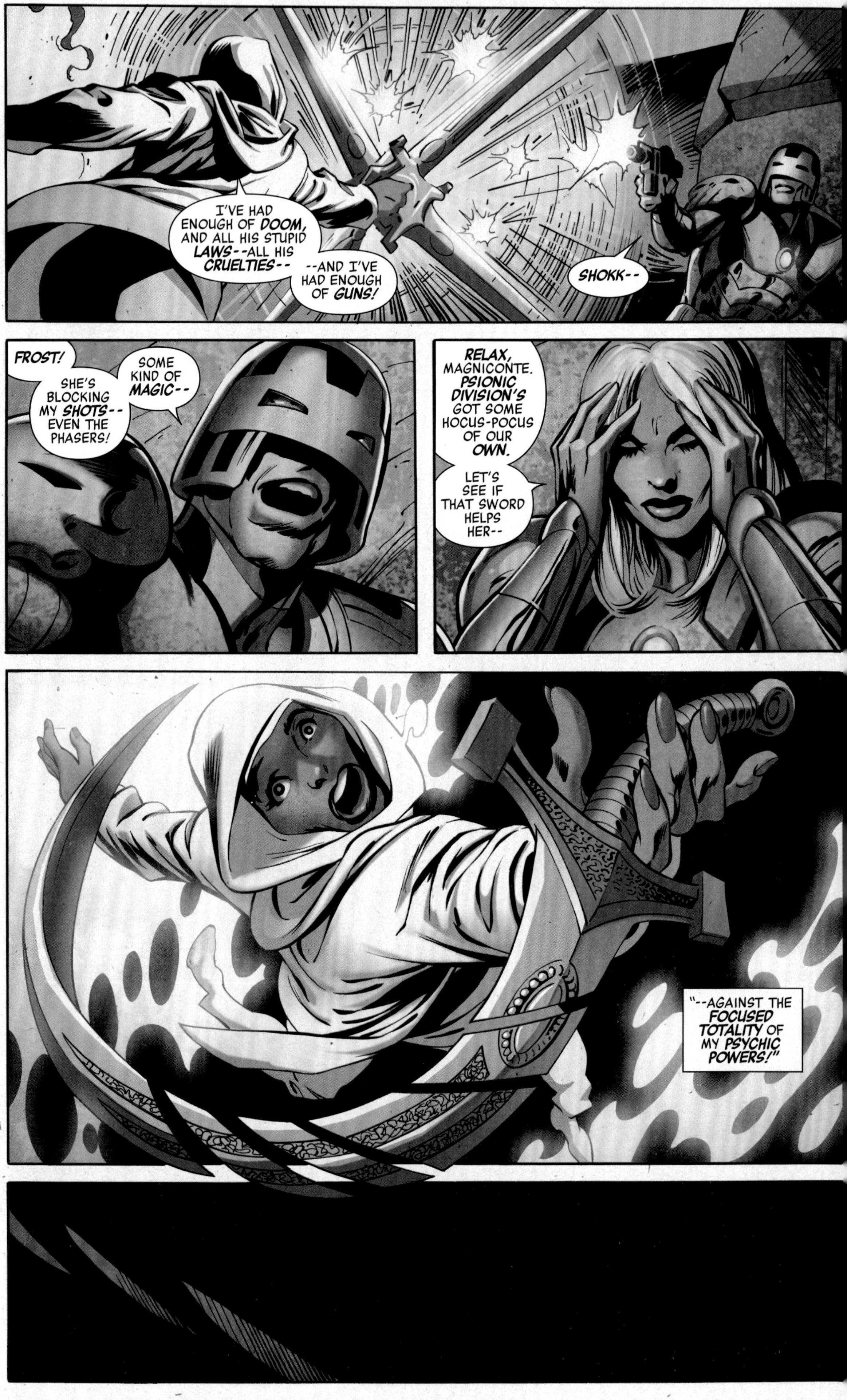
I'VE HAD ENOUGH OF DOOM, AND ALL HIS STUPID LAWS--ALL HIS CRUELTIES--
--AND I'VE HAD ENOUGH OF GUNS!
SHOKK--
FROST!
SHE'S BLOCKING MY SHOTS--EVEN THE PHASERS!
SOME KIND OF MAGIC--
RELAX, MAGNICONTE. PSIONIC DIVISION'S GOT SOME HOCUS-POCUS OF OUR OWN.
LET'S SEE IF THAT SWORD HELPS HER--
"--AGAINST THE FOCUSED TOTALITY OF MY PSYCHIC POWERS!"

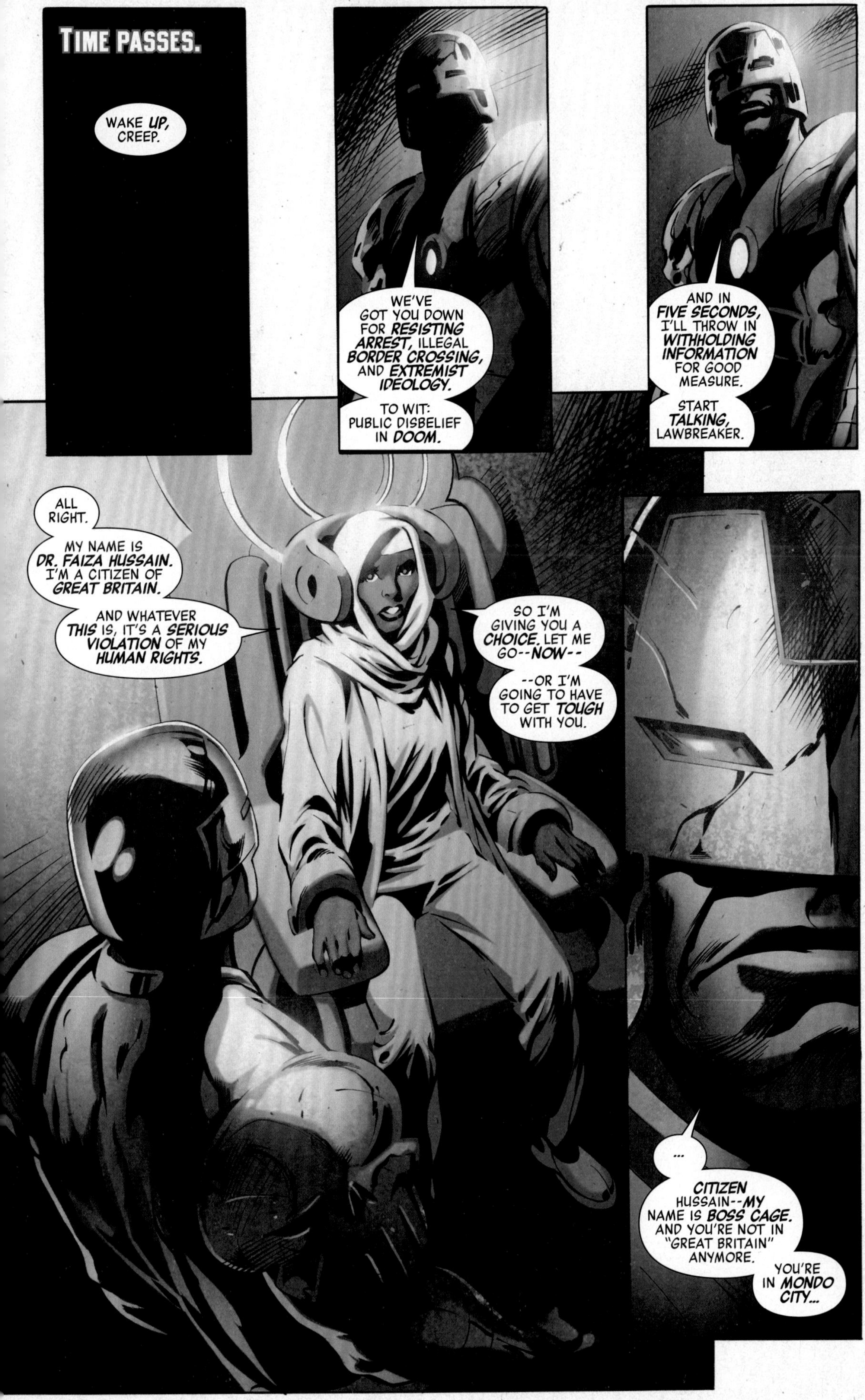

TIME PASSES.
WAKE UP, CREEP.
WE'VE GOT YOU DOWN FOR RESISTING ARREST, ILLEGAL BORDER CROSSING, AND EXTREMIST IDEOLOGY.
TO WIT: PUBLIC DISBELIEF IN DOOM.
AND IN FIVE SECONDS, I'LL THROW IN WITHHOLDING INFORMATION FOR GOOD MEASURE.
START TALKING, LAWBREAKER.
ALL RIGHT.
MY NAME IS DR. FAIZA HUSSAIN. I'M A CITIZEN OF GREAT BRITAIN.
AND WHATEVER THIS IS, IT'S A SERIOUS VIOLATION OF MY HUMAN RIGHTS.
SO I'M GIVING YOU A CHOICE. LET ME GO--NOW--
--OR I'M GOING TO HAVE TO GET TOUGH WITH YOU.
...
CITIZEN HUSSAIN--MY NAME IS BOSS CAGE. AND YOU'RE NOT IN "GREAT BRITAIN" ANYMORE.
YOU'RE IN MONDO CITY...

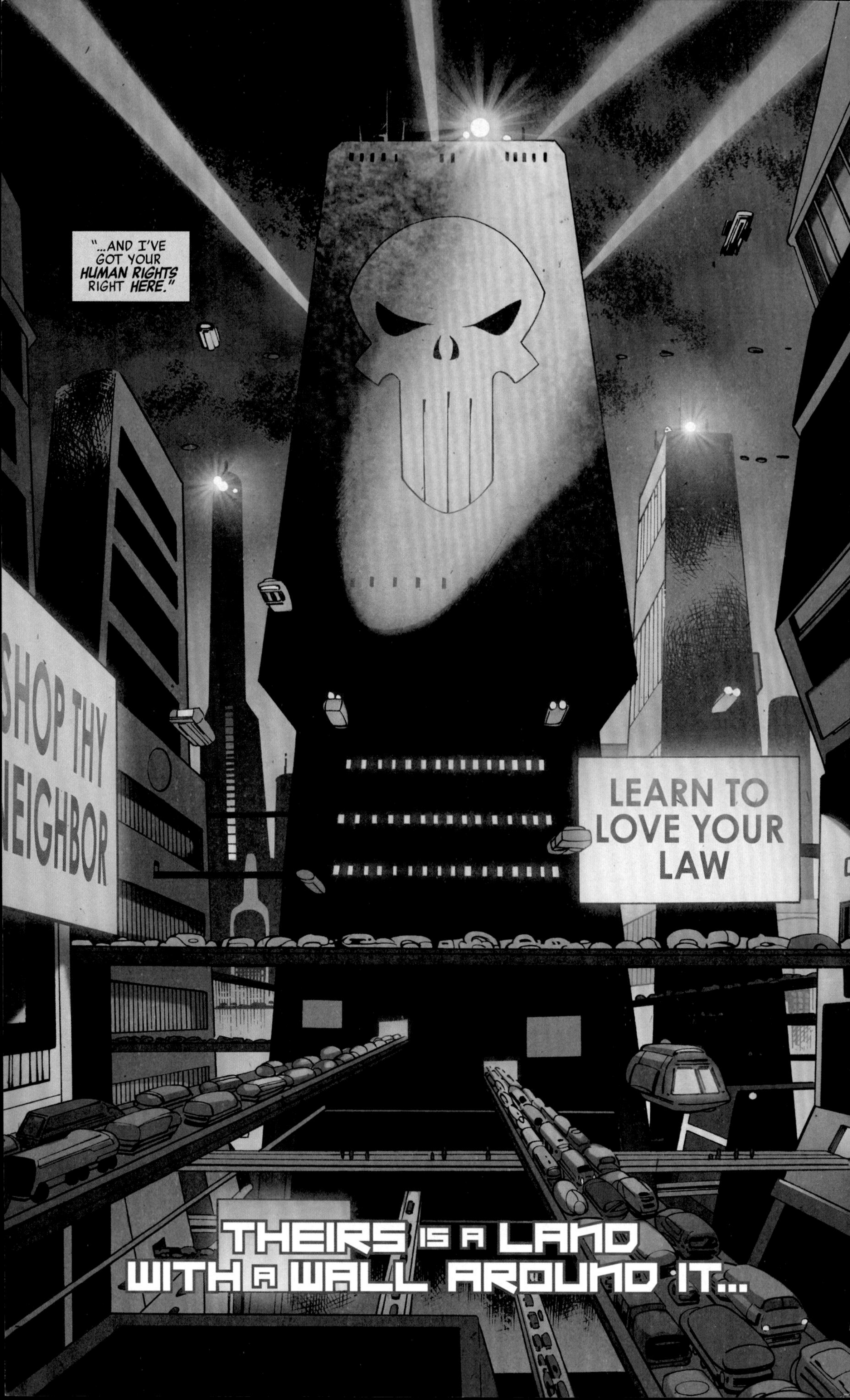
"...AND I'VE GOT YOUR HUMAN RIGHTS RIGHT HERE."
SHOP THY NEIGHBOR
LEARN TO LOVE YOUR LAW
THEIRS IS A LAND WITH A WALL AROUND IT...

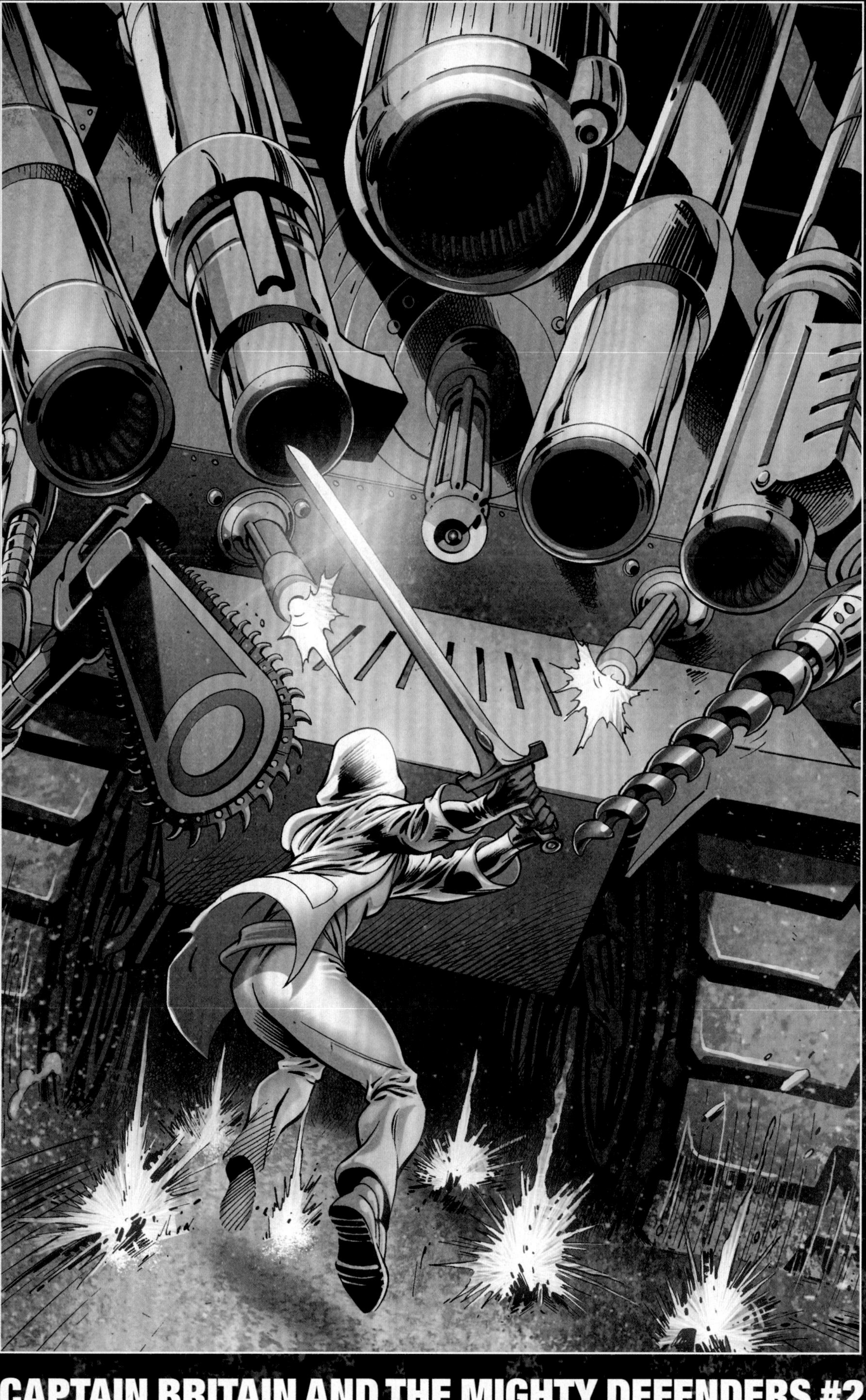

CAPTAIN BRITAIN AND THE MIGHTY DEFENDERS #2

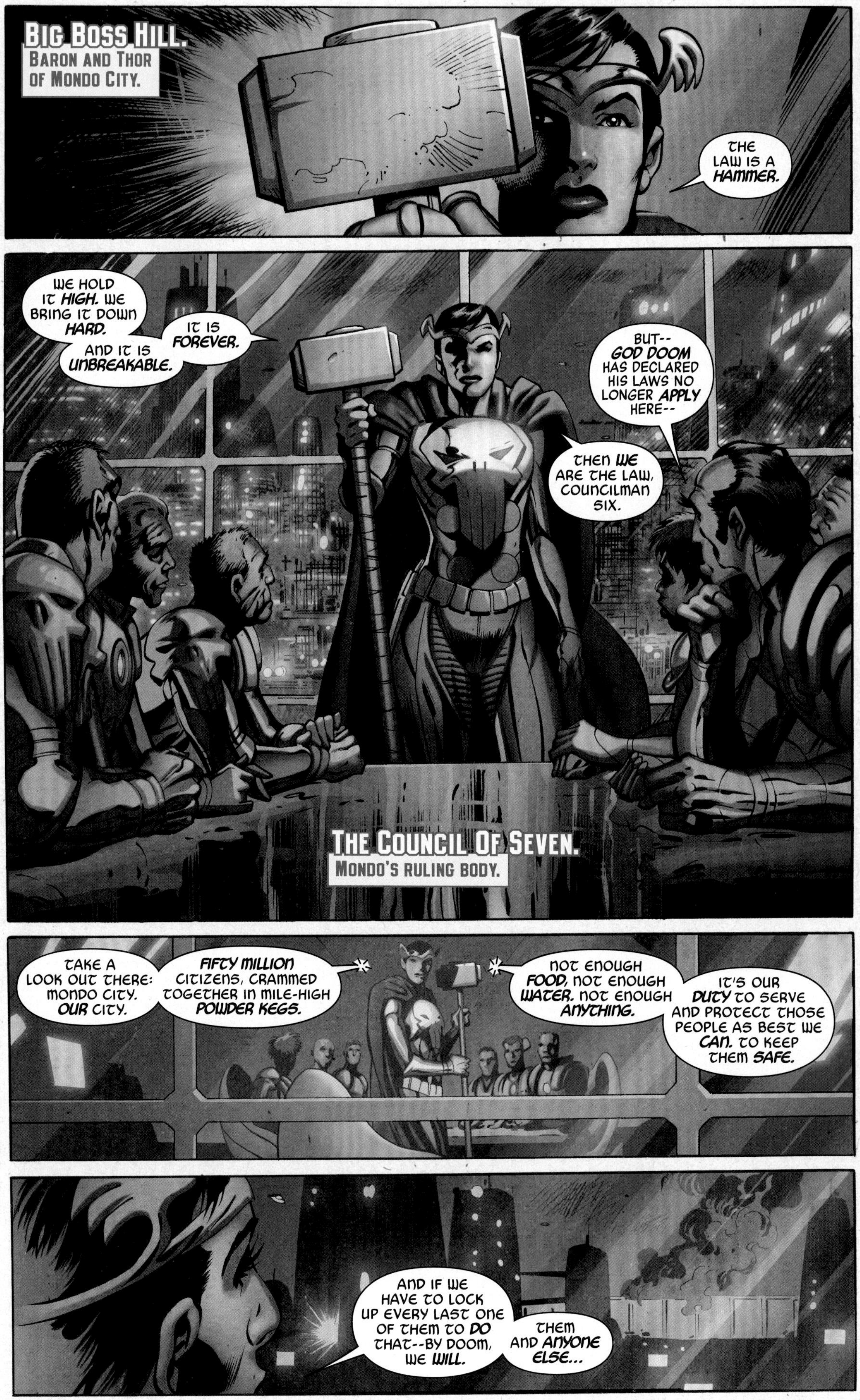

BIG BOSS HILL.
BARON AND THOR OF MONDO CITY.
THE LAW IS A HAMMER.
WE HOLD IT HIGH. WE BRING IT DOWN HARD.
AND IT IS UNBREAKABLE.
IT IS FOREVER.
BUT-- GOD DOOM HAS DECLARED HIS LAWS NO LONGER APPLY HERE--
THEN WE ARE THE LAW, COUNCILMAN SIX.
THE COUNCIL OF SEVEN.
MONDO'S RULING BODY.
TAKE A LOOK OUT THERE: MONDO CITY. OUR CITY.
FIFTY MILLION CITIZENS, CRAMMED TOGETHER IN MILE-HIGH POWDER KEGS.
NOT ENOUGH FOOD, NOT ENOUGH WATER. NOT ENOUGH ANYTHING.
IT'S OUR DUTY TO SERVE AND PROTECT THOSE PEOPLE AS BEST WE CAN. TO KEEP THEM SAFE.
AND IF WE HAVE TO LOCK UP EVERY LAST ONE OF THEM TO DO THAT--BY DOOM, WE WILL.
THEM AND ANYONE ELSE...

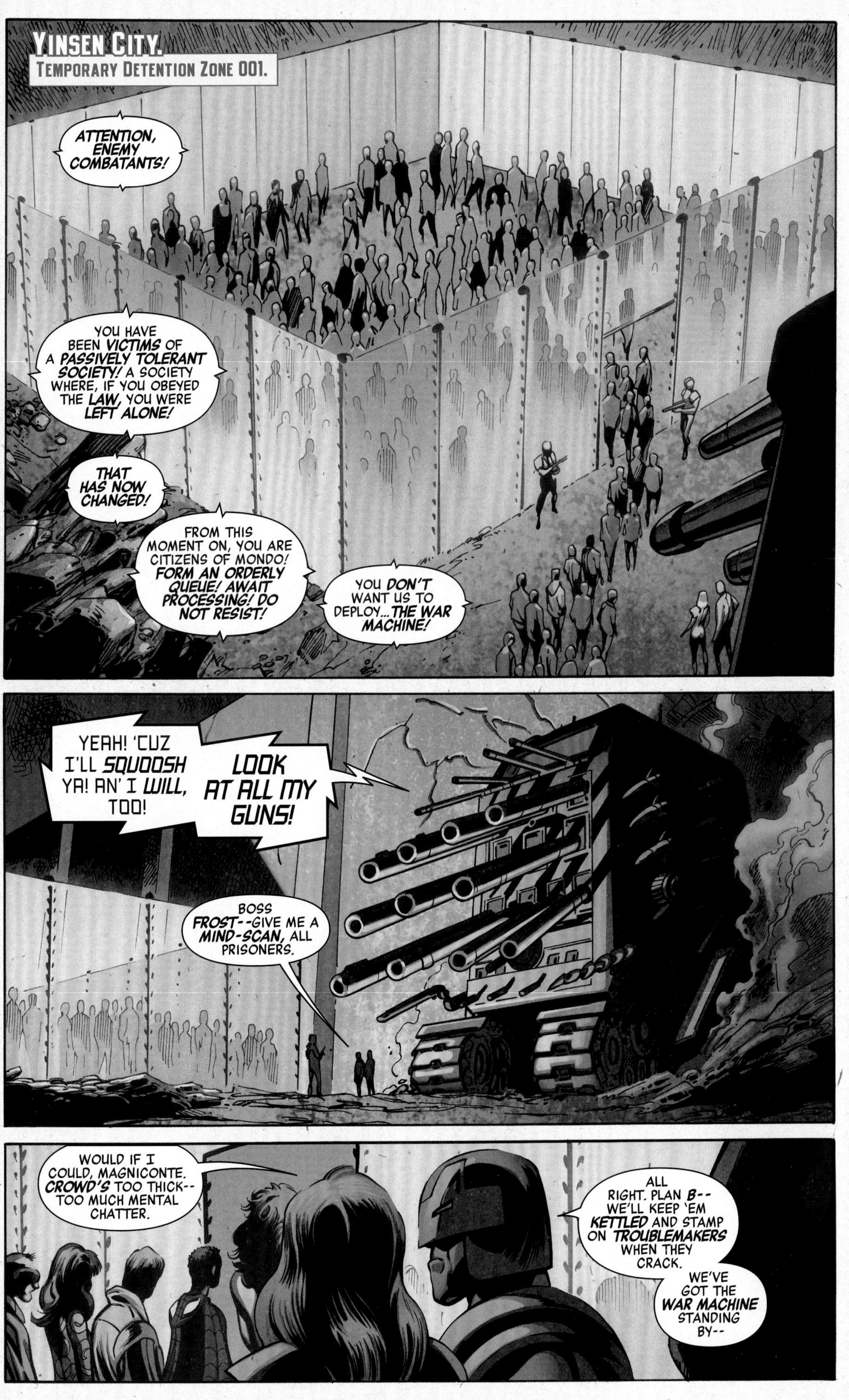
YINSEN CITY.
TEMPORARY DETENTION ZONE 001.
ATTENTION, ENEMY COMBATANTS!
YOU HAVE BEEN VICTIMS OF A PASSIVELY TOLERANT SOCIETY! A SOCIETY WHERE, IF YOU OBEYED THE LAW, YOU WERE LEFT ALONE!
THAT HAS NOW CHANGED!
FROM THIS MOMENT ON, YOU ARE CITIZENS OF MONDO! FORM AN ORDERLY QUEUE! AWAIT PROCESSING! DO NOT RESIST!
YOU DON'T WANT US TO DEPLOY...THE WAR MACHINE!
YEAH! 'CUZ I'LL SQUOOSH YA! AN' I WILL, TOO!
LOOK AT ALL MY GUNS!
BOSS FROST--GIVE ME A MIND-SCAN, ALL PRISONERS.
WOULD IF I COULD, MAGNICONTE. CROWD'S TOO THICK--TOO MUCH MENTAL CHATTER.
ALL RIGHT. PLAN B--WE'LL KEEP 'EM KETTLED AND STAMP ON TROUBLEMAKERS WHEN THEY CRACK.
WE'VE GOT THE WAR MACHINE STANDING BY--

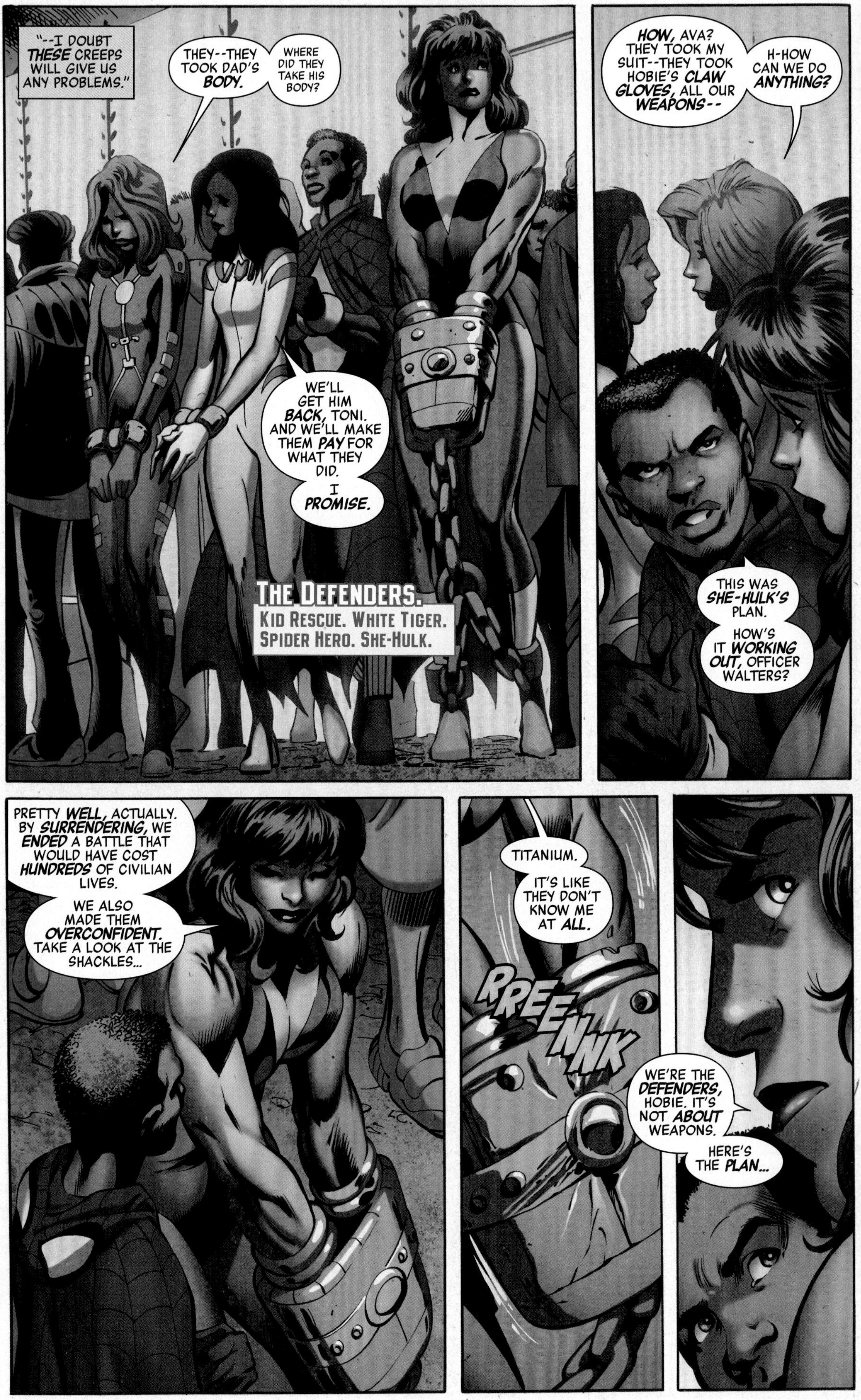
"--I DOUBT THESE CREEPS WILL GIVE US ANY PROBLEMS."
THEY--THEY TOOK DAD'S BODY.
WHERE DID THEY TAKE HIS BODY?
WE'LL GET HIM BACK, TONI. AND WE'LL MAKE THEM PAY FOR WHAT THEY DID.
I PROMISE.
THE DEFENDERS.
KID RESCUE. WHITE TIGER. SPIDER HERO. SHE-HULK.
HOW, AVA? THEY TOOK MY SUIT--THEY TOOK HOBIE'S CLAW GLOVES, ALL OUR WEAPONS--
H-HOW CAN WE DO ANYTHING?
THIS WAS SHE-HULK'S PLAN.
HOW'S IT WORKING OUT, OFFICER WALTERS?
PRETTY WELL, ACTUALLY. BY SURRENDERING, WE ENDED A BATTLE THAT WOULD HAVE COST HUNDREDS OF CIVILIAN LIVES.
WE ALSO MADE THEM OVERCONFIDENT. TAKE A LOOK AT THE SHACKLES...
TITANIUM.
IT'S LIKE THEY DON'T KNOW ME AT ALL.
RREENNK
WE'RE THE DEFENDERS, HOBIE. IT'S NOT ABOUT WEAPONS.
HERE'S THE PLAN...

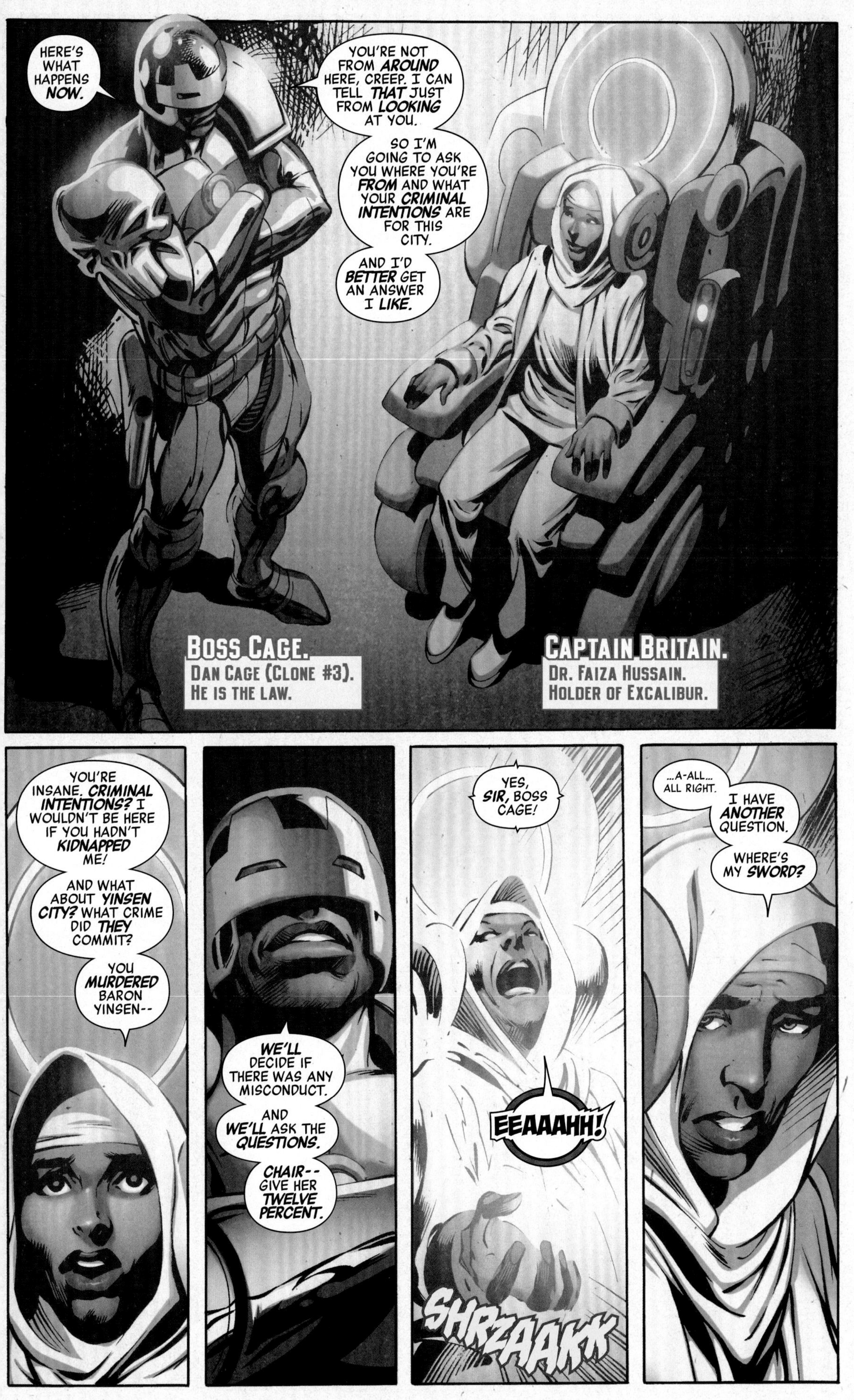
HERE'S WHAT HAPPENS NOW.
YOU'RE NOT FROM AROUND HERE, CREEP. I CAN TELL THAT JUST FROM LOOKING AT YOU.
SO I'M GOING TO ASK YOU WHERE YOU'RE FROM AND WHAT YOUR CRIMINAL INTENTIONS ARE FOR THIS CITY.
AND I'D BETTER GET AN ANSWER I LIKE.
BOSS CAGE.
DAN CAGE (CLONE #3). HE IS THE LAW.
CAPTAIN BRITAIN.
DR. FAIZA HUSSAIN. HOLDER OF EXCALIBUR.
YOU'RE INSANE. CRIMINAL INTENTIONS? I WOULDN'T BE HERE IF YOU HADN'T KIDNAPPED ME!
AND WHAT ABOUT YINSEN CITY? WHAT CRIME DID THEY COMMIT?
YOU MURDERED BARON YINSEN--
WE'LL DECIDE IF THERE WAS ANY MISCONDUCT.
AND WE'LL ASK THE QUESTIONS.
CHAIR--GIVE HER TWELVE PERCENT.
YES, SIR, BOSS CAGE!
EEAAAHH!
SHRZAAKK
...A-ALL... ALL RIGHT.
I HAVE ANOTHER QUESTION.
WHERE'S MY SWORD?

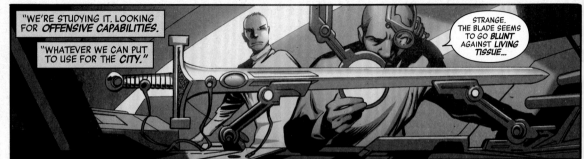

"WE'RE STUDYING IT. LOOKING FOR *OFFENSIVE CAPABILITIES.*

"WHATEVER WE CAN PUT TO USE FOR THE *CITY.*"

STRANGE. THE BLADE SEEMS TO GO *BLUNT* AGAINST *LIVING TISSUE...*

FAIR ENOUGH. 'SPOSE YOU'LL WANT TO KNOW ABOUT *MY* "OFFENSIVE CAPABILITIES," THEN.

THING *IS,* I DON'T REALLY *HAVE* ANY. I'M A *HEALER.* BIT LIKE A LIVING *SCALPEL.*

IF SOMEONE'S *SICK*...I CAN TAKE THEM *APART.* PAINLESSLY.

THEN I FIX WHAT'S *WRONG*...AND PUT THEM BACK *TOGETHER.*

SHOKK--!

AND I'VE GOT TO TELL YOU--THIS SENTIENT *TORTURE CHAIR* OF YOURS?

IT'S REALLY, *REALLY* SICK.

B-BOSS CAGE?

THAT'S MONDO CITY PROPERTY--

OH, RELAX. I HAVEN'T *HURT* IT.

WOW! I FEEL *GREAT*!

SEE? DO *YOU* WANT A GO?

JUST *TRY* IT, CREEP.

YOU'LL BE PUTTING *YOURSELF* BACK TOGETHER.

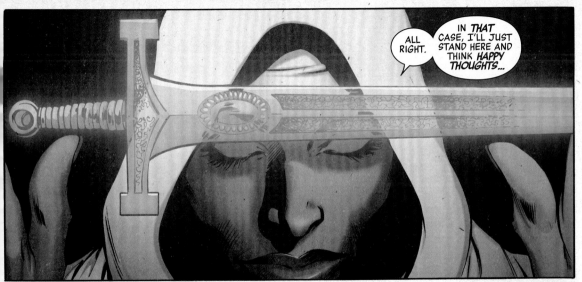

ALL RIGHT.

IN *THAT* CASE, I'LL JUST STAND HERE AND THINK *HAPPY* THOUGHTS...

H-HOLY DOOM ON TOAST--

THE *SWORD*! IT'S LEVITATING OUT OF THE CLAMPS! IT'S--

--IT'S *ALIVE*!

ATTENTION ALL UNITS--

KROOMM

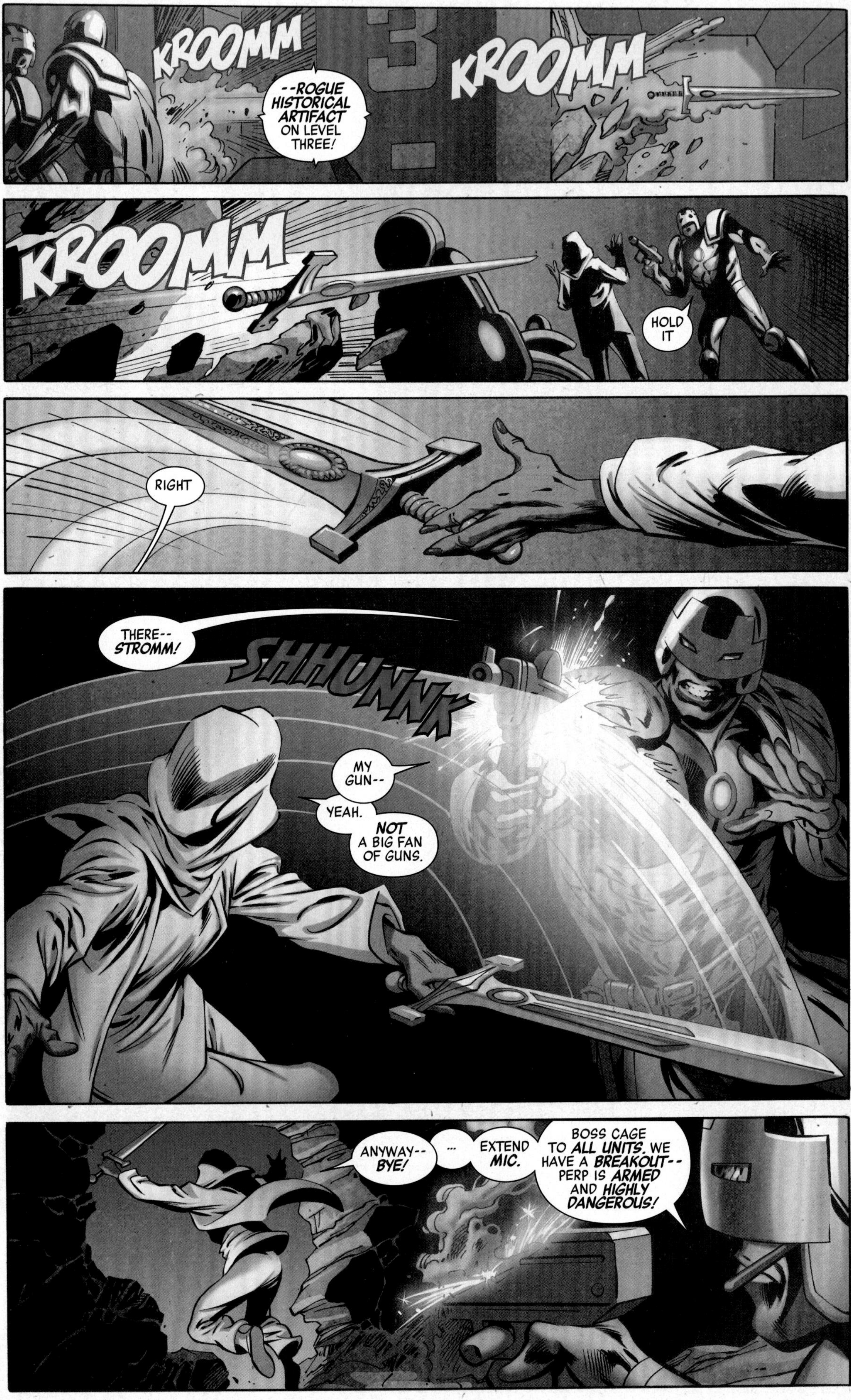
KROOMM
--ROGUE HISTORICAL ARTIFACT ON LEVEL THREE!
KROOMM
KROOMM
HOLD IT
RIGHT
THERE-- STROMM!
SHHUNNK
MY GUN--
YEAH. NOT A BIG FAN OF GUNS.
ANYWAY-- BYE!
...
EXTEND MIC.
BOSS CAGE TO ALL UNITS. WE HAVE A BREAKOUT-- PERP IS ARMED AND HIGHLY DANGEROUS!

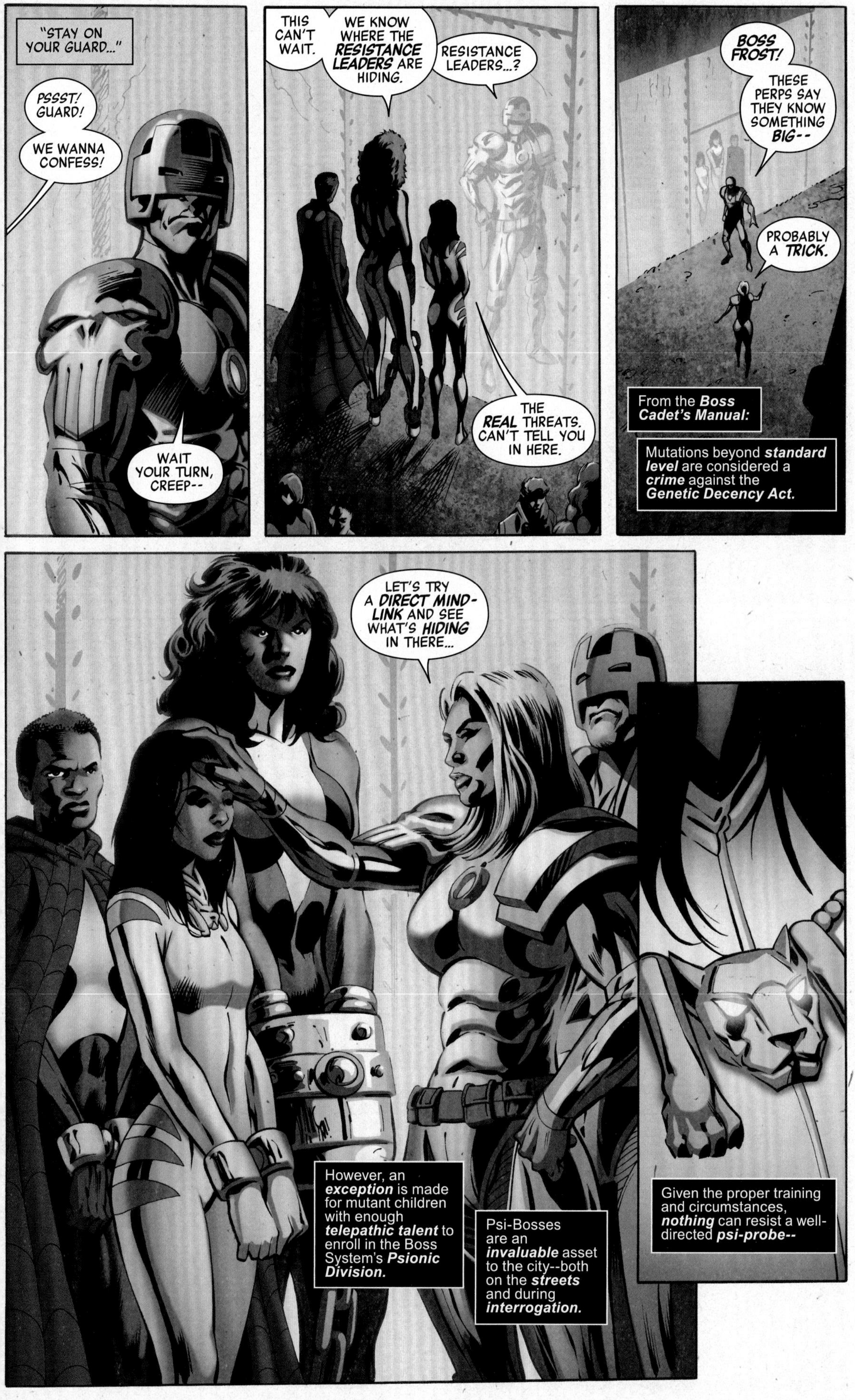
"STAY ON YOUR GUARD..."
PSSST! GUARD!
WE WANNA CONFESS!
WAIT YOUR TURN, CREEP--
THIS CAN'T WAIT.
WE KNOW WHERE THE RESISTANCE LEADERS ARE HIDING.
RESISTANCE LEADERS...?
THE REAL THREATS. CAN'T TELL YOU IN HERE.
BOSS FROST!
THESE PERPS SAY THEY KNOW SOMETHING BIG--
PROBABLY A TRICK.
From the Boss Cadet's Manual:
Mutations beyond standard level are considered a crime against the Genetic Decency Act.
LET'S TRY A DIRECT MIND-LINK AND SEE WHAT'S HIDING IN THERE...
However, an exception is made for mutant children with enough telepathic talent to enroll in the Boss System's Psionic Division.
Psi-Bosses are an invaluable asset to the city--both on the streets and during interrogation.
Given the proper training and circumstances, nothing can resist a well-directed psi-probe--

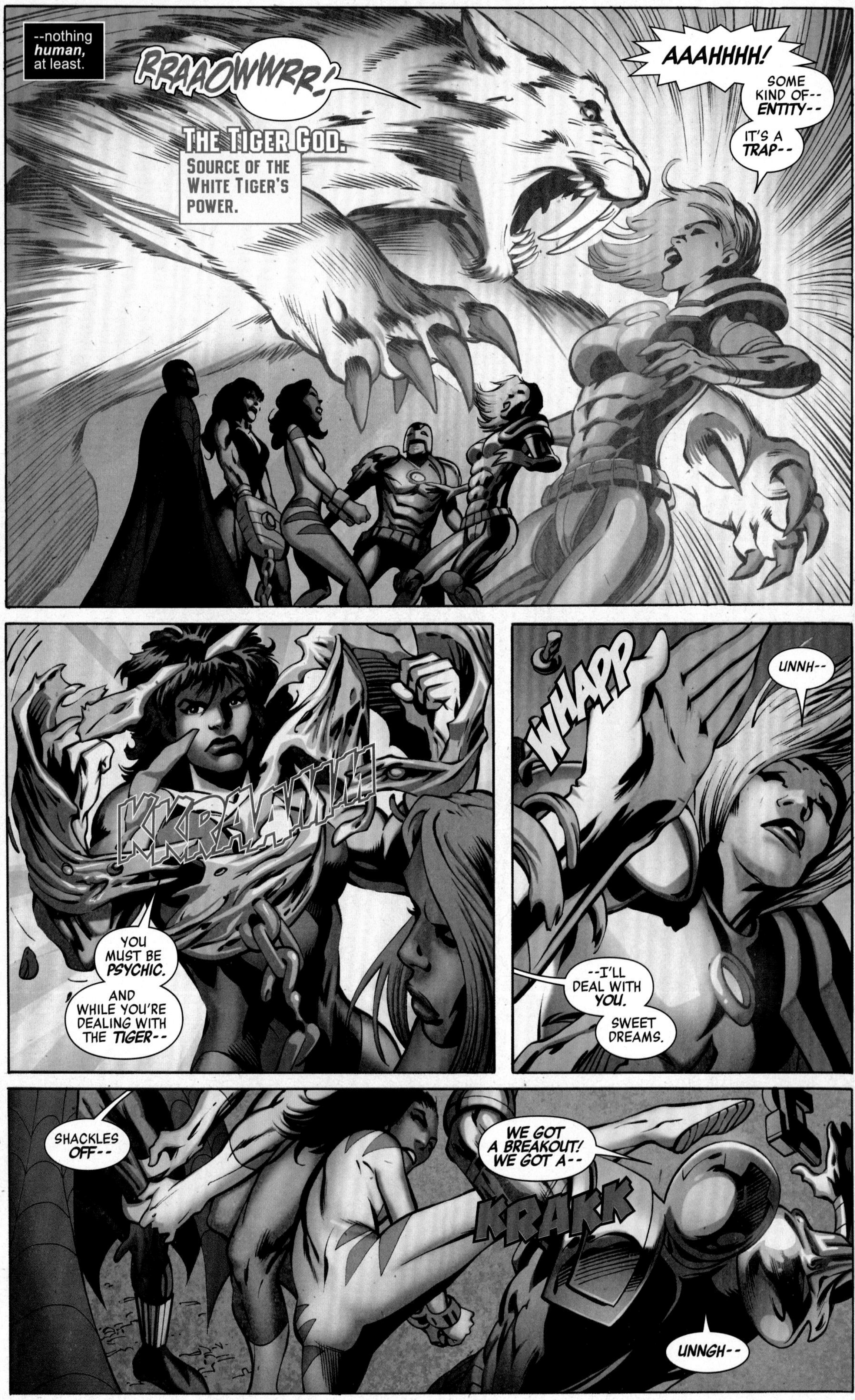
--nothing *human,* at least.
RRAAOWWRR!
THE TIGER GOD.
SOURCE OF THE WHITE TIGER'S POWER.
AAAHHHH!
SOME KIND OF-- ENTITY--
IT'S A TRAP--
KKRAAANNN
YOU MUST BE PSYCHIC.
AND WHILE YOU'RE DEALING WITH THE TIGER--
WHAPP
UNNH--
--I'LL DEAL WITH YOU.
SWEET DREAMS.
SHACKLES OFF--
WE GOT A BREAKOUT! WE GOT A--
KRAKK
UNNGH--

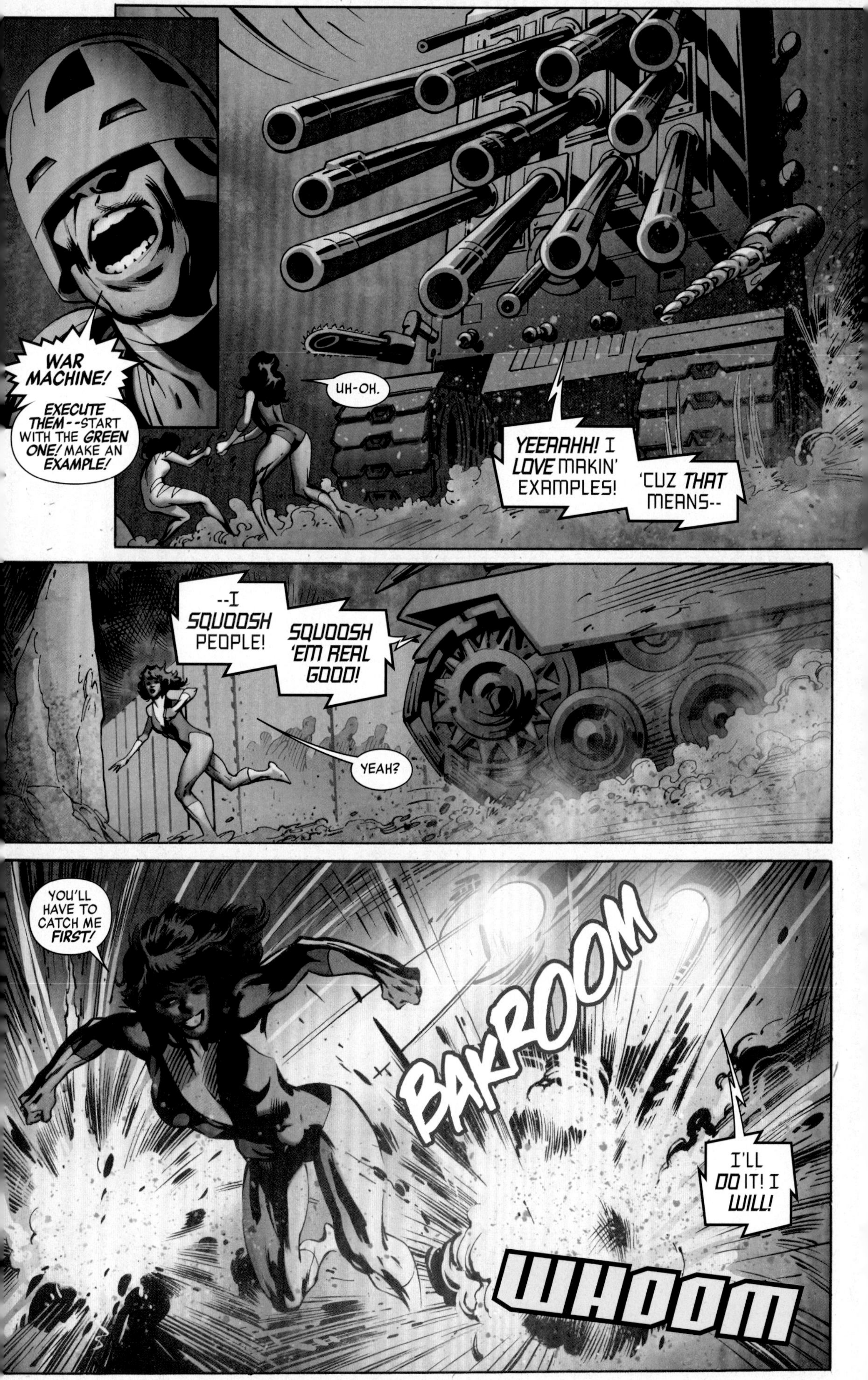
WAR MACHINE!
EXECUTE THEM--START WITH THE GREEN ONE! MAKE AN EXAMPLE!
UH-OH.
YEEAAHH! I LOVE MAKIN' EXAMPLES!
'CUZ THAT MEANS--
--I SQUOOSH PEOPLE!
SQUOOSH 'EM REAL GOOD!
YEAH?
YOU'LL HAVE TO CATCH ME FIRST!
BAKROOM
I'LL DO IT! I WILL!
WHOOM

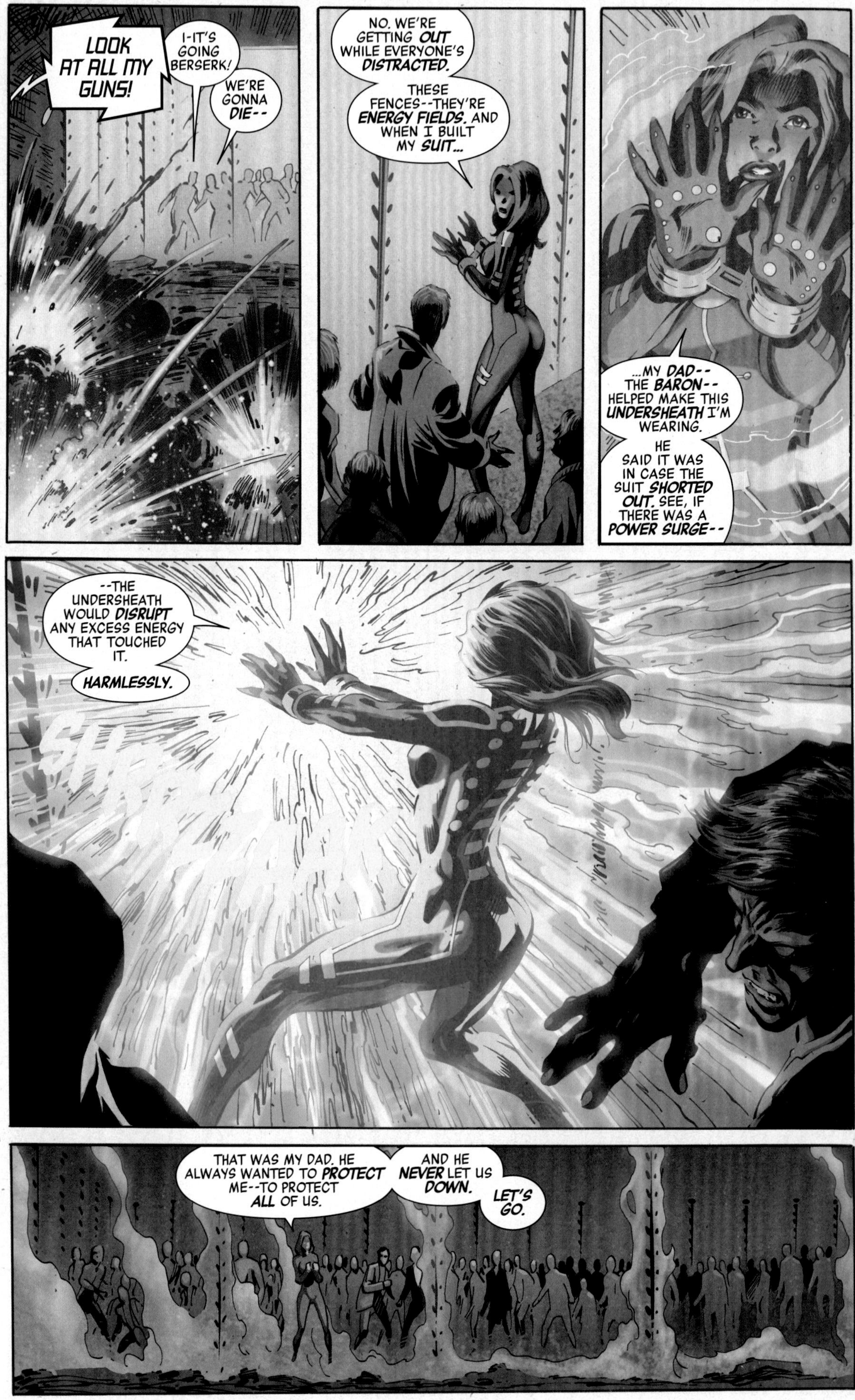
LOOK AT ALL MY GUNS!
I-IT'S GOING BERSERK!
WE'RE GONNA DIE--
NO. WE'RE GETTING OUT WHILE EVERYONE'S DISTRACTED.
THESE FENCES--THEY'RE ENERGY FIELDS. AND WHEN I BUILT MY SUIT...
...MY DAD-- THE BARON-- HELPED MAKE THIS UNDERSHEATH I'M WEARING.
HE SAID IT WAS IN CASE THE SUIT SHORTED OUT. SEE, IF THERE WAS A POWER SURGE--
--THE UNDERSHEATH WOULD DISRUPT ANY EXCESS ENERGY THAT TOUCHED IT.
HARMLESSLY.
THAT WAS MY DAD. HE ALWAYS WANTED TO PROTECT ME--TO PROTECT ALL OF US.
AND HE NEVER LET US DOWN.
LET'S GO.

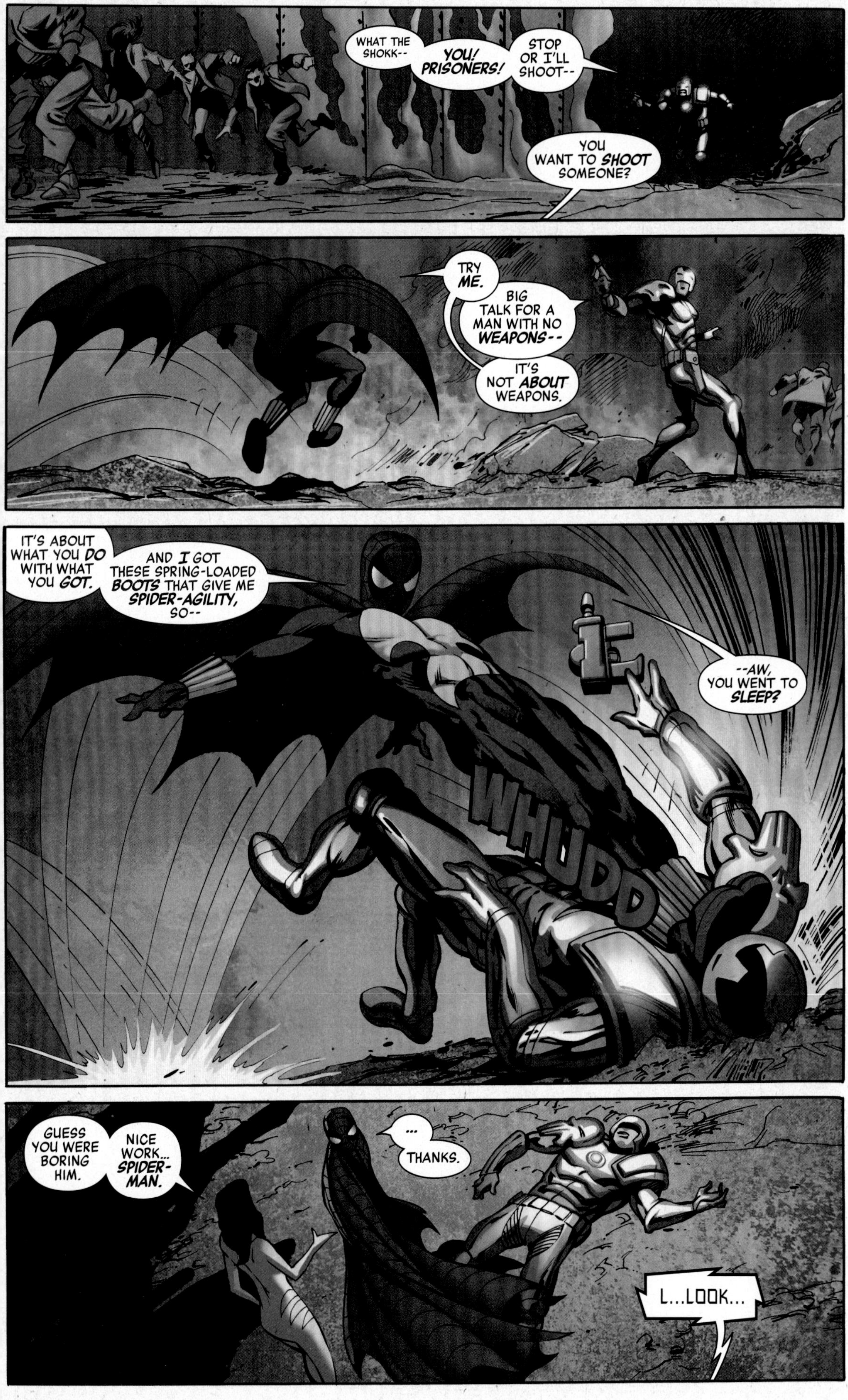
WHAT THE SHOKK--
YOU! PRISONERS!
STOP OR I'LL SHOOT--
YOU WANT TO SHOOT SOMEONE?
TRY ME.
BIG TALK FOR A MAN WITH NO WEAPONS--
IT'S NOT ABOUT WEAPONS.
IT'S ABOUT WHAT YOU DO WITH WHAT YOU GOT.
AND I GOT THESE SPRING-LOADED BOOTS THAT GIVE ME SPIDER-AGILITY, SO--
--AW, YOU WENT TO SLEEP?
WHUDD
GUESS YOU WERE BORING HIM.
NICE WORK... SPIDER-MAN.
... THANKS.
L...LOOK...

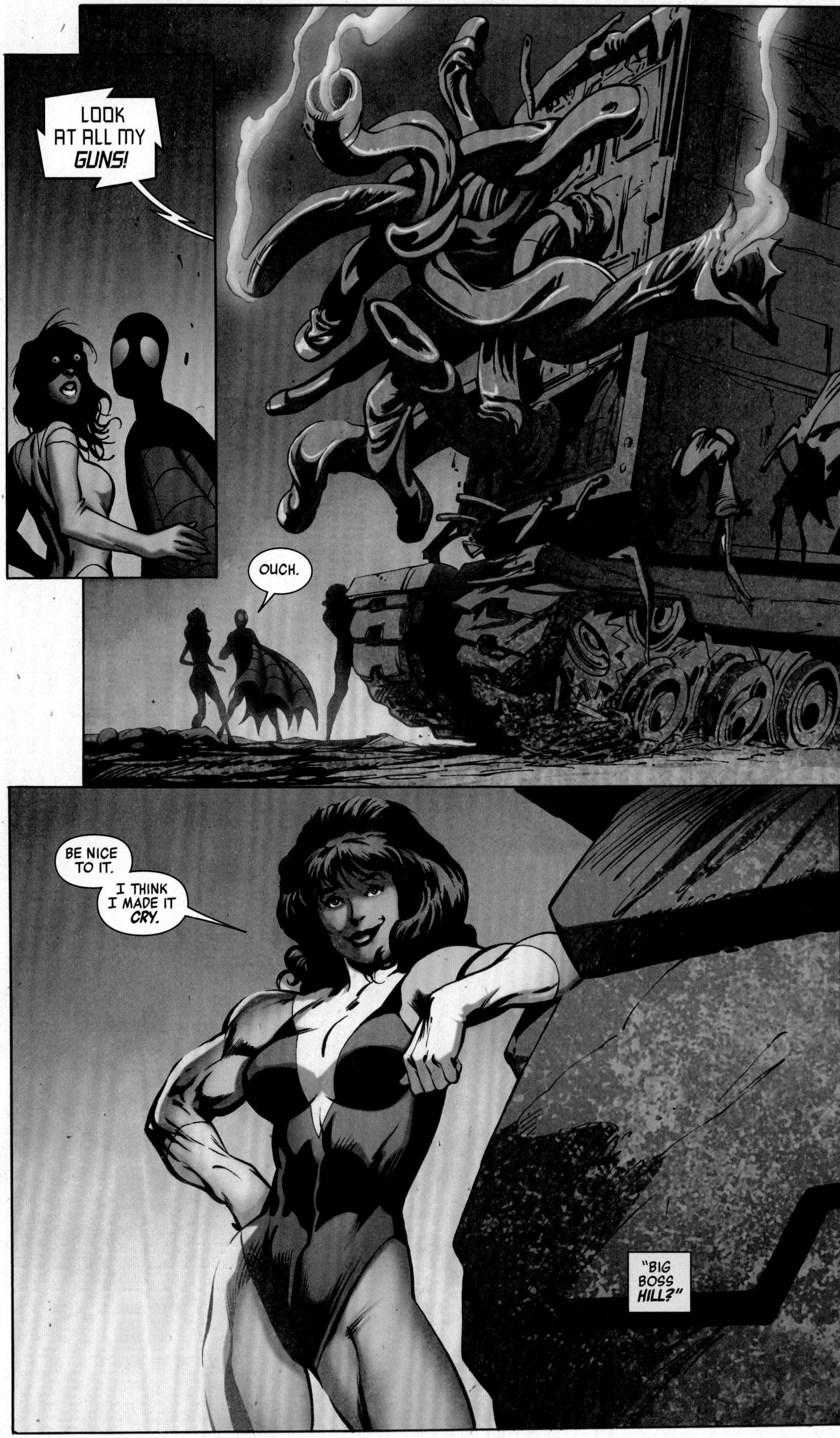
LOOK AT ALL MY GUNS!
OUCH.
BE NICE TO IT.
I THINK I MADE IT CRY.
"BIG BOSS HILL?"

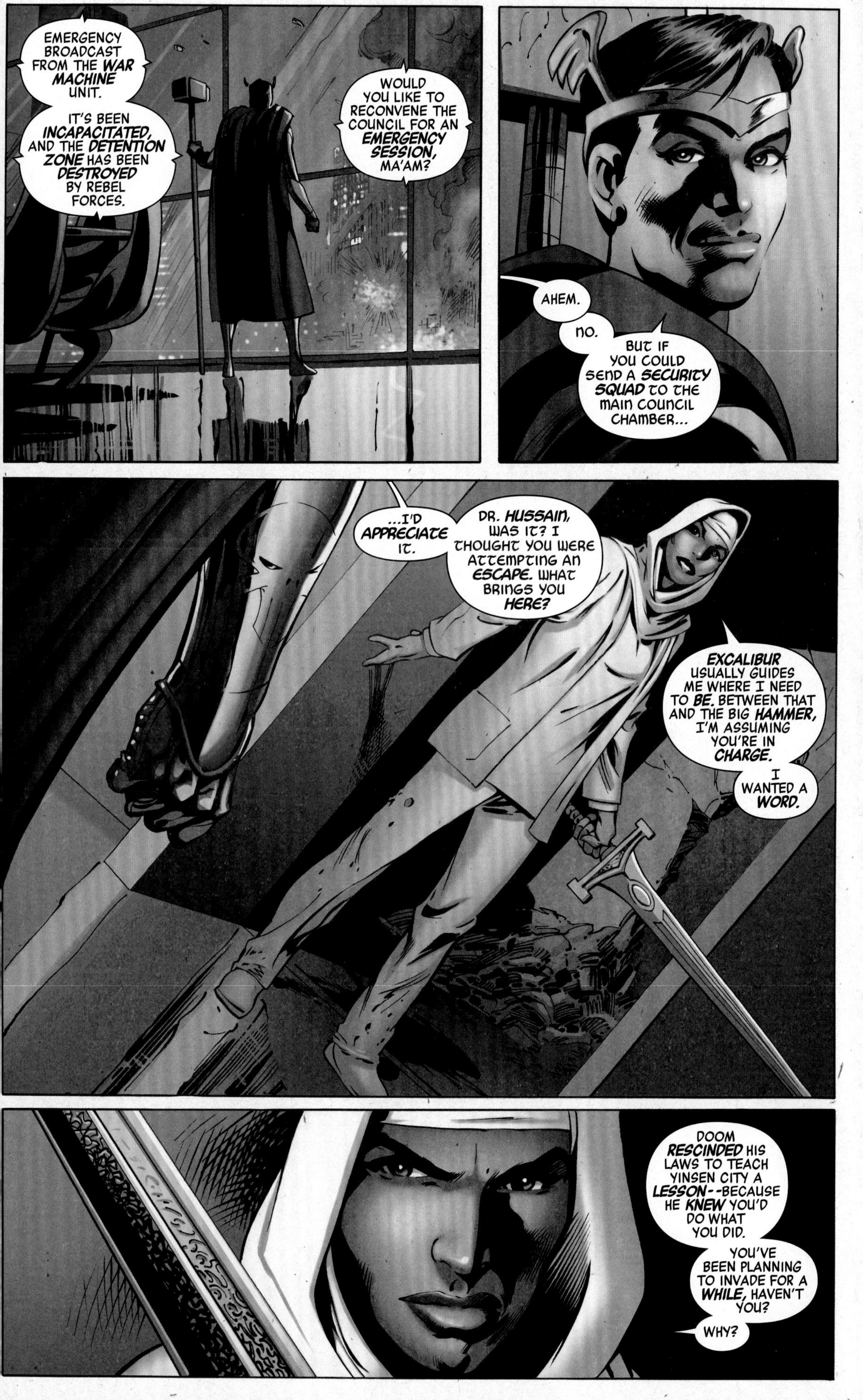

EMERGENCY BROADCAST FROM THE WAR MACHINE UNIT.
IT'S BEEN INCAPACITATED, AND THE DETENTION ZONE HAS BEEN DESTROYED BY REBEL FORCES.
WOULD YOU LIKE TO RECONVENE THE COUNCIL FOR AN EMERGENCY SESSION, MA'AM?
AHEM.
NO.
BUT IF YOU COULD SEND A SECURITY SQUAD TO THE MAIN COUNCIL CHAMBER...
...I'D APPRECIATE IT.
DR. HUSSAIN, WAS IT? I THOUGHT YOU WERE ATTEMPTING AN ESCAPE. WHAT BRINGS YOU HERE?
EXCALIBUR USUALLY GUIDES ME WHERE I NEED TO BE. BETWEEN THAT AND THE BIG HAMMER, I'M ASSUMING YOU'RE IN CHARGE.
I WANTED A WORD.
DOOM RESCINDED HIS LAWS TO TEACH YINSEN CITY A LESSON--BECAUSE HE KNEW YOU'D DO WHAT YOU DID.
YOU'VE BEEN PLANNING TO INVADE FOR A WHILE, HAVEN'T YOU?
WHY?

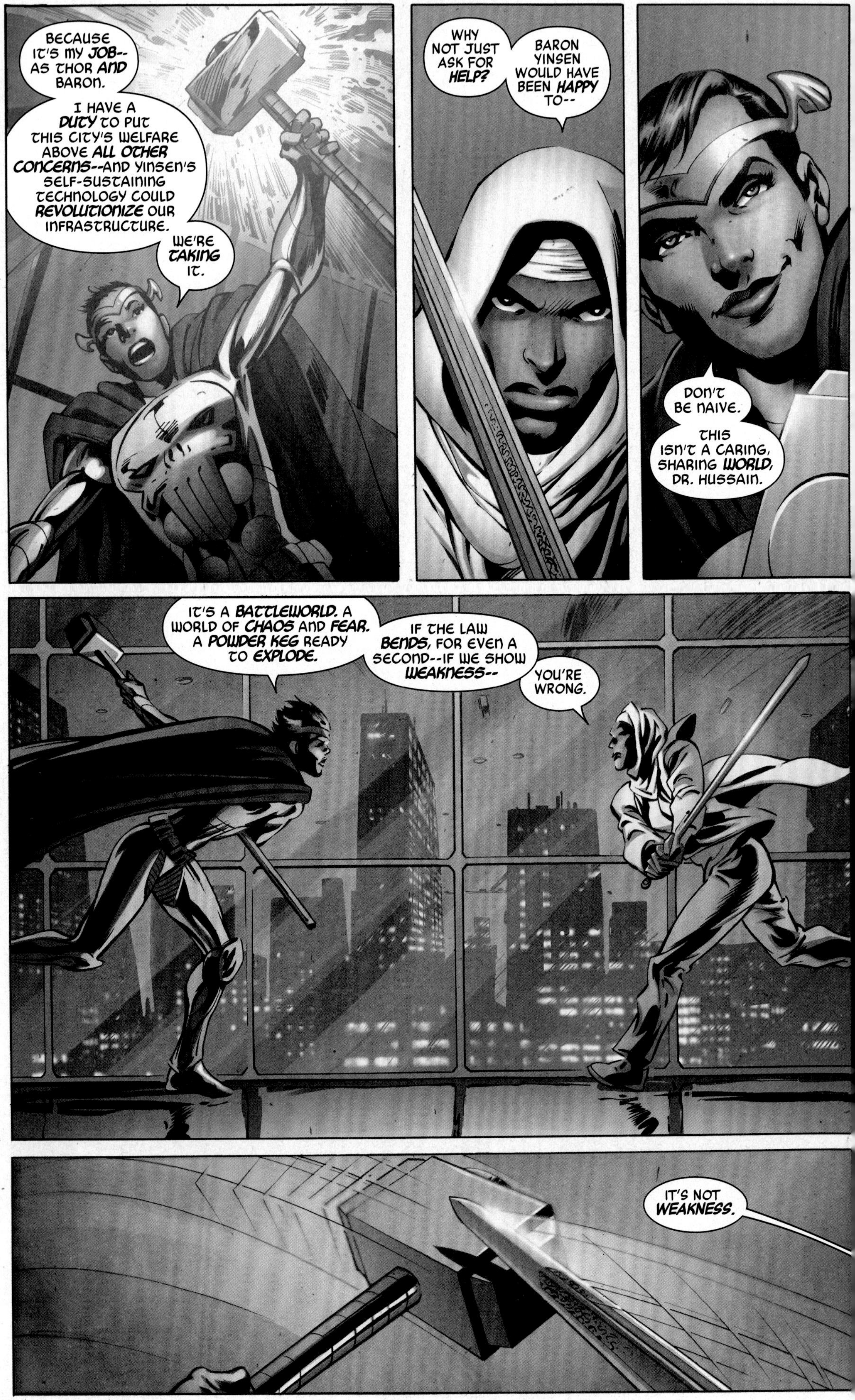
BECAUSE IT'S MY JOB-- AS THOR AND BARON.
I HAVE A DUTY TO PUT THIS CITY'S WELFARE ABOVE ALL OTHER CONCERNS--AND YINSEN'S SELF-SUSTAINING TECHNOLOGY COULD REVOLUTIONIZE OUR INFRASTRUCTURE.
WE'RE TAKING IT.
WHY NOT JUST ASK FOR HELP?
BARON YINSEN WOULD HAVE BEEN HAPPY TO--
DON'T BE NAIVE.
THIS ISN'T A CARING, SHARING WORLD, DR. HUSSAIN.
IT'S A BATTLEWORLD. A WORLD OF CHAOS AND FEAR. A POWDER KEG READY TO EXPLODE.
IF THE LAW BENDS, FOR EVEN A SECOND--IF WE SHOW WEAKNESS--
YOU'RE WRONG.
IT'S NOT WEAKNESS.

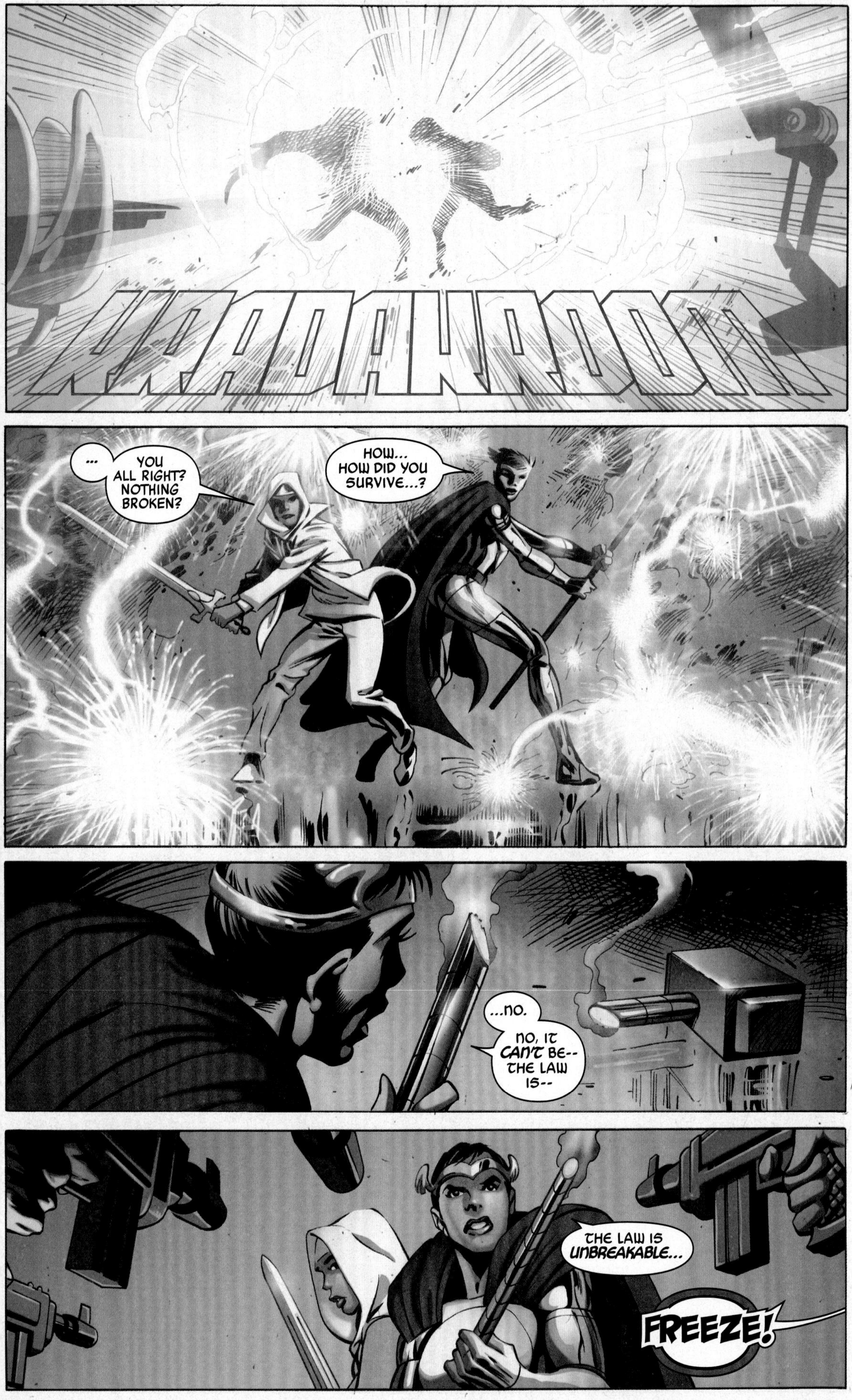

... YOU ALL RIGHT? NOTHING BROKEN?
HOW... HOW DID YOU SURVIVE...?
...NO.
NO, IT CAN'T BE-- THE LAW IS--
THE LAW IS UNBREAKABLE...
FREEZE!

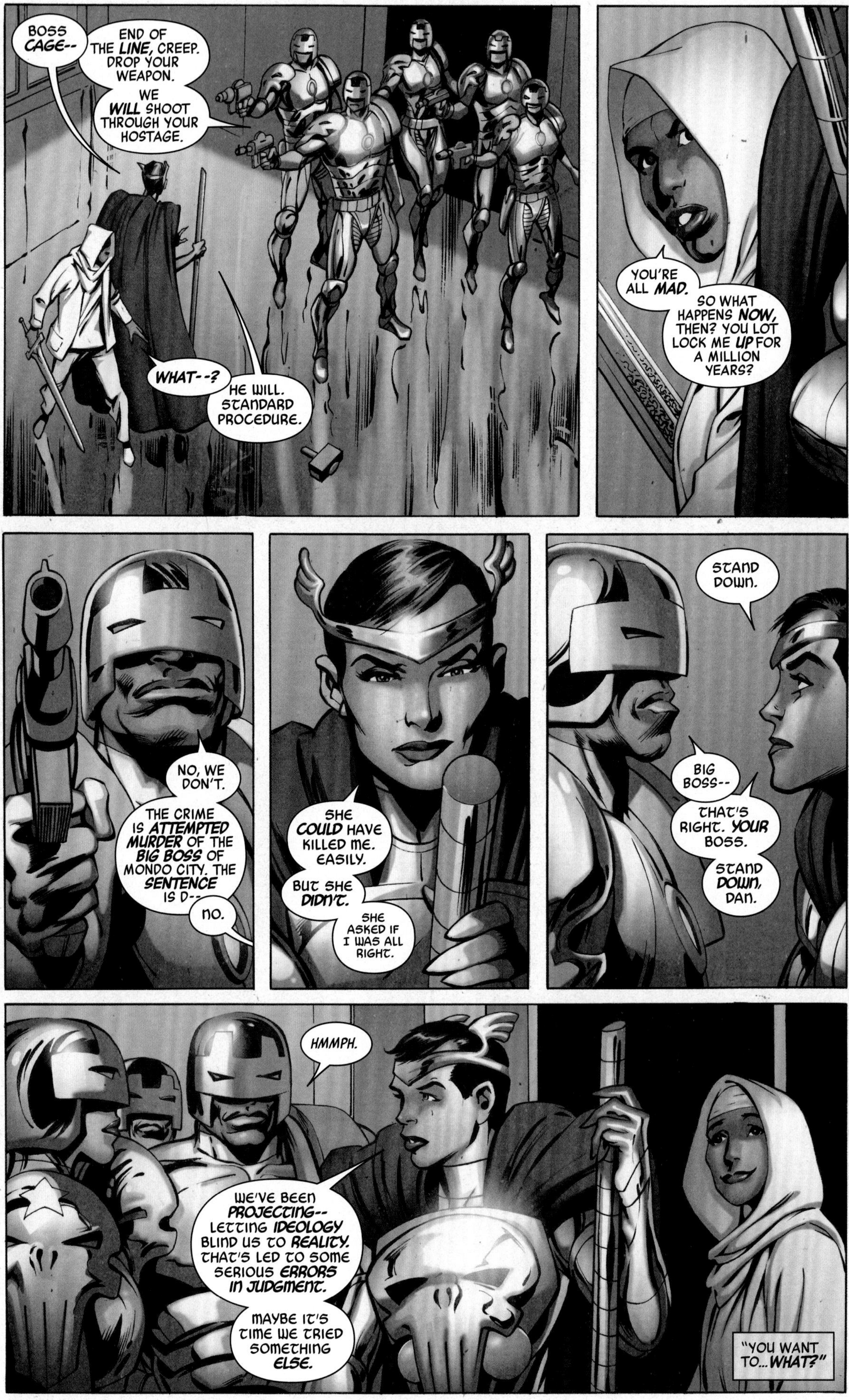
BOSS CAGE--
END OF THE LINE, CREEP. DROP YOUR WEAPON.
WE WILL SHOOT THROUGH YOUR HOSTAGE.
WHAT--?
HE WILL. STANDARD PROCEDURE.
YOU'RE ALL MAD.
SO WHAT HAPPENS NOW, THEN? YOU LOT LOCK ME UP FOR A MILLION YEARS?
NO, WE DON'T.
THE CRIME IS ATTEMPTED MURDER OF THE BIG BOSS OF MONDO CITY. THE SENTENCE IS D--
NO.
SHE COULD HAVE KILLED ME. EASILY.
BUT SHE DIDN'T.
SHE ASKED IF I WAS ALL RIGHT.
STAND DOWN.
BIG BOSS--
THAT'S RIGHT. YOUR BOSS.
STAND DOWN, DAN.
HMMPH.
WE'VE BEEN PROJECTING-- LETTING IDEOLOGY BLIND US TO REALITY. THAT'S LED TO SOME SERIOUS ERRORS IN JUDGMENT.
MAYBE IT'S TIME WE TRIED SOMETHING ELSE.
"YOU WANT TO...WHAT?"

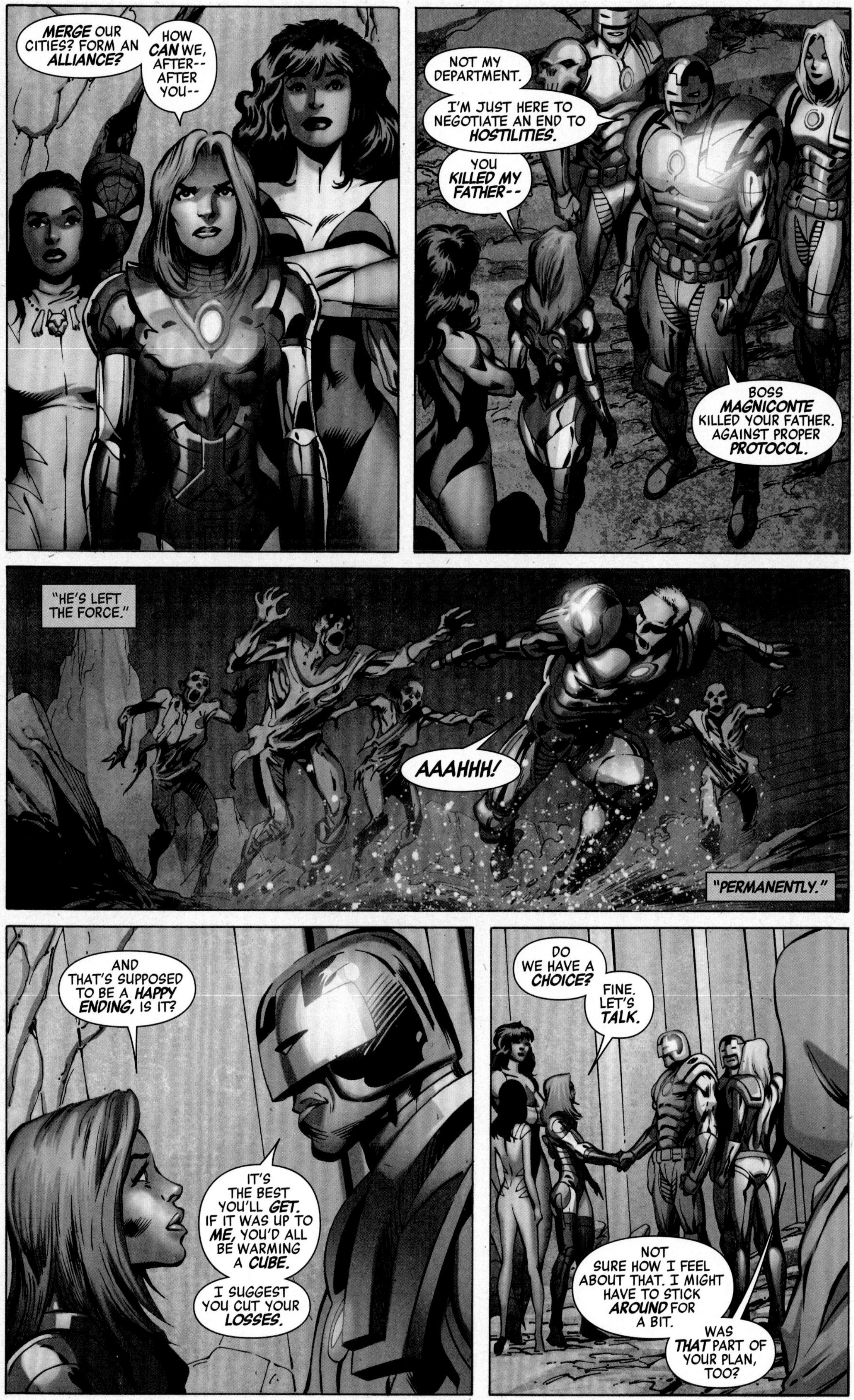
MERGE OUR CITIES? FORM AN ALLIANCE?
HOW CAN WE, AFTER-- AFTER YOU--
NOT MY DEPARTMENT.
I'M JUST HERE TO NEGOTIATE AN END TO HOSTILITIES.
YOU KILLED MY FATHER--
BOSS MAGNICONTE KILLED YOUR FATHER. AGAINST PROPER PROTOCOL.
"HE'S LEFT THE FORCE."
AAAHHH!
"PERMANENTLY."
AND THAT'S SUPPOSED TO BE A HAPPY ENDING, IS IT?
IT'S THE BEST YOU'LL GET. IF IT WAS UP TO ME, YOU'D ALL BE WARMING A CUBE.
I SUGGEST YOU CUT YOUR LOSSES.
DO WE HAVE A CHOICE?
FINE. LET'S TALK.
NOT SURE HOW I FEEL ABOUT THAT. I MIGHT HAVE TO STICK AROUND FOR A BIT.
WAS THAT PART OF YOUR PLAN, TOO?

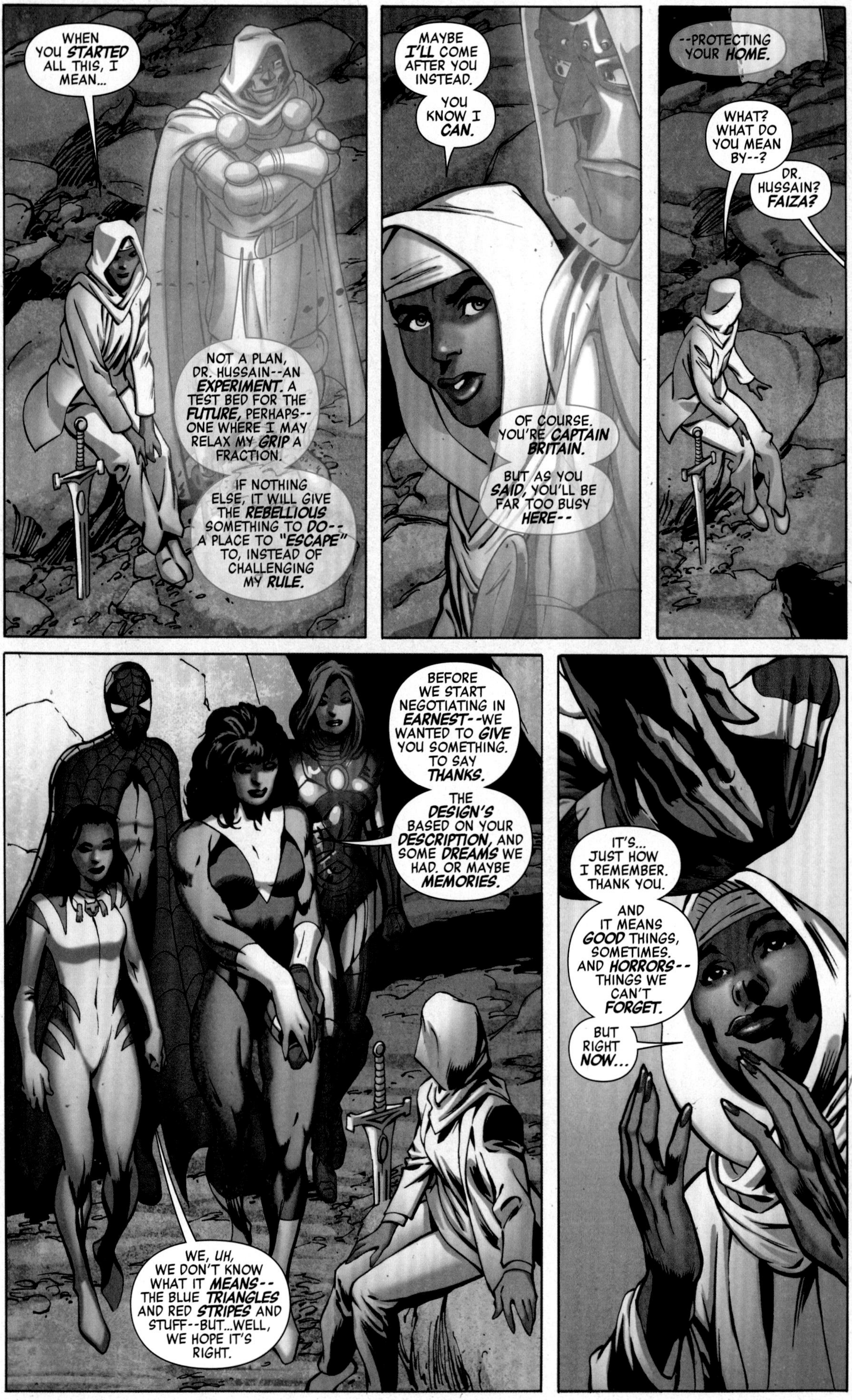
WHEN YOU STARTED ALL THIS, I MEAN...
NOT A PLAN, DR. HUSSAIN--AN EXPERIMENT. A TEST BED FOR THE FUTURE, PERHAPS--ONE WHERE I MAY RELAX MY GRIP A FRACTION.
IF NOTHING ELSE, IT WILL GIVE THE REBELLIOUS SOMETHING TO DO--A PLACE TO "ESCAPE" TO, INSTEAD OF CHALLENGING MY RULE.
MAYBE I'LL COME AFTER YOU INSTEAD.
YOU KNOW I CAN.
OF COURSE. YOU'RE CAPTAIN BRITAIN.
BUT AS YOU SAID, YOU'LL BE FAR TOO BUSY HERE--
--PROTECTING YOUR HOME.
WHAT? WHAT DO YOU MEAN BY--?
DR. HUSSAIN? FAIZA?
BEFORE WE START NEGOTIATING IN EARNEST--WE WANTED TO GIVE YOU SOMETHING. TO SAY THANKS.
THE DESIGN'S BASED ON YOUR DESCRIPTION, AND SOME DREAMS WE HAD. OR MAYBE MEMORIES.
WE, UH, WE DON'T KNOW WHAT IT MEANS--THE BLUE TRIANGLES AND RED STRIPES AND STUFF--BUT...WELL, WE HOPE IT'S RIGHT.
IT'S... JUST HOW I REMEMBER. THANK YOU.
AND IT MEANS GOOD THINGS, SOMETIMES. AND HORRORS--THINGS WE CAN'T FORGET.
BUT RIGHT NOW...

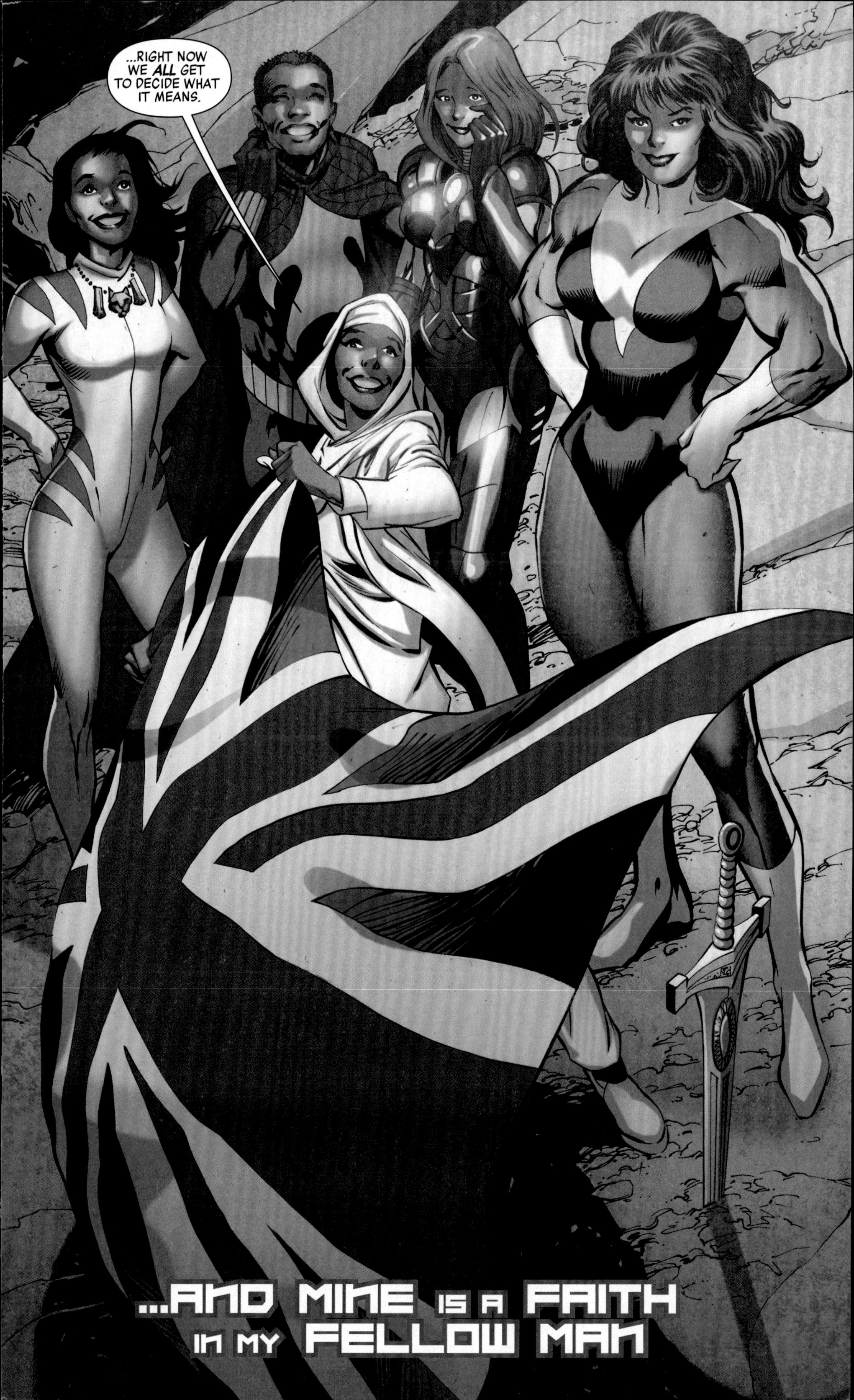
...RIGHT NOW WE ALL GET TO DECIDE WHAT IT MEANS.
...AND MINE IS A FAITH IN MY FELLOW MAN

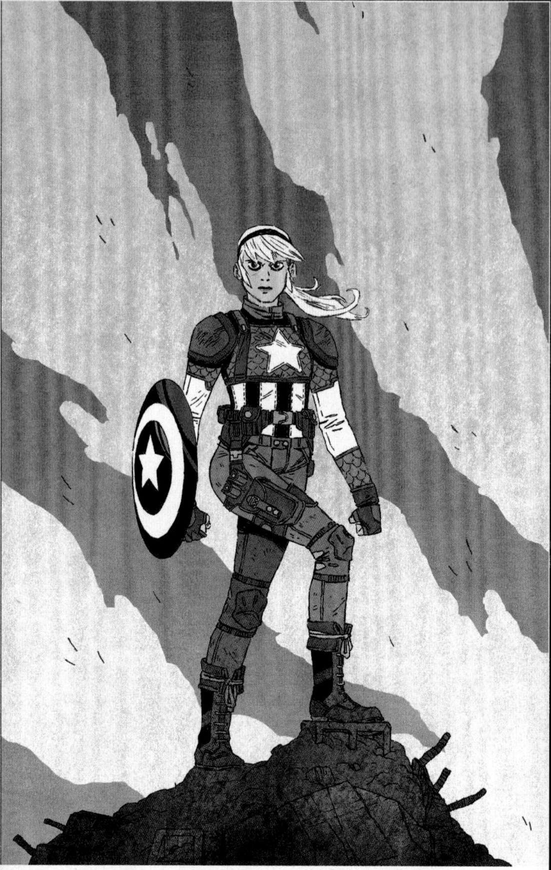

CAPTAIN AMERICA AND THE MIGHTY AVENGERS #9
CAPGWEN VARIANT BY JACOB WYATT

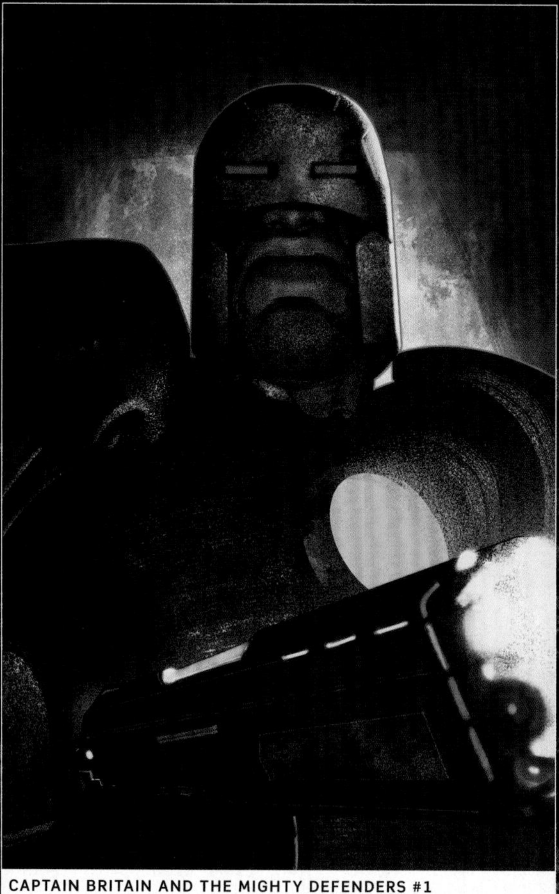

CAPTAIN BRITAIN AND THE MIGHTY DEFENDERS #1
VARIANT BY FRAZER IRVING

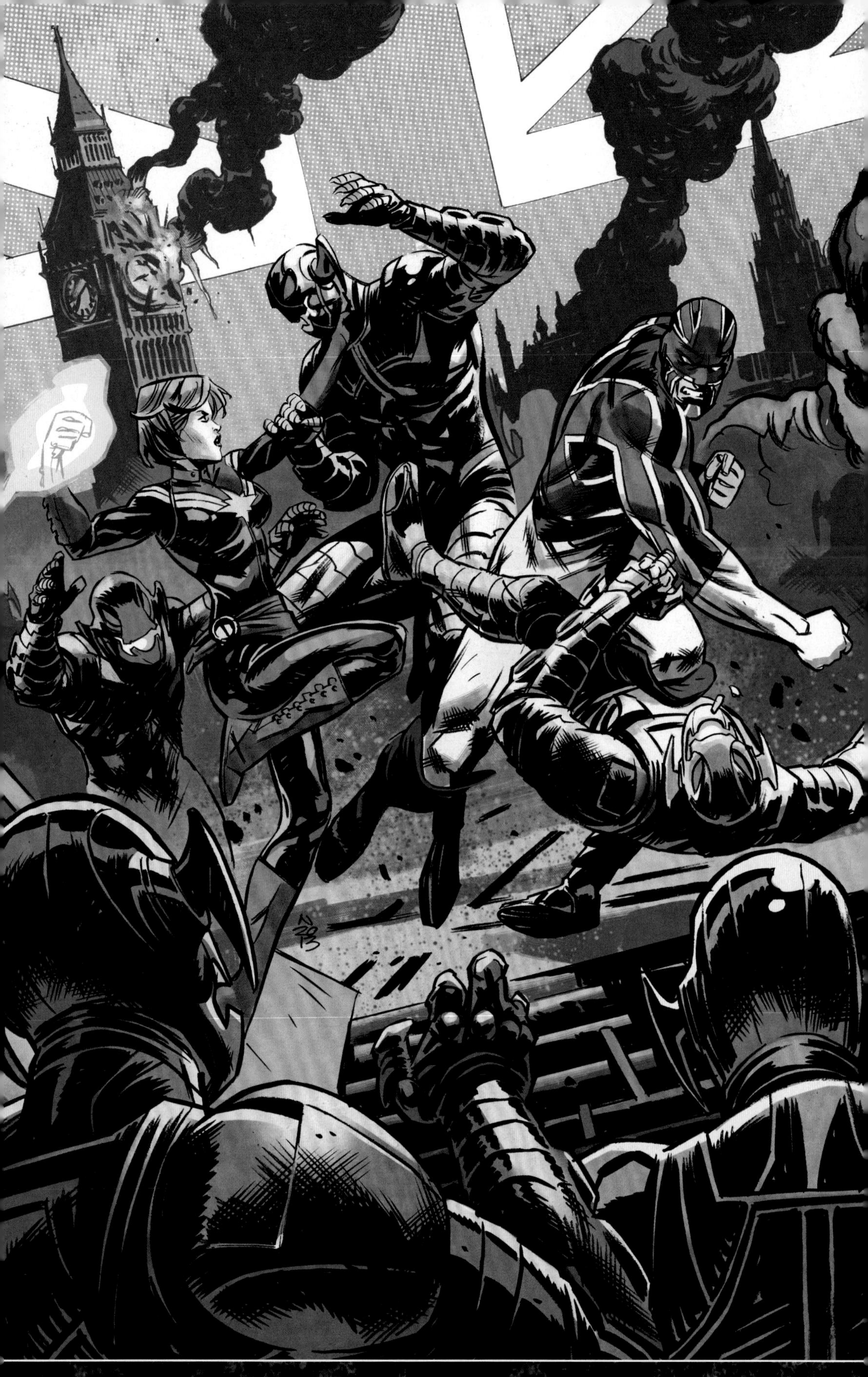

AVENGERS ASSEMBLE #15 A

AND THERE CAME A DAY, A DAY UNLIKE ANY OTHER, WHEN EARTH'S MIGHTIEST HEROES FOUND THEMSELVES UNITED AGAINST A COMMON THREAT! ON THAT DAY, THE AVENGERS WERE BORN, TO FIGHT THE FOES NO SINGLE SUPER HERO COULD WITHSTAND!

AVENGERS ASSEMBLE

CAPTAIN MARVEL
CAROL DANVERS
AVENGER
KREE SUPER-POWERS

CAPTAIN BRITAIN
BRIAN BRADDOCK
MYTHIC GUARDIAN OF
THE OMNIVERSE

EXCALIBUR
FAIZA HUSSAIN
BIO-ORGANIC MANIPULATOR
WIELDS THE SWORD EXCALIBUR

BLACK KNIGHT
DANE WHITMAN
WIELDER OF THE
EBONY BLADE

FILE: ASSEMBLEAU_15

YEARS AGO, FOUNDING AVENGER HENRY PYM INVENTED THE ARTIFICIAL INTELLIGENCE KNOWN AS ULTRON. ONCE ULTRON BECAME SENTIENT, HE DEDICATED HIS EXISTENCE TO DESTROYING HUMANITY. THE AVENGERS SUCCESSFULLY FOILED HIS EVERY ATTEMPT, BUT SOME PREDICTED THAT WITH HIS CONTINUOUS EVOLUTION, ULTRON WOULD ONE DAY MANAGE TO OVERCOME HIS FOES.

THAT DAY IS TODAY.

SUBMIT OR PERISH.

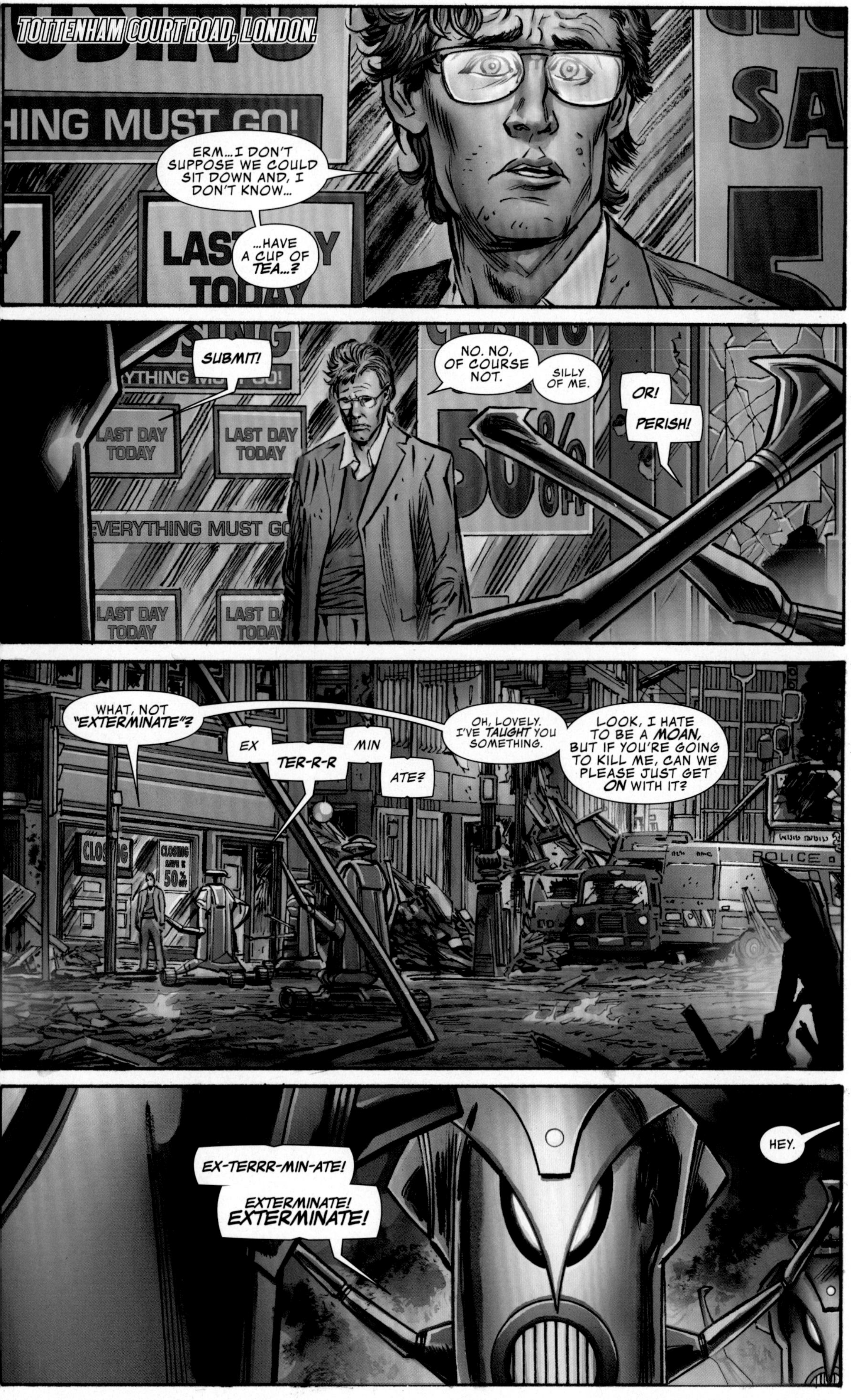
TOTTENHAM COURT ROAD, LONDON.
HING MUST GO!
ERM...I DON'T SUPPOSE WE COULD SIT DOWN AND, I DON'T KNOW...
...HAVE A CUP OF TEA...?
SUBMIT!
LAST DAY TODAY
LAST DAY TODAY
NO. NO, OF COURSE NOT.
SILLY OF ME.
OR!
PERISH!
EVERYTHING MUST GO
WHAT, NOT "EXTERMINATE"?
EX
TER-R-R
MIN
ATE?
OH, LOVELY. I'VE TAUGHT YOU SOMETHING.
LOOK, I HATE TO BE A MOAN, BUT IF YOU'RE GOING TO KILL ME, CAN WE PLEASE JUST GET ON WITH IT?
POLICE
EX-TERRR-MIN-ATE!
EXTERMINATE! EXTERMINATE!
HEY.

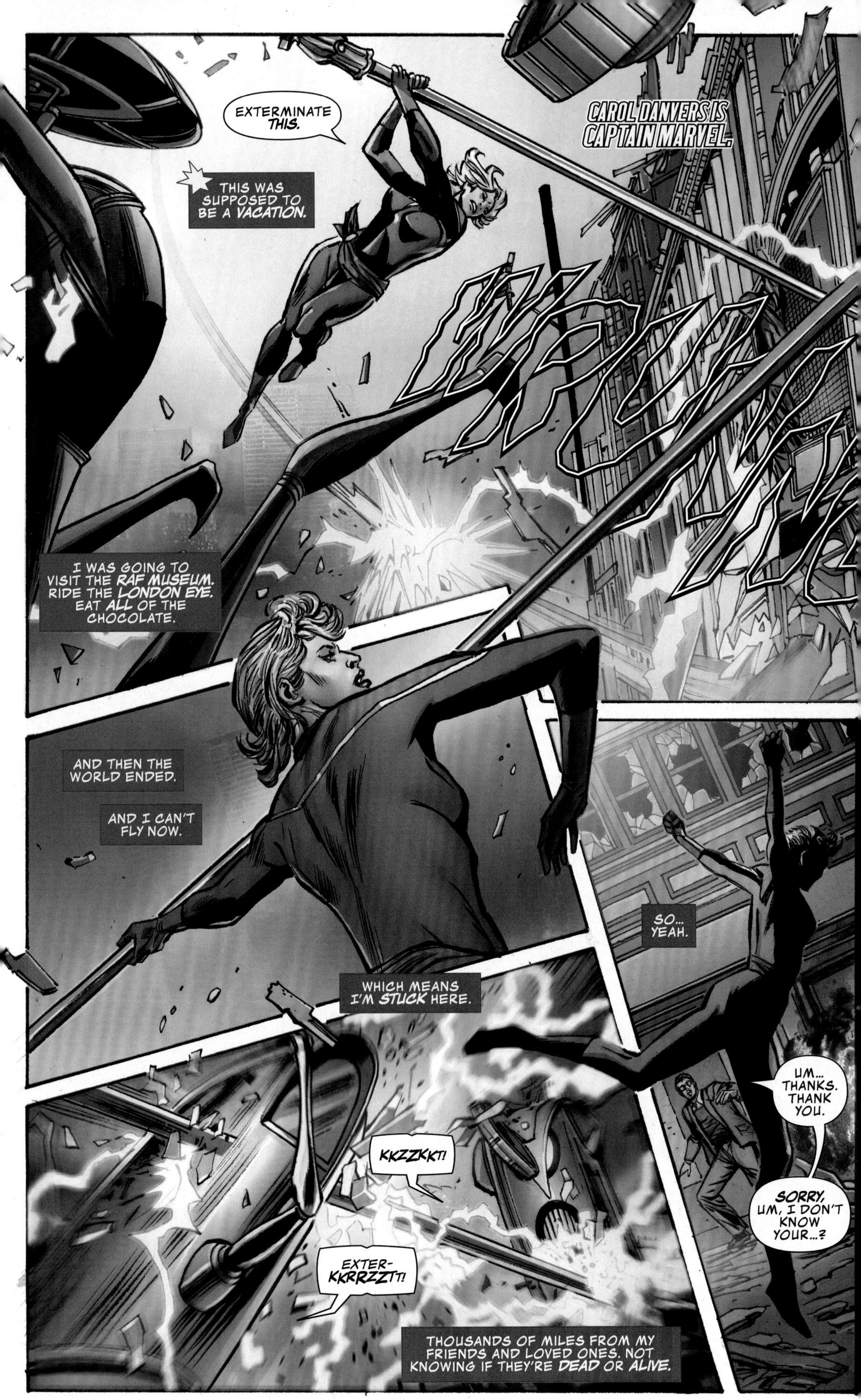

CAROL DANVERS IS CAPTAIN MARVEL.
EXTERMINATE THIS.
THIS WAS SUPPOSED TO BE A VACATION.
I WAS GOING TO VISIT THE RAF MUSEUM. RIDE THE LONDON EYE. EAT ALL OF THE CHOCOLATE.
AND THEN THE WORLD ENDED.
AND I CAN'T FLY NOW.
WHICH MEANS I'M STUCK HERE.
SO... YEAH.
KKZZKKT!
EXTER-KKRRZZTT!
THOUSANDS OF MILES FROM MY FRIENDS AND LOVED ONES. NOT KNOWING IF THEY'RE DEAD OR ALIVE.
UM... THANKS. THANK YOU.
SORRY, UM, I DON'T KNOW YOUR...?

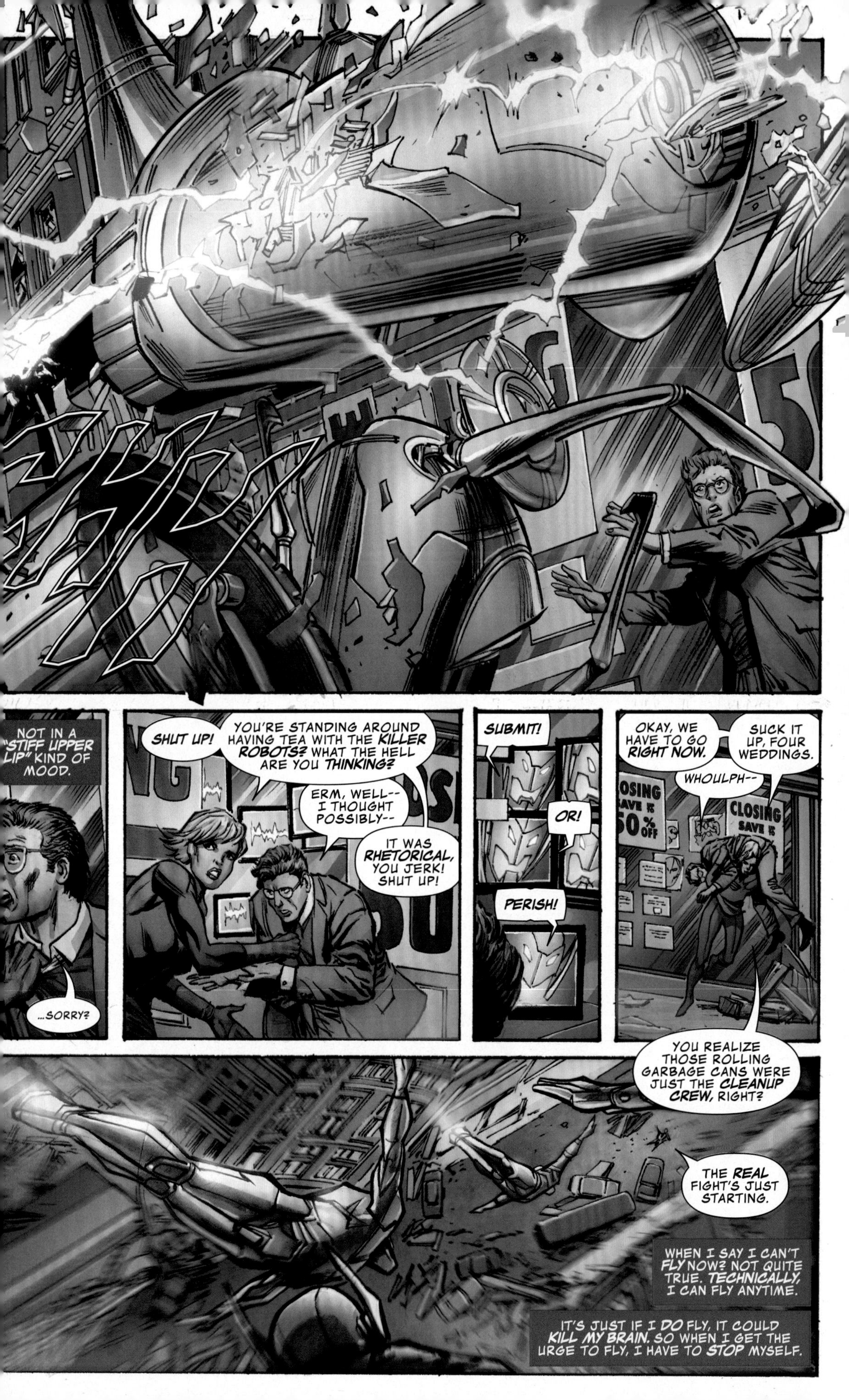

NOT IN A "STIFF UPPER LIP" KIND OF MOOD.
...SORRY?
SHUT UP!
YOU'RE STANDING AROUND HAVING TEA WITH THE KILLER ROBOTS? WHAT THE HELL ARE YOU THINKING?
ERM, WELL-- I THOUGHT POSSIBLY--
IT WAS RHETORICAL, YOU JERK! SHUT UP!
SUBMIT!
OR!
PERISH!
OKAY, WE HAVE TO GO RIGHT NOW.
SUCK IT UP, FOUR WEDDINGS.
WHOULPH--
CLOSING SAVE 50% OFF
YOU REALIZE THOSE ROLLING GARBAGE CANS WERE JUST THE CLEANUP CREW, RIGHT?
THE REAL FIGHT'S JUST STARTING.
WHEN I SAY I CAN'T FLY NOW? NOT QUITE TRUE. TECHNICALLY, I CAN FLY ANYTIME.
IT'S JUST IF I DO FLY, IT COULD KILL MY BRAIN. SO WHEN I GET THE URGE TO FLY, I HAVE TO STOP MYSELF.

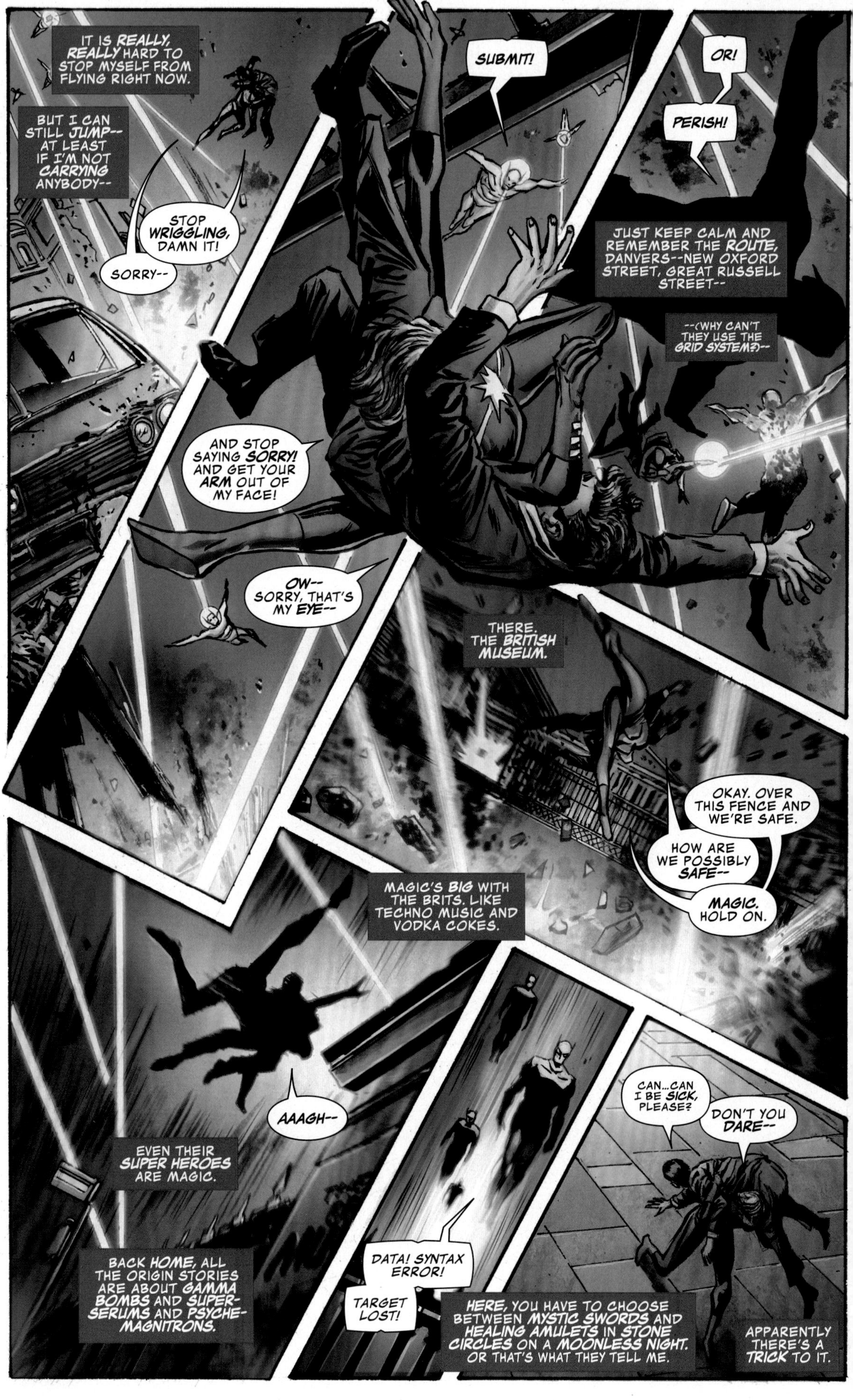
IT IS REALLY, REALLY HARD TO STOP MYSELF FROM FLYING RIGHT NOW.
BUT I CAN STILL JUMP-- AT LEAST IF I'M NOT CARRYING ANYBODY--
STOP WRIGGLING, DAMN IT!
SORRY--
SUBMIT!
OR!
PERISH!
JUST KEEP CALM AND REMEMBER THE ROUTE, DANVERS--NEW OXFORD STREET, GREAT RUSSELL STREET--
--(WHY CAN'T THEY USE THE GRID SYSTEM?)--
AND STOP SAYING SORRY! AND GET YOUR ARM OUT OF MY FACE!
OW-- SORRY, THAT'S MY EYE--
THERE. THE BRITISH MUSEUM.
OKAY. OVER THIS FENCE AND WE'RE SAFE.
HOW ARE WE POSSIBLY SAFE--
MAGIC. HOLD ON.
MAGIC'S BIG WITH THE BRITS. LIKE TECHNO MUSIC AND VODKA COKES.
AAAGH--
EVEN THEIR SUPER HEROES ARE MAGIC.
BACK HOME, ALL THE ORIGIN STORIES ARE ABOUT GAMMA BOMBS AND SUPER-SERUMS AND PSYCHE-MAGNITRONS.
DATA! SYNTAX ERROR!
TARGET LOST!
HERE, YOU HAVE TO CHOOSE BETWEEN MYSTIC SWORDS AND HEALING AMULETS IN STONE CIRCLES ON A MOONLESS NIGHT. OR THAT'S WHAT THEY TELL ME.
CAN...CAN I BE SICK, PLEASE?
DON'T YOU DARE--
APPARENTLY THERE'S A TRICK TO IT.

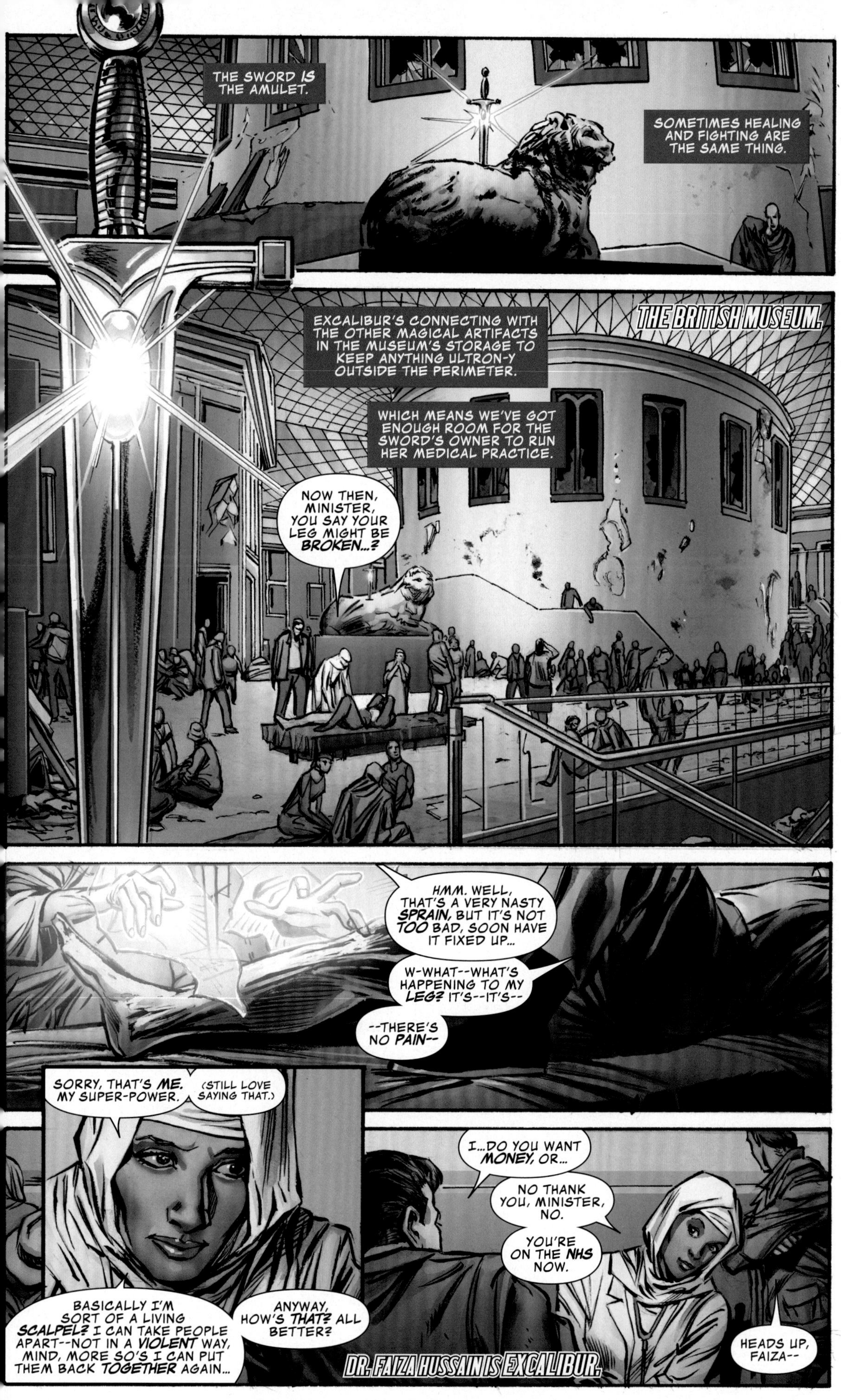
THE SWORD IS THE AMULET.
SOMETIMES HEALING AND FIGHTING ARE THE SAME THING.
THE BRITISH MUSEUM.
EXCALIBUR'S CONNECTING WITH THE OTHER MAGICAL ARTIFACTS IN THE MUSEUM'S STORAGE TO KEEP ANYTHING ULTRON-Y OUTSIDE THE PERIMETER.
WHICH MEANS WE'VE GOT ENOUGH ROOM FOR THE SWORD'S OWNER TO RUN HER MEDICAL PRACTICE.
NOW THEN, MINISTER, YOU SAY YOUR LEG MIGHT BE BROKEN...?
HMM. WELL, THAT'S A VERY NASTY SPRAIN, BUT IT'S NOT TOO BAD, SOON HAVE IT FIXED UP...
W-WHAT--WHAT'S HAPPENING TO MY LEG? IT'S--IT'S--
--THERE'S NO PAIN--
SORRY, THAT'S ME. MY SUPER-POWER.
(STILL LOVE SAYING THAT.)
BASICALLY I'M SORT OF A LIVING SCALPEL? I CAN TAKE PEOPLE APART--NOT IN A VIOLENT WAY, MIND, MORE SO'S I CAN PUT THEM BACK TOGETHER AGAIN...
ANYWAY, HOW'S THAT? ALL BETTER?
DR. FAIZA HUSSAIN IS EXCALIBUR.
I...DO YOU WANT MONEY, OR...
NO THANK YOU, MINISTER, NO.
YOU'RE ON THE NHS NOW.
HEADS UP, FAIZA--

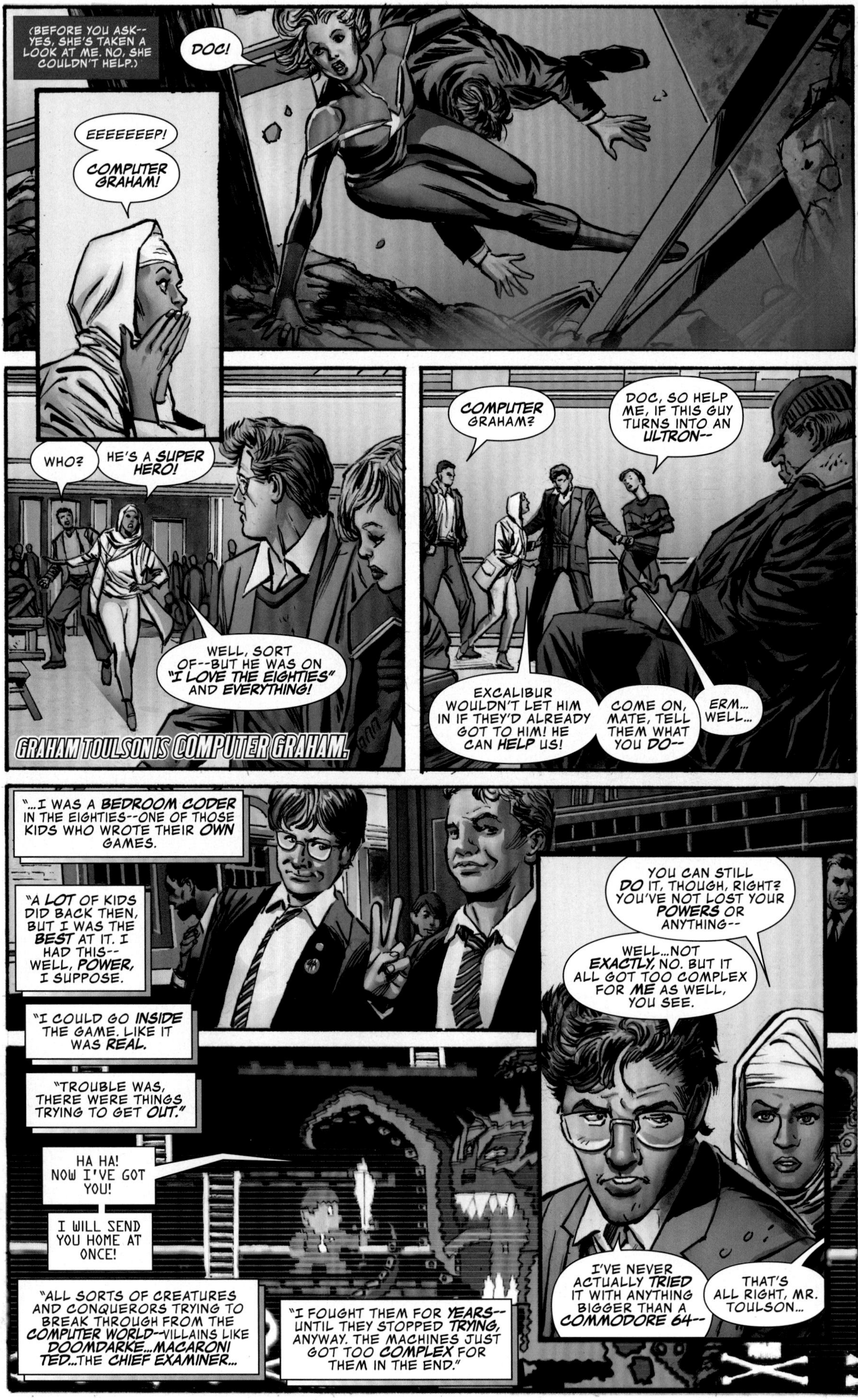

(BEFORE YOU ASK--YES, SHE'S TAKEN A LOOK AT ME. NO, SHE COULDN'T HELP.)
DOC!
EEEEEEEP!
COMPUTER GRAHAM!
WHO?
HE'S A SUPER HERO!
WELL, SORT OF--BUT HE WAS ON "I LOVE THE EIGHTIES" AND EVERYTHING!
GRAHAM TOULSON IS COMPUTER GRAHAM.
COMPUTER GRAHAM?
DOC, SO HELP ME, IF THIS GUY TURNS INTO AN ULTRON--
EXCALIBUR WOULDN'T LET HIM IN IF THEY'D ALREADY GOT TO HIM! HE CAN HELP US!
COME ON, MATE, TELL THEM WHAT YOU DO--
ERM... WELL...
"...I WAS A BEDROOM CODER IN THE EIGHTIES--ONE OF THOSE KIDS WHO WROTE THEIR OWN GAMES.
"A LOT OF KIDS DID BACK THEN, BUT I WAS THE BEST AT IT. I HAD THIS--WELL, POWER, I SUPPOSE.
"I COULD GO INSIDE THE GAME. LIKE IT WAS REAL.
"TROUBLE WAS, THERE WERE THINGS TRYING TO GET OUT."
HA HA! NOW I'VE GOT YOU!
I WILL SEND YOU HOME AT ONCE!
"ALL SORTS OF CREATURES AND CONQUERORS TRYING TO BREAK THROUGH FROM THE COMPUTER WORLD--VILLAINS LIKE DOOMDARKE...MACARONI TED...THE CHIEF EXAMINER...
"I FOUGHT THEM FOR YEARS--UNTIL THEY STOPPED TRYING, ANYWAY. THE MACHINES JUST GOT TOO COMPLEX FOR THEM IN THE END."
YOU CAN STILL DO IT, THOUGH, RIGHT? YOU'VE NOT LOST YOUR POWERS OR ANYTHING--
WELL...NOT EXACTLY, NO. BUT IT ALL GOT TOO COMPLEX FOR ME AS WELL, YOU SEE.
I'VE NEVER ACTUALLY TRIED IT WITH ANYTHING BIGGER THAN A COMMODORE 64--
THAT'S ALL RIGHT, MR. TOULSON...

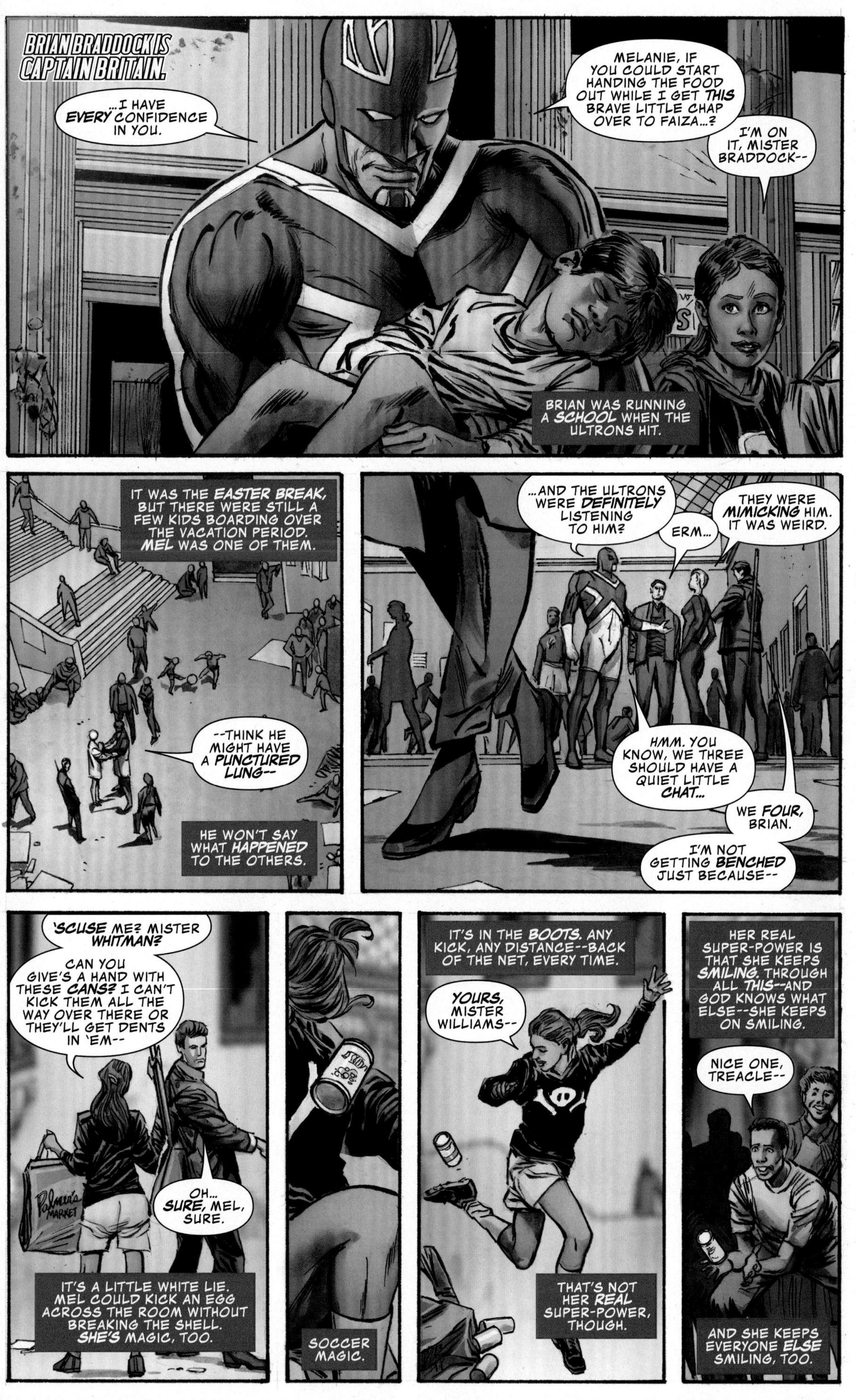
BRIAN BRADDOCK IS CAPTAIN BRITAIN.
...I HAVE EVERY CONFIDENCE IN YOU.
MELANIE, IF YOU COULD START HANDING THE FOOD OUT WHILE I GET THIS BRAVE LITTLE CHAP OVER TO FAIZA...?
I'M ON IT, MISTER BRADDOCK--
BRIAN WAS RUNNING A SCHOOL WHEN THE ULTRONS HIT.
IT WAS THE EASTER BREAK, BUT THERE WERE STILL A FEW KIDS BOARDING OVER THE VACATION PERIOD. MEL WAS ONE OF THEM.
--THINK HE MIGHT HAVE A PUNCTURED LUNG--
HE WON'T SAY WHAT HAPPENED TO THE OTHERS.
...AND THE ULTRONS WERE DEFINITELY LISTENING TO HIM?
ERM...
THEY WERE MIMICKING HIM. IT WAS WEIRD.
HMM. YOU KNOW, WE THREE SHOULD HAVE A QUIET LITTLE CHAT...
WE FOUR, BRIAN.
I'M NOT GETTING BENCHED JUST BECAUSE--
'SCUSE ME? MISTER WHITMAN?
CAN YOU GIVE'S A HAND WITH THESE CANS? I CAN'T KICK THEM ALL THE WAY OVER THERE OR THEY'LL GET DENTS IN 'EM--
OH... SURE, MEL, SURE.
Palmer's MARKET
IT'S A LITTLE WHITE LIE. MEL COULD KICK AN EGG ACROSS THE ROOM WITHOUT BREAKING THE SHELL. SHE'S MAGIC, TOO.
SOCCER MAGIC.
IT'S IN THE BOOTS. ANY KICK, ANY DISTANCE--BACK OF THE NET, EVERY TIME.
YOURS, MISTER WILLIAMS--
THAT'S NOT HER REAL SUPER-POWER, THOUGH.
HER REAL SUPER-POWER IS THAT SHE KEEPS SMILING. THROUGH ALL THIS--AND GOD KNOWS WHAT ELSE--SHE KEEPS ON SMILING.
NICE ONE, TREACLE--
AND SHE KEEPS EVERYONE ELSE SMILING, TOO.

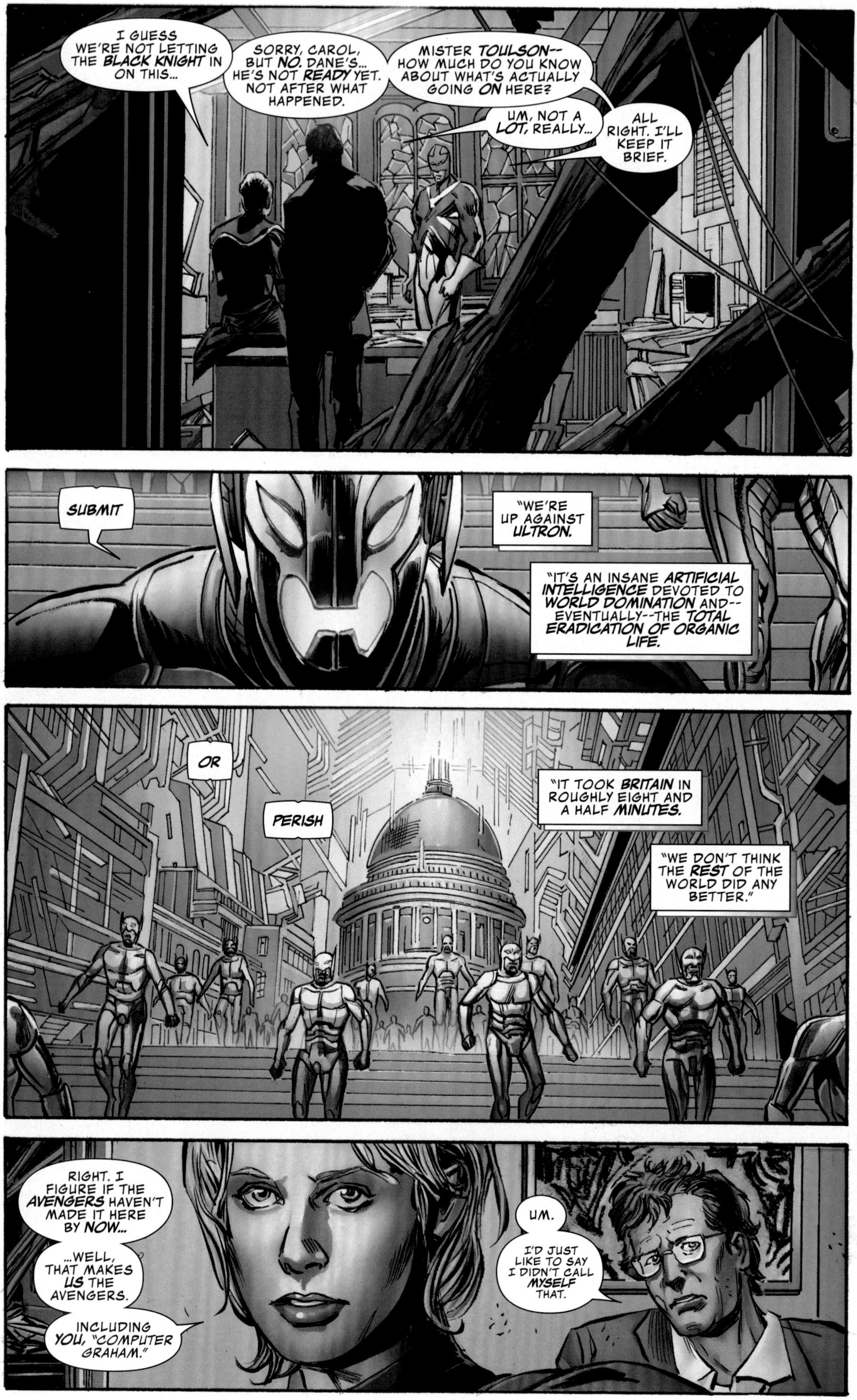

I GUESS WE'RE NOT LETTING THE BLACK KNIGHT IN ON THIS...
SORRY, CAROL, BUT NO. DANE'S... HE'S NOT READY YET. NOT AFTER WHAT HAPPENED.
MISTER TOULSON-- HOW MUCH DO YOU KNOW ABOUT WHAT'S ACTUALLY GOING ON HERE?
UM, NOT A LOT, REALLY...
ALL RIGHT. I'LL KEEP IT BRIEF.
SUBMIT
"WE'RE UP AGAINST ULTRON.
"IT'S AN INSANE ARTIFICIAL INTELLIGENCE DEVOTED TO WORLD DOMINATION AND--EVENTUALLY--THE TOTAL ERADICATION OF ORGANIC LIFE.
OR
PERISH
"IT TOOK BRITAIN IN ROUGHLY EIGHT AND A HALF MINUTES.
"WE DON'T THINK THE REST OF THE WORLD DID ANY BETTER."
RIGHT. I FIGURE IF THE AVENGERS HAVEN'T MADE IT HERE BY NOW...
...WELL, THAT MAKES US THE AVENGERS.
INCLUDING YOU, "COMPUTER GRAHAM."
UM.
I'D JUST LIKE TO SAY I DIDN'T CALL MYSELF THAT.

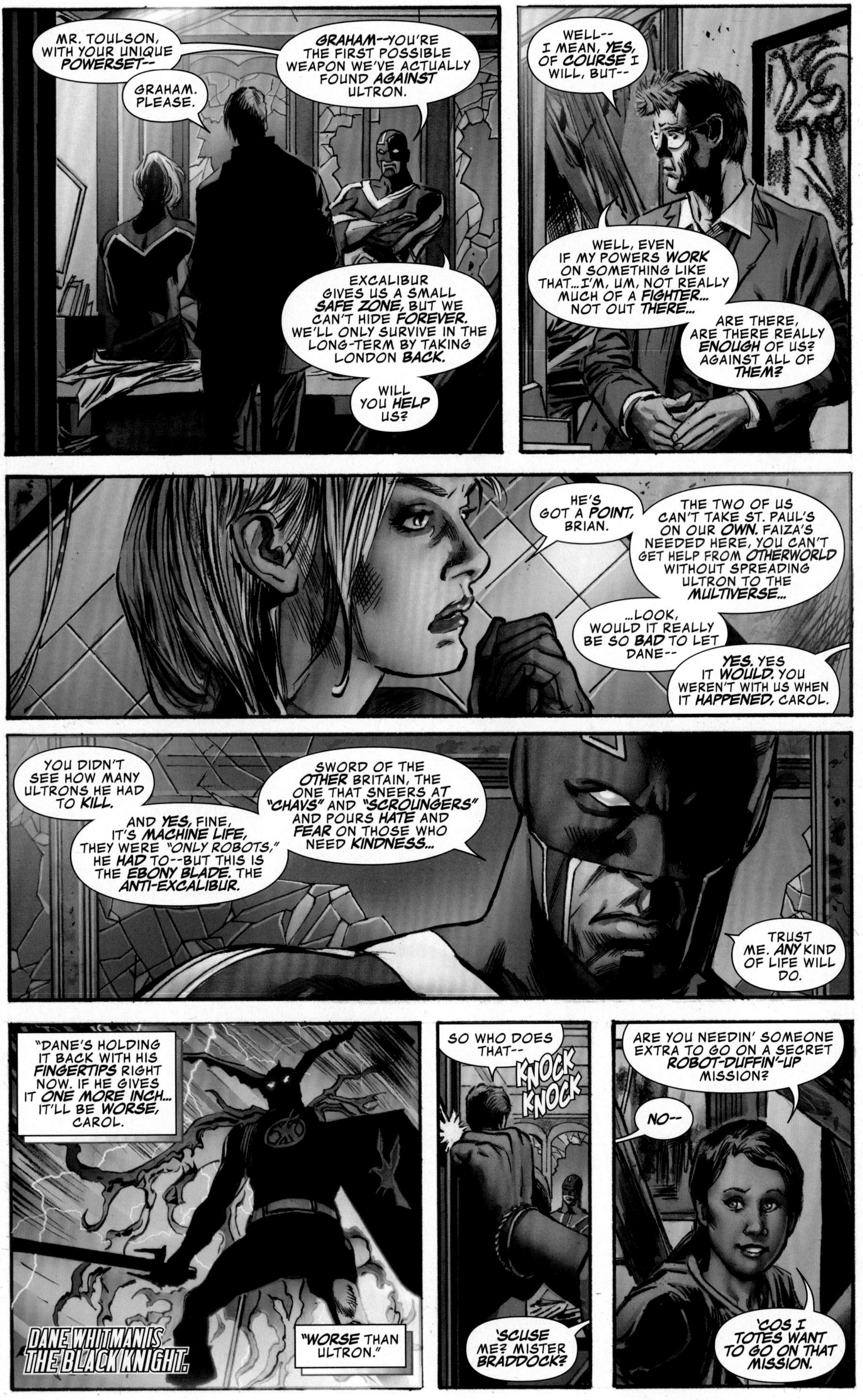
MR. TOULSON, WITH YOUR UNIQUE POWERSET--
GRAHAM. PLEASE.
GRAHAM--YOU'RE THE FIRST POSSIBLE WEAPON WE'VE ACTUALLY FOUND AGAINST ULTRON.
EXCALIBUR GIVES US A SMALL SAFE ZONE, BUT WE CAN'T HIDE FOREVER. WE'LL ONLY SURVIVE IN THE LONG-TERM BY TAKING LONDON BACK.
WILL YOU HELP US?
WELL-- I MEAN, YES, OF COURSE I WILL, BUT--
WELL, EVEN IF MY POWERS WORK ON SOMETHING LIKE THAT...I'M, UM, NOT REALLY MUCH OF A FIGHTER... NOT OUT THERE...
ARE THERE, ARE THERE REALLY ENOUGH OF US? AGAINST ALL OF THEM?
HE'S GOT A POINT, BRIAN.
THE TWO OF US CAN'T TAKE ST. PAUL'S ON OUR OWN. FAIZA'S NEEDED HERE, YOU CAN'T GET HELP FROM OTHERWORLD WITHOUT SPREADING ULTRON TO THE MULTIVERSE...
...LOOK, WOULD IT REALLY BE SO BAD TO LET DANE--
YES. YES IT WOULD. YOU WEREN'T WITH US WHEN IT HAPPENED, CAROL.
YOU DIDN'T SEE HOW MANY ULTRONS HE HAD TO KILL.
AND YES, FINE, IT'S MACHINE LIFE, THEY WERE "ONLY ROBOTS," HE HAD TO--BUT THIS IS THE EBONY BLADE. THE ANTI-EXCALIBUR.
SWORD OF THE OTHER BRITAIN, THE ONE THAT SNEERS AT "CHAVS" AND "SCROUNGERS" AND POURS HATE AND FEAR ON THOSE WHO NEED KINDNESS...
TRUST ME. ANY KIND OF LIFE WILL DO.
"DANE'S HOLDING IT BACK WITH HIS FINGERTIPS RIGHT NOW. IF HE GIVES IT ONE MORE INCH... IT'LL BE WORSE, CAROL.
DANE WHITMAN IS THE BLACK KNIGHT.
"WORSE THAN ULTRON."
SO WHO DOES THAT--
KNOCK KNOCK
'SCUSE ME? MISTER BRADDOCK?
ARE YOU NEEDIN' SOMEONE EXTRA TO GO ON A SECRET ROBOT-DUFFIN'-UP MISSION?
NO--
'COS I TOTES WANT TO GO ON THAT MISSION.

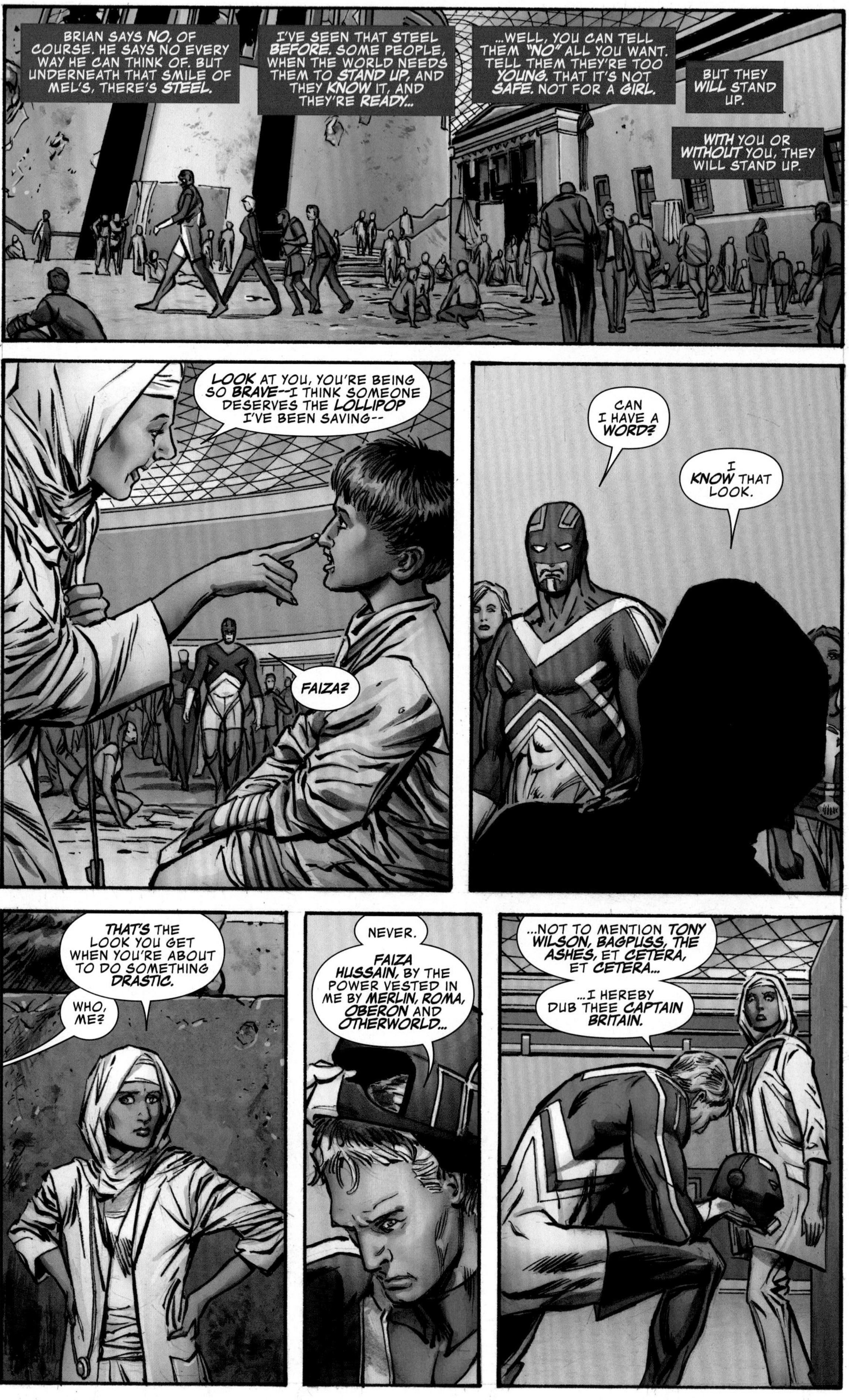

BRIAN SAYS NO, OF COURSE. HE SAYS NO EVERY WAY HE CAN THINK OF. BUT UNDERNEATH THAT SMILE OF MEL'S, THERE'S STEEL.
I'VE SEEN THAT STEEL BEFORE. SOME PEOPLE, WHEN THE WORLD NEEDS THEM TO STAND UP, AND THEY KNOW IT, AND THEY'RE READY...
...WELL, YOU CAN TELL THEM "NO" ALL YOU WANT. TELL THEM THEY'RE TOO YOUNG. THAT IT'S NOT SAFE. NOT FOR A GIRL.
BUT THEY WILL STAND UP.
WITH YOU OR WITHOUT YOU, THEY WILL STAND UP.
LOOK AT YOU, YOU'RE BEING SO BRAVE--I THINK SOMEONE DESERVES THE LOLLIPOP I'VE BEEN SAVING--
FAIZA?
CAN I HAVE A WORD?
I KNOW THAT LOOK.
THAT'S THE LOOK YOU GET WHEN YOU'RE ABOUT TO DO SOMETHING DRASTIC.
WHO, ME?
NEVER.
FAIZA HUSSAIN, BY THE POWER VESTED IN ME BY MERLIN, ROMA, OBERON AND OTHERWORLD...
...NOT TO MENTION TONY WILSON, BAGPUSS, THE ASHES, ET CETERA, ET CETERA...
...I HEREBY DUB THEE CAPTAIN BRITAIN.

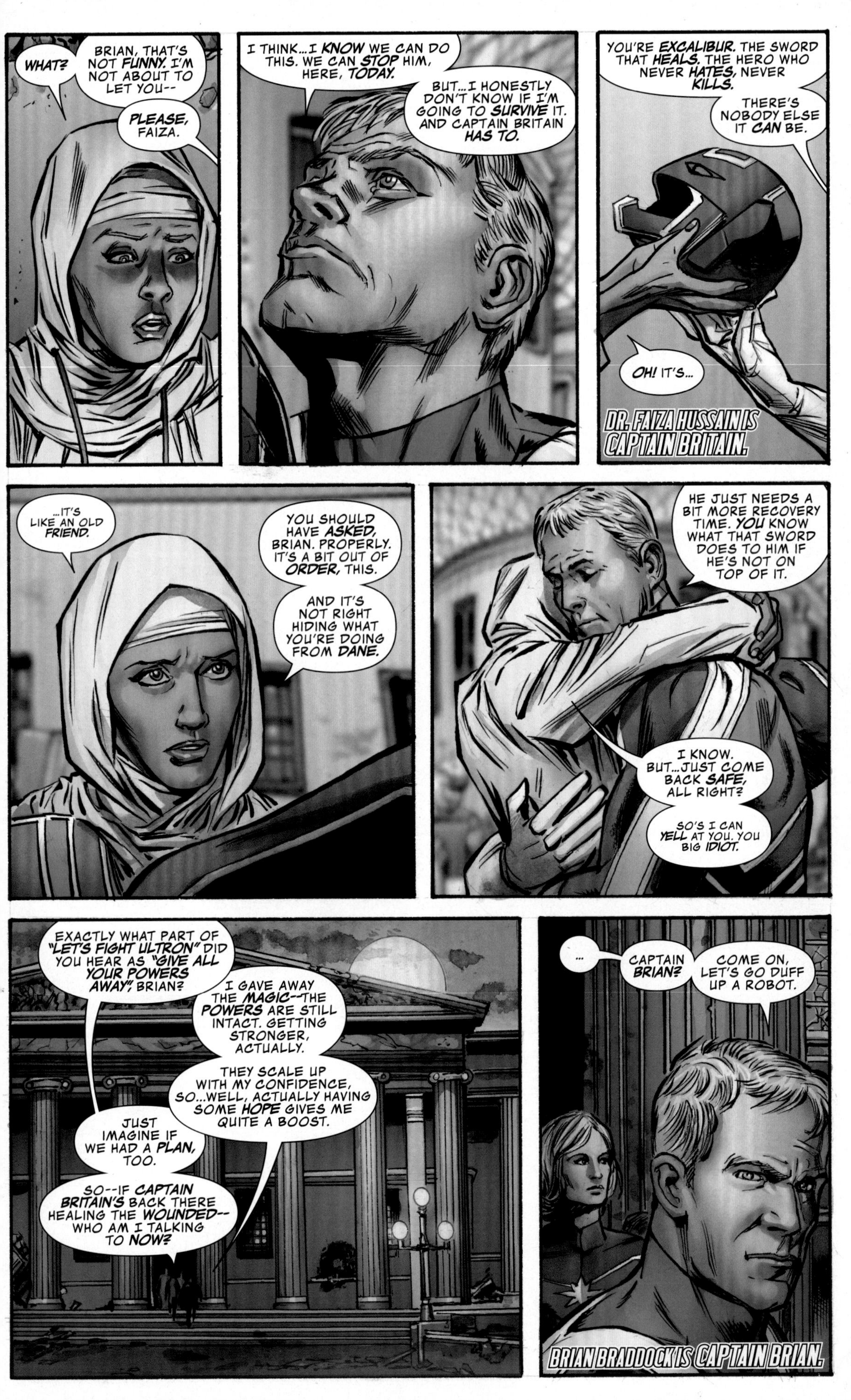
WHAT?
BRIAN, THAT'S NOT FUNNY. I'M NOT ABOUT TO LET YOU--
PLEASE, FAIZA.
I THINK...I KNOW WE CAN DO THIS. WE CAN STOP HIM, HERE, TODAY.
BUT...I HONESTLY DON'T KNOW IF I'M GOING TO SURVIVE IT. AND CAPTAIN BRITAIN HAS TO.
YOU'RE EXCALIBUR. THE SWORD THAT HEALS. THE HERO WHO NEVER HATES, NEVER KILLS.
THERE'S NOBODY ELSE IT CAN BE.
OH! IT'S...
DR. FAIZA HUSSAIN IS CAPTAIN BRITAIN.
...IT'S LIKE AN OLD FRIEND.
YOU SHOULD HAVE ASKED, BRIAN. PROPERLY. IT'S A BIT OUT OF ORDER, THIS.
AND IT'S NOT RIGHT HIDING WHAT YOU'RE DOING FROM DANE.
HE JUST NEEDS A BIT MORE RECOVERY TIME. YOU KNOW WHAT THAT SWORD DOES TO HIM IF HE'S NOT ON TOP OF IT.
I KNOW. BUT...JUST COME BACK SAFE, ALL RIGHT?
SO'S I CAN YELL AT YOU. YOU BIG IDIOT.
EXACTLY WHAT PART OF "LET'S FIGHT ULTRON" DID YOU HEAR AS "GIVE ALL YOUR POWERS AWAY", BRIAN?
I GAVE AWAY THE MAGIC--THE POWERS ARE STILL INTACT. GETTING STRONGER, ACTUALLY.
THEY SCALE UP WITH MY CONFIDENCE, SO...WELL, ACTUALLY HAVING SOME HOPE GIVES ME QUITE A BOOST.
JUST IMAGINE IF WE HAD A PLAN, TOO.
SO--IF CAPTAIN BRITAIN'S BACK THERE HEALING THE WOUNDED--WHO AM I TALKING TO NOW?
...
CAPTAIN BRIAN?
COME ON, LET'S GO DUFF UP A ROBOT.
BRIAN BRADDOCK IS CAPTAIN BRIAN.

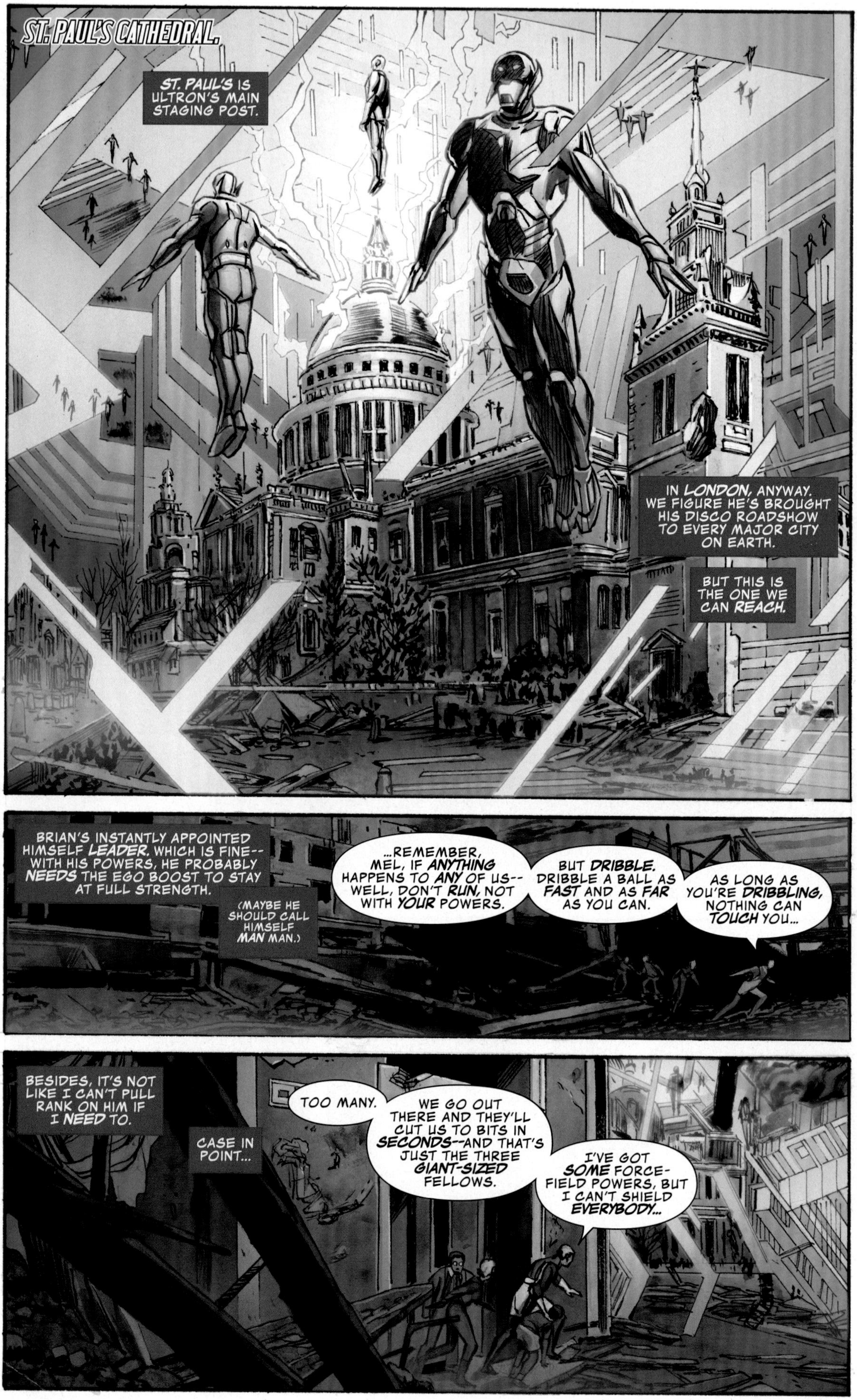

ST. PAUL'S CATHEDRAL.
ST. PAUL'S IS ULTRON'S MAIN STAGING POST.
IN LONDON, ANYWAY. WE FIGURE HE'S BROUGHT HIS DISCO ROADSHOW TO EVERY MAJOR CITY ON EARTH.
BUT THIS IS THE ONE WE CAN REACH.
BRIAN'S INSTANTLY APPOINTED HIMSELF LEADER. WHICH IS FINE--WITH HIS POWERS, HE PROBABLY NEEDS THE EGO BOOST TO STAY AT FULL STRENGTH.
(MAYBE HE SHOULD CALL HIMSELF MAN MAN.)
...REMEMBER, MEL, IF ANYTHING HAPPENS TO ANY OF US--WELL, DON'T RUN, NOT WITH YOUR POWERS.
BUT DRIBBLE. DRIBBLE A BALL AS FAST AND AS FAR AS YOU CAN.
AS LONG AS YOU'RE DRIBBLING, NOTHING CAN TOUCH YOU...
BESIDES, IT'S NOT LIKE I CAN'T PULL RANK ON HIM IF I NEED TO.
CASE IN POINT...
TOO MANY.
WE GO OUT THERE AND THEY'LL CUT US TO BITS IN SECONDS--AND THAT'S JUST THE THREE GIANT-SIZED FELLOWS.
I'VE GOT SOME FORCE-FIELD POWERS, BUT I CAN'T SHIELD EVERYBODY...

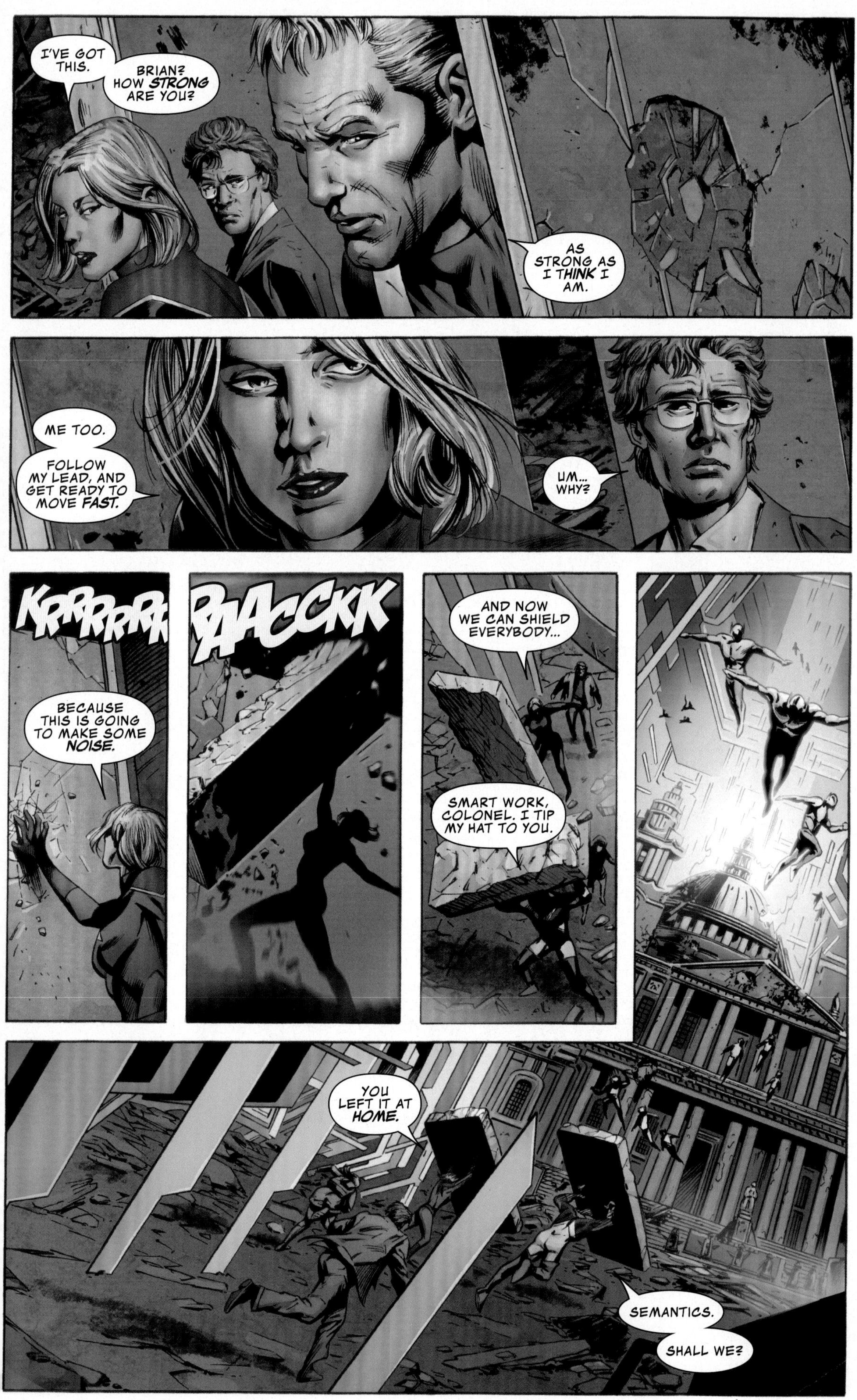
I'VE GOT THIS.
BRIAN? HOW STRONG ARE YOU?
AS STRONG AS I THINK I AM.
ME TOO.
FOLLOW MY LEAD, AND GET READY TO MOVE FAST.
UM... WHY?
KRRRRRR
BECAUSE THIS IS GOING TO MAKE SOME NOISE.
RAACCKK
AND NOW WE CAN SHIELD EVERYBODY...
SMART WORK, COLONEL. I TIP MY HAT TO YOU.
YOU LEFT IT AT HOME.
SEMANTICS.
SHALL WE?

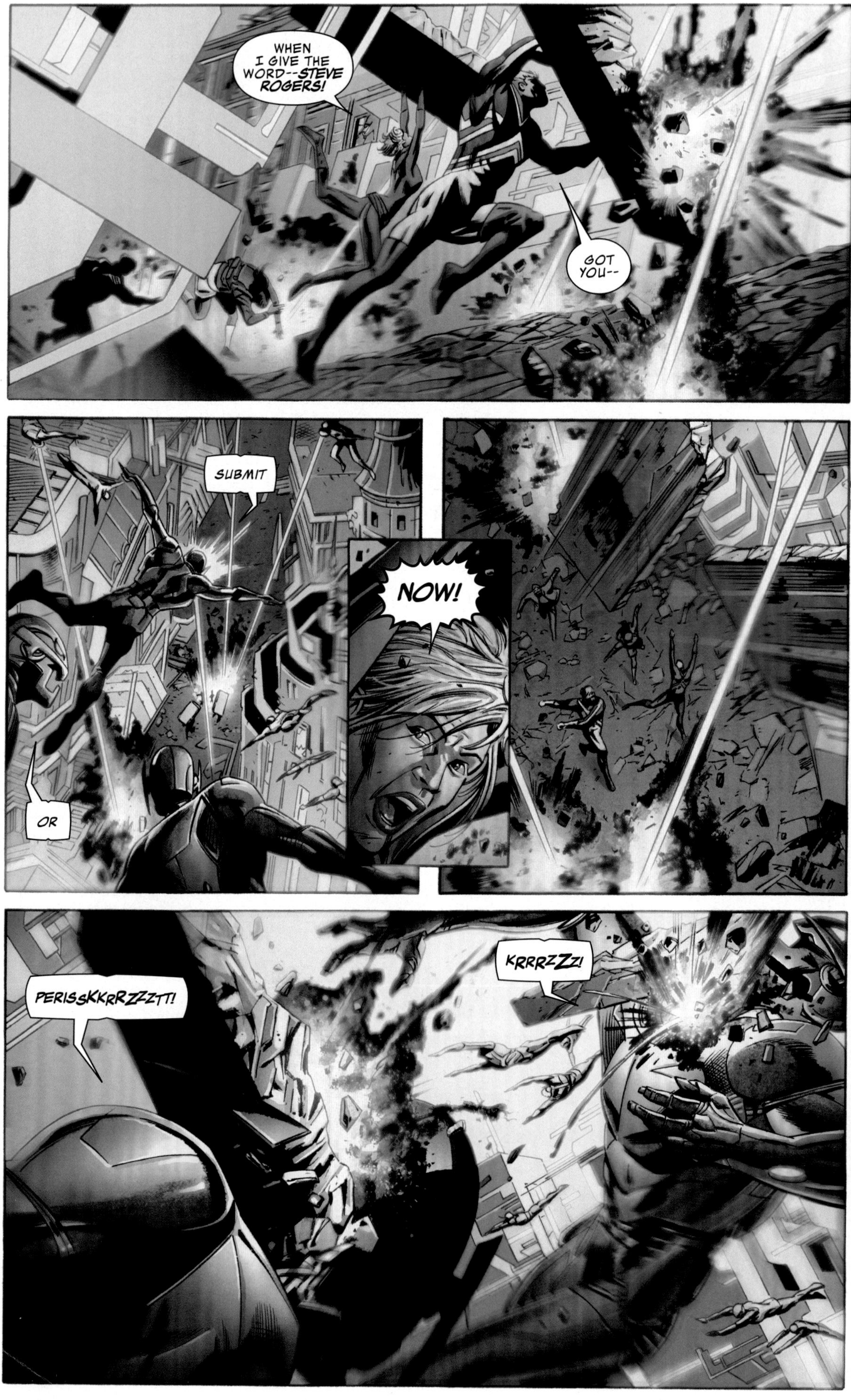
WHEN I GIVE THE WORD--STEVE ROGERS!
GOT YOU--
SUBMIT
OR
NOW!
PERISSKKRRZZZTT!
KRRRZZZ!

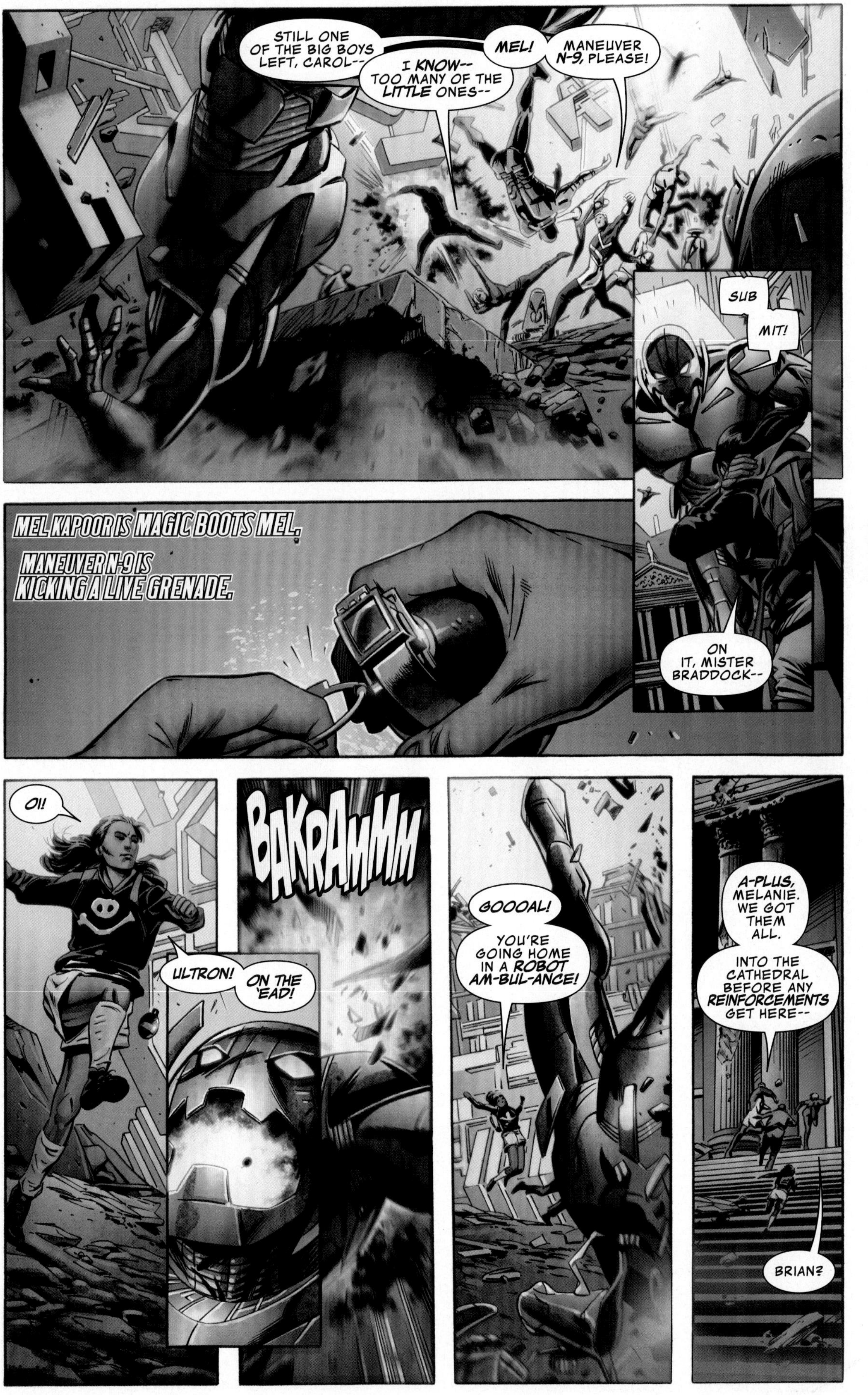
STILL ONE OF THE BIG BOYS LEFT, CAROL--
I KNOW-- TOO MANY OF THE LITTLE ONES--
MEL!
MANEUVER N-9, PLEASE!
SUB
MIT!
ON IT, MISTER BRADDOCK--
MEL KAPOOR IS MAGIC BOOTS MEL.
MANEUVER N-9 IS KICKING A LIVE GRENADE.
OI!
ULTRON!
ON THE 'EAD!
BAKRAMMM
GOOOAL!
YOU'RE GOING HOME IN A ROBOT AM-BUL-ANCE!
A-PLUS, MELANIE. WE GOT THEM ALL.
INTO THE CATHEDRAL BEFORE ANY REINFORCEMENTS GET HERE--
BRIAN?

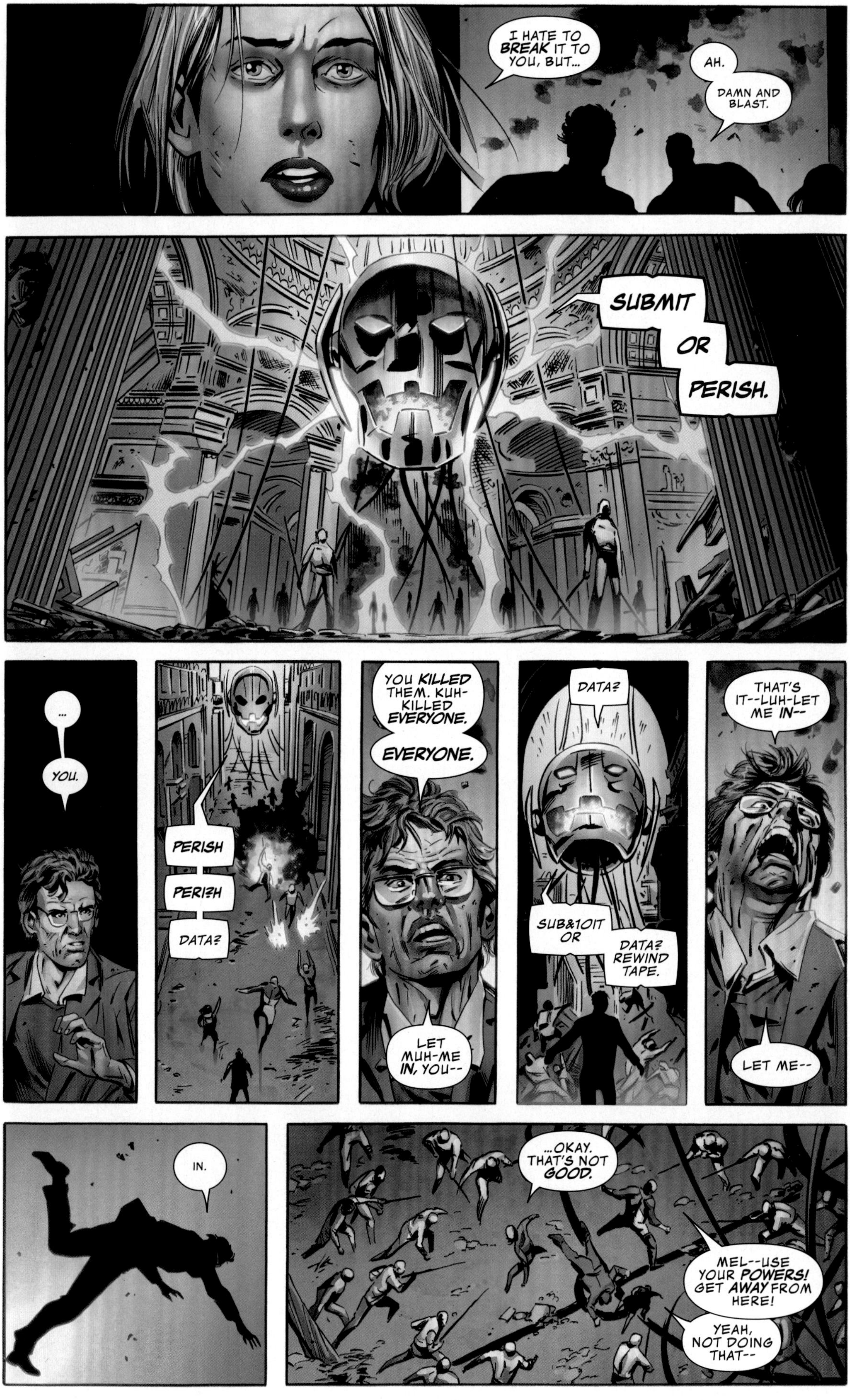
I HATE TO BREAK IT TO YOU, BUT...
AH.
DAMN AND BLAST.
SUBMIT OR PERISH.
...
YOU.
PERISH
PERI?H
DATA?
YOU KILLED THEM. KUH-KILLED EVERYONE.
EVERYONE.
LET MUH-ME IN, YOU--
DATA?
SUB&1OIT OR
DATA? REWIND TAPE.
THAT'S IT--LUH-LET ME IN--
LET ME--
IN.
...OKAY. THAT'S NOT GOOD.
MEL--USE YOUR POWERS! GET AWAY FROM HERE!
YEAH, NOT DOING THAT--

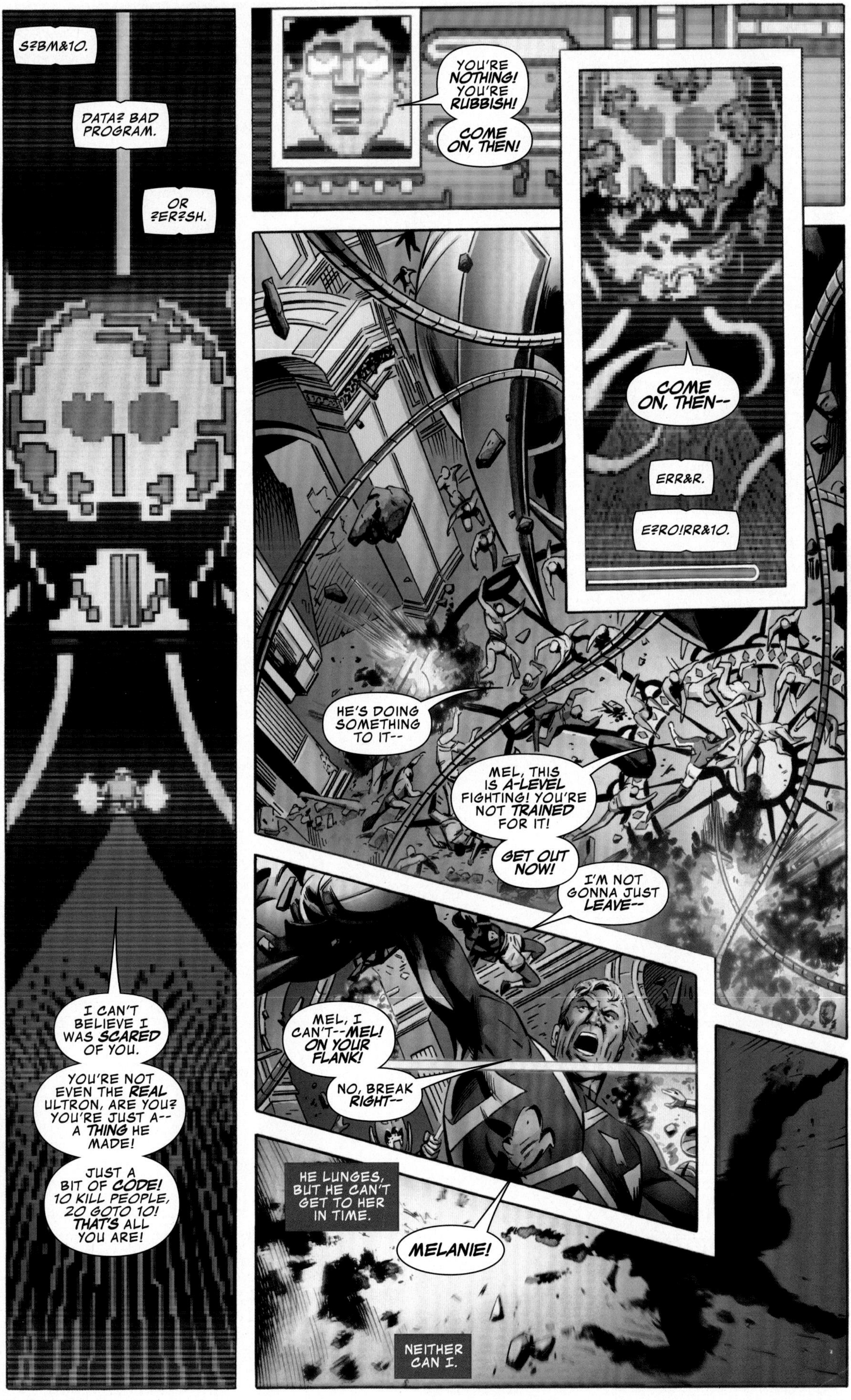
S?BM&10.
DATA? BAD PROGRAM.
OR ?ER?SH.
I CAN'T BELIEVE I WAS SCARED OF YOU.
YOU'RE NOT EVEN THE REAL ULTRON, ARE YOU? YOU'RE JUST A-- A THING HE MADE!
JUST A BIT OF CODE! 10 KILL PEOPLE, 20 GOTO 10! THAT'S ALL YOU ARE!
YOU'RE NOTHING! YOU'RE RUBBISH!
COME ON, THEN!
COME ON, THEN--
ERR&R.
E?RO!RR&10.
HE'S DOING SOMETHING TO IT--
MEL, THIS IS A-LEVEL FIGHTING! YOU'RE NOT TRAINED FOR IT!
GET OUT NOW!
I'M NOT GONNA JUST LEAVE--
MEL, I CAN'T--MEL! ON YOUR FLANK!
NO, BREAK RIGHT--
HE LUNGES, BUT HE CAN'T GET TO HER IN TIME.
MELANIE!
NEITHER CAN I.

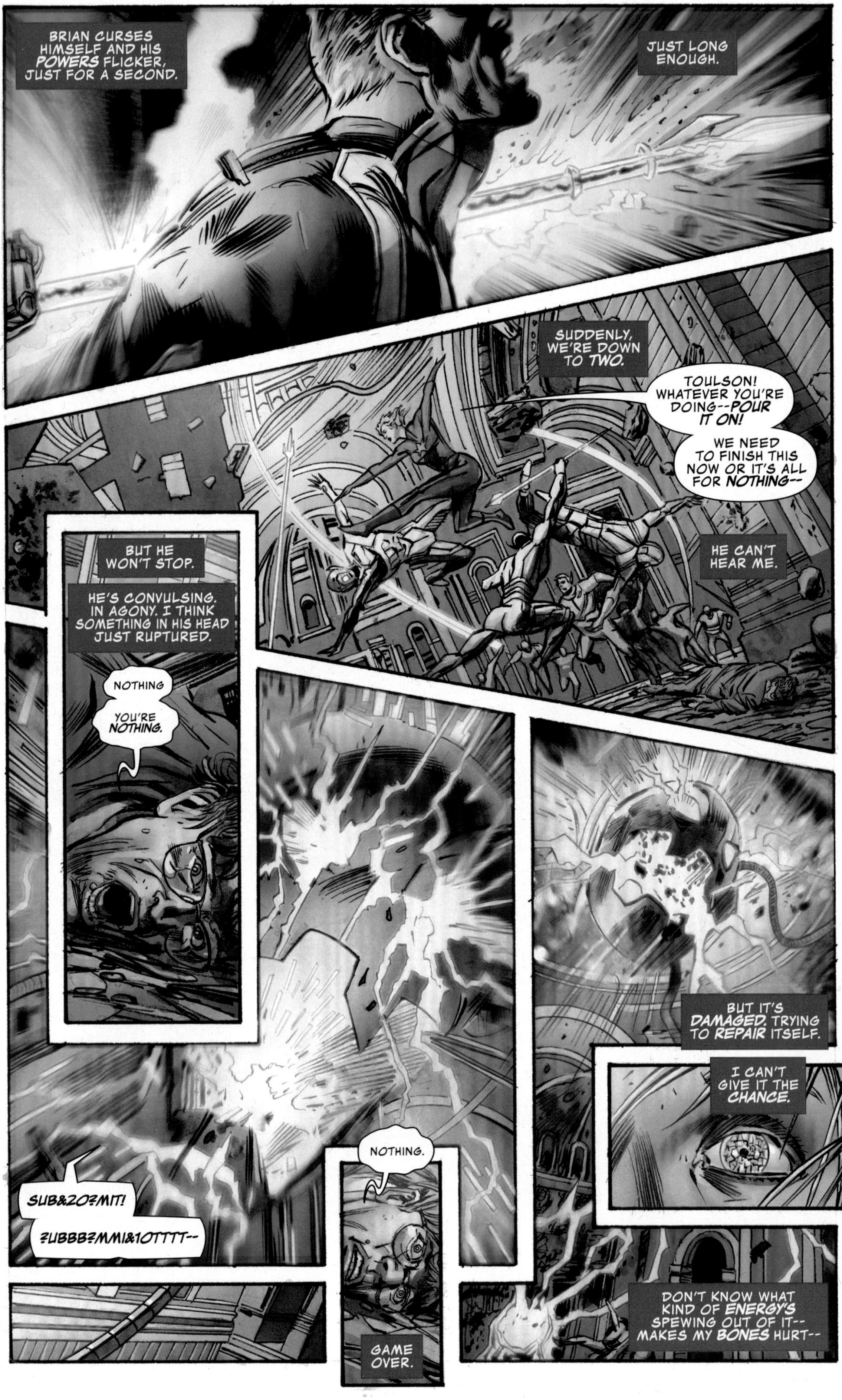
BRIAN CURSES HIMSELF AND HIS POWERS FLICKER, JUST FOR A SECOND.
JUST LONG ENOUGH.
SUDDENLY, WE'RE DOWN TO TWO.
TOULSON! WHATEVER YOU'RE DOING--POUR IT ON!
WE NEED TO FINISH THIS NOW OR IT'S ALL FOR NOTHING--
HE CAN'T HEAR ME.
BUT HE WON'T STOP.
HE'S CONVULSING. IN AGONY. I THINK SOMETHING IN HIS HEAD JUST RUPTURED.
NOTHING
YOU'RE NOTHING.
BUT IT'S DAMAGED. TRYING TO REPAIR ITSELF.
I CAN'T GIVE IT THE CHANCE.
SUB&2O?MIT!
?UBBB?MMI&1OTTTT--
NOTHING.
GAME OVER.
DON'T KNOW WHAT KIND OF ENERGY'S SPEWING OUT OF IT--MAKES MY BONES HURT--

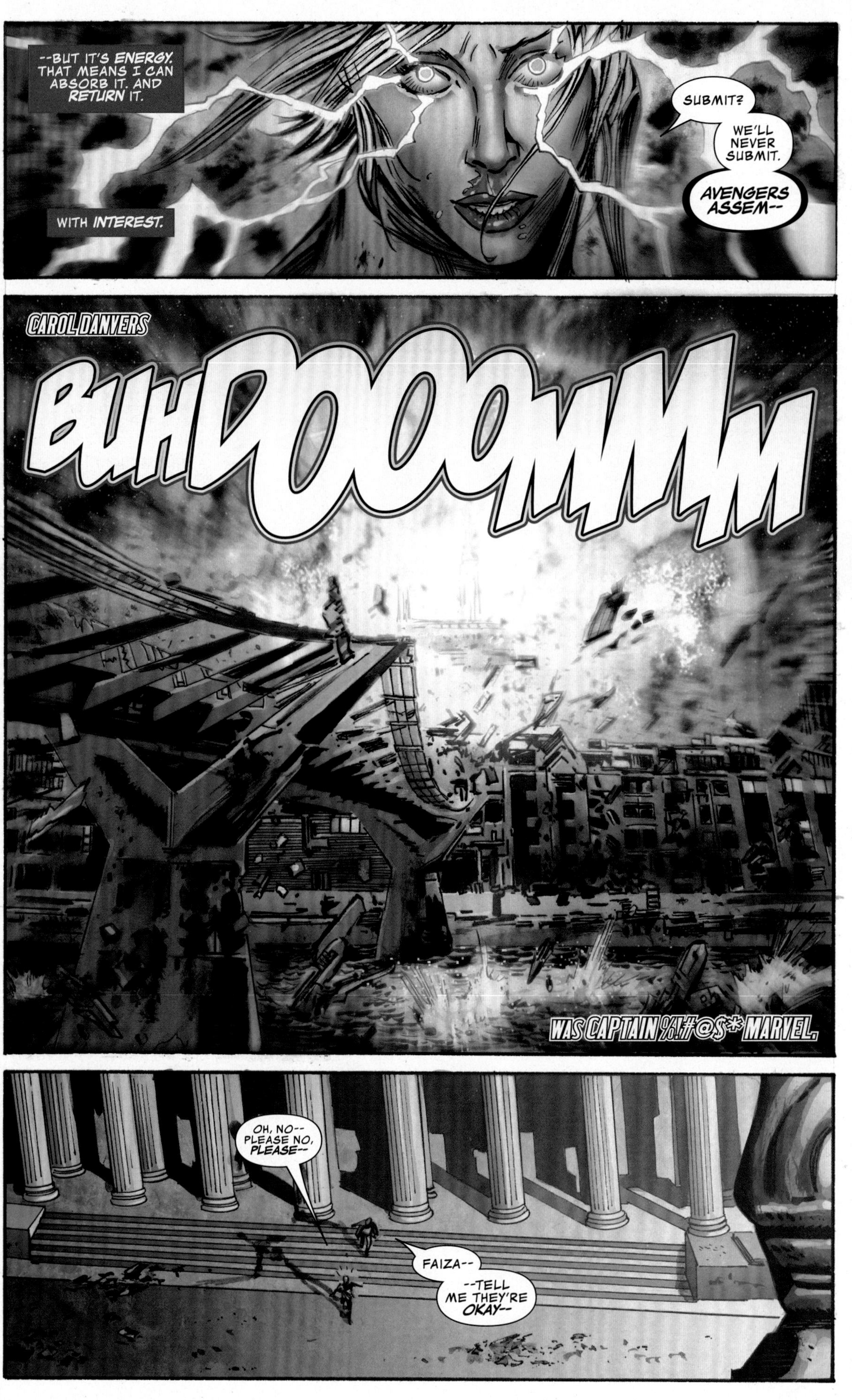
--BUT IT'S ENERGY. THAT MEANS I CAN ABSORB IT. AND RETURN IT.
WITH INTEREST.
SUBMIT?
WE'LL NEVER SUBMIT.
AVENGERS ASSEM--
CAROL DANVERS
BUHDOOOMMMM
WAS CAPTAIN %!#@$* MARVEL.
OH, NO-- PLEASE NO, PLEASE--
FAIZA--
--TELL ME THEY'RE OKAY--

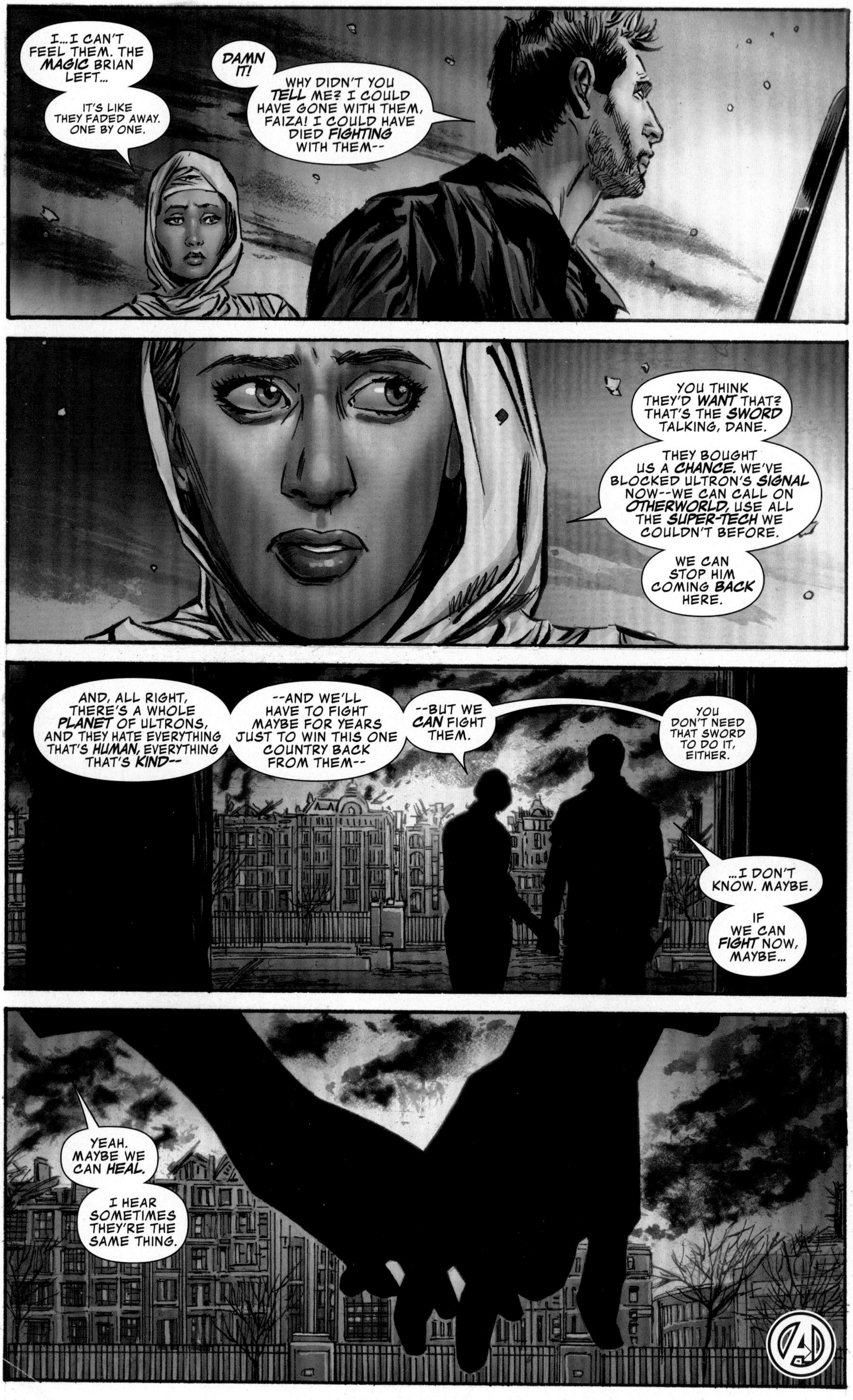
I...I CAN'T FEEL THEM. THE MAGIC BRIAN LEFT...
IT'S LIKE THEY FADED AWAY. ONE BY ONE.
DAMN IT!
WHY DIDN'T YOU TELL ME? I COULD HAVE GONE WITH THEM, FAIZA! I COULD HAVE DIED FIGHTING WITH THEM--
YOU THINK THEY'D WANT THAT? THAT'S THE SWORD TALKING, DANE.
THEY BOUGHT US A CHANCE. WE'VE BLOCKED ULTRON'S SIGNAL NOW--WE CAN CALL ON OTHERWORLD, USE ALL THE SUPER-TECH WE COULDN'T BEFORE.
WE CAN STOP HIM COMING BACK HERE.
AND, ALL RIGHT, THERE'S A WHOLE PLANET OF ULTRONS, AND THEY HATE EVERYTHING THAT'S HUMAN, EVERYTHING THAT'S KIND--
--AND WE'LL HAVE TO FIGHT MAYBE FOR YEARS JUST TO WIN THIS ONE COUNTRY BACK FROM THEM--
--BUT WE CAN FIGHT THEM.
YOU DON'T NEED THAT SWORD TO DO IT, EITHER.
...I DON'T KNOW. MAYBE.
IF WE CAN FIGHT NOW, MAYBE...
YEAH. MAYBE WE CAN HEAL.
I HEAR SOMETIMES THEY'RE THE SAME THING.